Organizational Rhetoric

To our families of origin and our families of affiliation.

—M. F. H. and D. J. F.

Organizational Rhetoric

Situations and Strategies

Mary F. Hoffman

University of Wisconsin-Eau Claire

Debra J. Ford

University of Kansas School of Nursing

Los Angeles | London | New Delhi
Singapore | Washington DC

For information:

SAGE Publications, Inc.
2455 Teller Road
Thousand Oaks,
    California 91320
E-mail: order@sagepub.com

SAGE Publications India Pvt. Ltd.
B 1/I 1 Mohan Cooperative
    Industrial Area
Mathura Road, New Delhi 110 044
India

SAGE Publications Ltd.
1 Oliver's Yard
55 City Road
London EC1Y 1SP
United Kingdom

SAGE Publications
    Asia-Pacific Pte. Ltd.
33 Pekin Street #02-01
Far East Square
Singapore 048763

Printed in the United States of America

Library of Congress Cataloging-in-Publication Data

Hoffman, Mary F. (Mary Frances)
Organizational rhetoric : situations and strategies/Mary F. Hoffman, Debra J. Ford.
    p. cm.
Includes bibliographical references and index.
ISBN 978-1-4129-5668-0 (cloth)
ISBN 978-1-4129-5669-7 (pbk.)
    1. Communication in organizations. I. Ford, Debra J. II. Title.

HD30.3.H59 2010
808'.06665—dc22   2009023867

This book is printed on acid-free paper.

09   10   11   12   13   10   9   8   7   6   5   4   3   2   1

Acquisitions Editor:	Todd R. Armstrong
Assistant Editor:	Aja Baker
Editorial Assistant:	Nathan Davidson
Production Editor:	Brittany Bauhaus
Copy Editor:	Teresa Herlinger
Typesetter:	C&M Digitals (P) Ltd.
Proofreader:	Sally Jaskold
Indexer:	Diggs Publication Services, Inc.
Cover Designer:	Janet Kiesel
Marketing Manager:	Jennifer Reed Banando

Brief Contents

Preface   xiii

Acknowledgments   xix

Chapter 1: Organizations and
            Rhetoric in Contemporary Culture   1
Chapter 2: Identifying Rhetorical Strategies in
            Organizational Rhetoric   23
Chapter 3: Rhetorical Situations in Organizations   55
Chapter 4: Critical Approaches to Organizational Rhetoric   77
Chapter 5: Evaluating and Critiquing Organizational Rhetoric   103
Chapter 6: Identity Creation and Maintenance Rhetoric   119
Chapter 7: Rhetoric About Issues   139
Chapter 8: Rhetoric About Organizational Risk   163
Chapter 9: Crisis Rhetoric   185
Chapter 10: Organizational Rhetoric for Internal Audiences   209

Epilogue: The Ancient Art of Rhetoric in a Complex
          Organizational World   233
Appendix: Worksheets for Analyzing Organizational Rhetoric   237
References   245
Index   259
About the Authors   267

Detailed Contents

Preface   xiii

Acknowledgments   xix

**Chapter 1: Organizations and Rhetoric in
    Contemporary Culture**   1
   Defining Rhetoric
   Defining Organization
   Defining Organizational Rhetoric
   Understanding Organizational Rhetoric
   Characteristics of Organizational Rhetoric
      Speaker
      Situation
      Audiences
      Message
   Reasons for Studying Organizational Rhetoric
      Organizations Are a Powerful Force in Society
      Organizations Produce a Great Deal of Rhetoric
   Goals for Studying Organizational Rhetoric
   Practical Outcomes of Studying Organizational Rhetoric
   A Process for Analyzing Organizational Rhetoric
   Conclusion

**Chapter 2: Identifying Rhetorical Strategies in
    Organizational Rhetoric**   23
   Canon of Invention
      Ethos in Traditional Rhetoric
      Ethos in Organizational Rhetoric
      Pathos in Traditional Rhetoric
      *Pathos in Organizational Rhetoric: Needs,
         Values, and Identification*

Logos in Traditional Rhetoric
Logos in Organizational Rhetoric: Inductive and
   Deductive Reasoning
Interdependence of Ethos, Pathos, and Logos
Evidence in Organizational Rhetoric
Canon of Organization in Organizational Rhetoric
Canon of Style in Organizational Rhetoric
Canon of Delivery in Organizational Rhetoric
Interdependence of Invention, Organization, Style,
   and Delivery in Organizational Rhetoric
Canon of Memory in Organizational Rhetoric
Special Situations and Rhetorical Strategies
Conclusion
Worksheet for Identifying Rhetorical Strategies in
   Organizational Texts

Chapter 3: Rhetorical Situations in Organizations   **55**
The Importance of Context in Rhetoric
Two Perspectives on Rhetorical Situations
   Bitzer's Perspective: Situations Call for Rhetoric
   Using Bitzer's Perspective in Organizations
   Vatz's Perspective: Rhetoric Creates Situations
   Using Vatz's Perspective in Organizations
The Rhetorical Situation in Organizational Rhetoric
   Organizational Exigencies
   Audiences in Organizational Rhetoric
   Constraints and Assets in Organizational Rhetoric
Researching the Rhetorical Situation
   Using Published Sources
   Conducting Primary Research
Conclusion
Case Study: A Showdown Over Power in Texas
   Case Study References
Worksheet for Describing Rhetorical
   Situations in Organizations

Chapter 4: Critical Approaches to Organizational Rhetoric   **77**
Historical Overview
Key Ideas in Critical Approaches to Organization
   Studies and Organizational Rhetoric
   Discourse of Suspicion and the Construction of Power
   Ideology

Hegemony and Whose Meaning "Wins"
Corporate Voice
"The" Public
Summary of Key Concepts in Critical Theory/Perspectives
Making Choices: Ethics and Organizational Rhetoric
Conclusion
Note

**Chapter 5: Evaluating and Critiquing
Organizational Rhetoric**   **103**
Two Approaches to Analyzing Organizational Rhetoric
An Evaluative Approach
A Critical Approach
Conclusion
Worksheet for Conducting an Evaluative Reading
Worksheet for Conducting a Critical Reading

Chapter 6: Identity Creation and Maintenance Rhetoric   **119**
The Foundation for Identity Rhetoric:
Organizational Identity
Identity Building Rhetoric
The Rhetorical Situation for Identity Building
Rhetorical Strategies for Identity Building
Identity Maintenance Rhetoric
The Rhetorical Situation for Identity Maintenance Rhetoric
Rhetorical Strategies for Identity Maintenance
Evaluating and Critiquing Identity Creation and
Maintenance Rhetoric
Conclusion
Case Study: "Who Says the Internet Is
Only for Young People?" Identity and Disaster Relief
Case Study Questions
Case Study References

Chapter 7: Rhetoric About Issues   **139**
Defining Issues and Issue Management in Organizations
Foundation for Understanding Issues Rhetoric:
Issue Life Cycles
Potential Status
Imminent Status
Current Status
Critical Status
Dormant Status

Issue Management: The Rhetorical Situation
    Exigencies
    Audiences
    Constraints and Assets
Strategies for Rhetoric About Issues
    Claims and Evidence in Rhetoric About Issues
    Values Advocacy in Rhetoric About Issues
    Credibility Strategies in Rhetoric About Issues
Evaluating and Critiquing Rhetoric About Issues
Conclusion
Case Study: Menu Labeling—Healthy Idea or Big Brother?
    Case Study Questions
    Case Study References

Chapter 8: Rhetoric About Organizational Risk   **163**
Defining Risk in Organizations
Foundations for Understanding Risk Rhetoric
    Risk Perception Frames
    The Elaboration Likelihood Model of Persuasion
The Rhetorical Situation for Risk Rhetoric
    Exigencies
    Audiences
    Constraints and Assets
Strategies for Rhetoric About Risk
    Organizational Credibility
    Values Advocacy
    Claims and Evidence
    Community Participation
    Stylistic Strategies
Evaluating and Critiquing Rhetoric About Risk
Conclusion
Case Study: No Bodies in My Backyard
    Case Study Questions
    Case Study References

Chapter 9: Crisis Rhetoric   **185**
Defining Rhetoric About Crisis
Foundation for Understanding Crisis Rhetoric:
    Life Cycle of a Crisis
    Pre-Crisis Stage
    Crisis Response Stage
    Post-Crisis Stage

Crisis Management: The Rhetorical Situation
    Exigencies
    Audiences
    Constraints
Strategies in Crisis Rhetoric
    Instructional Strategies
    Apologia Strategies
    Dissociation Strategies
    Crisis Strategies in Combination
Evaluating and Critiquing Organizational Rhetoric
   About Crisis
Conclusion
Case Study: The Perfect Storm
    Case Study Questions
    Case Study References

Chapter 10: Organizational Rhetoric for Internal Audiences   **209**
The Rhetorical Situation in Internal Organizational Rhetoric
    Exigencies, Audiences, and Constraints for
        Organizational Socialization
    Exigencies, Audiences, and Constraints for
        Reinforcement and Retention
    Exigencies, Audiences, and Constraints for
        Organizational Change
    External Challenges, Internal Exigencies: Situations Requiring
        Member Advocacy
Rhetorical Strategies for Internal Messages
    Rhetorical Strategies for Socialization
    Rhetorical Strategies for Reinforcement and Retention
    Rhetorical Strategies for Organizational Change
    Rhetorical Strategies for Identity, Issue, Risk,
        and Crisis Situations
Evaluating and Critiquing Internal Organizational Rhetoric
Conclusion
Case Study: A New Record—Transitioning to Electronic
   Medical Records
    Case Study Questions
    Case Study References

**Epilogue: The Ancient Art of Rhetoric in a
Complex Organizational World**   **233**
    Rhetoric in a Globalized Organizational World
    Corporate Rhetoric in Nonprofit Organizations
    Traditional Rhetorical Strategies in Contemporary Forms
    The Environment as Situation and Strategy

Appendix: Worksheets for Analyzing Organizational Rhetoric   **237**
    Worksheet for Identifying Rhetorical Strategies in
        Organizational Texts
    Worksheet for Describing Rhetorical Situations
        in Organizations
    Worksheet for Conducting an Evaluative Reading
    Worksheet for Conducting a Critical Reading

References   **245**

Index   **259**

About the Authors   **267**

Preface

Organizational messages confront us every day: Public universities lobby state legislatures for financial support. A bank that made wise decisions prior to the subprime mortgage crisis wants to differentiate itself from other banks that are struggling. Media companies want listeners to stop downloading music without paying for it. A community's parks and recreation office seeks support from voters for tax funding that will support improvements in green spaces. An energy company wants customers to believe that the solutions it develops will solve our world's energy problems. A small, locally owned grocery store seeks to reassure customers that it is safe to shop there after a murder takes place in the store. Your employer asks that you work hard to make decisions in the best interest of the organization. And the list could go on and on.

These messages appear online, on television and radio, on billboards, and in print media every day, 24/7, around the world. All multinational corporations, nongovernmental organizations (NGOs), trade associations, large and small not-for-profit organizations, religious organizations, and locally owned companies—in other words, organizations of all sizes and missions—at some point want to promote their identity, manage an issue, resolve a crisis, or recruit and retain employees and volunteers.

All of these messages are rhetoric—they strategically use symbols to influence thoughts, feelings, or behaviors. In many cases, these messages are produced as part of large campaigns by public relations and other communication professionals working in close coordination with management teams. However, even very small organizations with limited and generalist staff create these types of messages in order to promote their goals to various publics and audiences.

A key aspect of many of these types of organizational messages is that they often are not attributed to an individual (e.g., "Verizon said today . . ."), or the individual clearly is speaking on behalf of the organization, not on behalf of him- or herself (e.g., CEOs or public relations professionals). These messages are designed to promote an organization's interests, sometimes (not always) at the expense of the interests of others involved in a situation. Given the immense influence that organizations have in our daily lives (Deetz, 1995), it is important to have a set of skills for slicing into the possible meanings of such messages in order to draw our own conclusions about them. Therefore, the purpose of this book is to provide a systematic approach to analyzing and critiquing organizational rhetoric.

❖ WHAT THIS BOOK DOES

The perspective offered in this book is rooted in an ancient tradition of rhetorical analysis, but is focused on using that tradition to understand messages created by central players in contemporary society—corporate and non-profit organizations. Because the organization is a different kind of speaker (a multitude of people-in-one)—a speaker whom you could argue really only "exists" legally, who faces different constraints than an individual, who often draws upon much larger resources than an individual does, and who wields considerable influence in our daily lives—we need to pay particular attention to this area of rhetoric.

This book teaches students and citizens how to pay careful, critical attention to organizational messages, particularly those not attributed to any particular individual. Creators of public relations messages will also find that this textbook provides a strong background in the strategies used to develop and critique public relations messages.

The following are examples of the types of questions students will learn to consider when examining rhetoric:

- What appears to be the organization's goals for the message?
- Which rhetorical (persuasive) language and action strategies is the organization using to achieve its goal?
- Does the rhetoric seem well-designed to meet its goal?
- What is the organization *not* saying?
- What voices may be marginalized by the organization's message?
- To the extent it is possible to judge independently of the organization, what does the organization appear to be up to?
- Does the organization appear to be wielding its influence fairly and ethically?

Considering such questions will allow individuals to make judgments and decisions using more complete information than they might otherwise. Many organizational rhetoric and public relations scholars have laid the foundation for this area of study in their research (for a comprehensive review, see Meisenbach & McMillan, 2006). The purpose of this book is to make those tools and research results accessible to the student/citizen.

❖ WHAT THIS BOOK DOES NOT DO

This is not a traditional organizational communication textbook that provides broad, overarching perspectives for many of the types of messages or functions that are associated with organizations. For example, we do not address conversations that take place among members of organizations. We also do not address researcher-initiated texts, such as transcripts that result from interviews or focus groups. While the analytical process we discuss can be applied usefully to those texts, they are not the focus of this book. Those broader perspectives are addressed by traditional organizational communication textbooks (e.g., see Conrad & Poole, 2005; Eisenberg, Goodall, & Tretheway, 2007; Miller, 2006).

This book also is not a public relations theory textbook, nor is it a textbook about public relations strategy development. For example, we do not discuss how to develop a campaign to promote a nonprofit organization's fundraiser. Those PR theory and design approaches are addressed more usefully and comprehensively by more traditional PR textbooks (i.e., see Heath & Coombs, 2006).

❖ ORGANIZATION OF THE BOOK

We take an integrated theoretical approach to each of the content areas by incorporating into our discussion the major contributions of various rhetorical, organizational rhetoric, public relations, and organizational communication scholars. Our goal is to present research findings and recommendations relevant to the analysis of organizational messages. In the first part of the book, we explain a process for analyzing organizational rhetoric, grounded in rhetorical, organizational, and public relations theory. In each chapter of the second part of the book, you will find:

- Foundational concepts for understanding each content area;

- Components of the rhetorical situation as applied to each content area;

- Strategies applicable to each content area, as supported by research;

- Questions for students to ask while evaluating and critiquing organizational rhetoric representative of that content area; and

- A case study with questions to exemplify each content area.

In addition to critical aids provided in each chapter, an appendix provides four worksheets designed to assist students in analyzing any organizational artifact of interest.

In order to achieve these goals, the book follows an overarching model we call the *process for analyzing organizational rhetoric* (see Figure P.1). This model is adapted from Ford (1999) and presented to demonstrate the relationship of the components in the process of analyzing, evaluating, and critiquing organizational rhetoric, thereby demonstrating the relationships of the chapters to each other. It is not unlike models developed by Campbell and Burkholder (1997) and Rowland (2008) and discussed by Foss (2004). However, it is unique in that it clearly illustrates the integration of commonly occurring rhetorical strategies and situations faced by organizations into a broader process of rhetorical criticism. It also incorporates principles of conducting a critical reading of organizational rhetoric with the more commonly described principles of conducting an evaluative reading of organizational rhetoric.

Each chapter begins with the model. The section to which the particular chapter applies is highlighted in the model to facilitate understanding of the flow of the process, and thus the book, as a whole. Chapters 1–5 explain the overarching process and the individual steps for conducting rhetorical criticism of organizational rhetoric. Chapter 2 deliberately is designed as a longer chapter in comparison to the other eight. The content is cumulative and integrated, so it is best presented as a whole. Chapters 6 through 10 feature the particular sets of commonly recurring rhetorical situations and strategies faced by organizations, and include case studies and discussion questions. The epilogue briefly introduces emerging areas of organizational rhetoric research that are ripe for analysis.

❖ TEACHING AND LEARNING TOOLS FOR FACULTY AND STUDENTS

To assist both students and instructors a variety of teaching/learning tools are incorporated throughout the book. As a student or an

Figure P.1: Process for Analyzing Organizational Rhetoric (Overall)

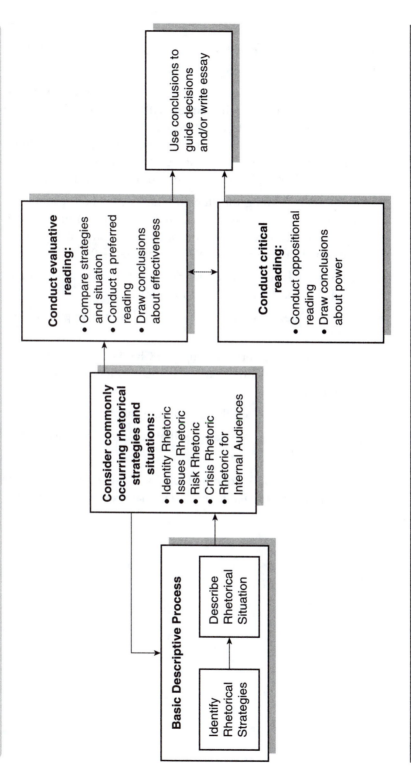

SOURCE: Adapted from Ford (1999).

instructor, take advantage of these tips to gain the most from your time and energy:

- The *process for analyzing organizational rhetoric* model appears at the beginning of each chapter with the chapter's primary purpose highlighted to assist you in following the overarching process while focusing on each chapter's specific content. Think of the model of these stages as a search history when surfing the Web; it helps you keep your place in the process.

- Worksheets outlining the steps of analysis for both evaluative and critical readings are included in the appendix. You may find it helpful to make copies of the worksheets because they should be used with the case materials in Chapters 6–10.

- Case materials (context summaries and texts) for analysis are included for each case outlined in Chapters 6–10.

- Discussion questions follow each case for classroom or preparation activities.

- "Look boxes" are inserted throughout Chapter 2 to help students understand and identify particular rhetorical strategies as they are introduced.

- Key terms are italicized throughout the chapters.

- Have fun exploring the strategies that organizations use to influence all of us!

By the end of the book, students should have a solid understanding of rhetorical analysis as applied to organizational texts in contemporary contexts.

Acknowledgments

As with all books, we could not have completed this manuscript without the assistance of many people.

From Mary

Thanks to my former colleagues at Texas State University-San Marcos, particularly textbook mentors Timothy Mottet and Steven Beebe for their encouragement and advice. Thanks also to all of the graduate and undergraduate students in 8 years of classes on organizational rhetoric. They provided great examples, and pushed me to think about the best educational approach to the topic. I offer special thanks to Dorothy Collins, who introduced me to the topic of risk rhetoric, and Renee Cowan, whose motivation ensured other important projects were not neglected as I worked on this book.

Thanks also to my new colleagues at the University of Wisconsin-Eau Claire, especially Judy Gatlin and Ellen Hon, who patiently helped a new chair learn the ropes at the same time that she completed a textbook project.

I offer personal thanks to my parents, Joy and Arnie Hoffman; to my dinner-night family, Rick Gonzalez, Lynn Ellison, and Tim Mottet; and to my friends Ann Burnette and Rey Garcia, Marian and Steve Houser, Lisa and Brian Furler, and Renee and D. C. Cowan, who made sure I had some fun once in a while.

From Debbie

I would like to thank Rita Clifford, Associate Dean, for her constant support of a project that Mary and I had proposed before Rita hired me in my role as assistant dean at the University of Kansas School of Nursing Office of Student Affairs. Without Rita's, Dean Karen Miller's, and Associate Dean Cindy Teel's support of this project as a part of my new responsibilities, this book would not exist today. I also thank the staff and faculty in the Office of Student Affairs who helped in many ways, probably without realizing it: Alice Debauche, Adam Keener, Elizabeth Leach, Barbara Leeds, Carolyn Ross, Cyndie Schudel, Jeanne Schott, Debbie Stratton, and Susan Tanzie.

Thank you to Joann Keyton for introducing us to Todd Armstrong as newer scholars who had something to offer the discipline. To my friends and family who put up with me during this process for over 2 years, there are no words: Dorothy Graham, Robert and Constance Graham, Sandra, Robert, Jefferson, and Jordan Vlasnik, Rosetta Ford, Dawn Ford, Corine and Paul Wegener, JoAnn and Bryant Paradis, Barbara and Ed Thompson, Barbara and Tracy Shelanskey, Dorothy Perrin, Mary Ann Danielson, Scott Myers, Elaine Dean, Patricia Martin, Tracy Russo, Mary Banwart, Mary Gambino, Judith Warren, Nelda Godfrey, Sara Cooke, Sandra Sanchez, and Jenny Ford. And last, thank you to my husband, Jayson Ford, *without whom.*

From Both of Us

We both would like to thank Robert C. Rowland for introducing us to the field of organizational rhetoric. His courses taught us how we could combine our interests in rhetoric with our interests in organizations and their influence in the world. We also thank Todd Armstrong for shepherding our idea into a full-blown book. His assistant, Aja Baker, was very helpful in aiding us with the logistics of producing this book. We thank our reviewers for their careful and thoughtful comments: Josh Boyd (*Purdue University*), George Cheney (*The University of Utah and the University of Waikato*), H. L. Goodall, Jr. (*Arizona State University*), Keith M. Hearit (*Western Michigan University*), Robert L. Heath (*University of Houston*), John M. Jones (*Pepperdine University*), Jill Jordan McMillan (*Wake Forest University*), Rebecca J. Meisenbach (*University of Missouri*), Maribeth S. Metzler (*University of Cincinnati*), and Bonita Dostal Neff (*Valparaiso University*). Together, we would also like to thank Ryan Bisel for his helpful feedback, and our students who constantly challenge our thinking and who inspired us to write this book. The book is a far better product because of all of their input.

1

Organizations and Rhetoric in Contemporary Culture

❖ ❖ ❖

Figure 1.1   Process for Analyzing Organizational Rhetoric (Introduction)

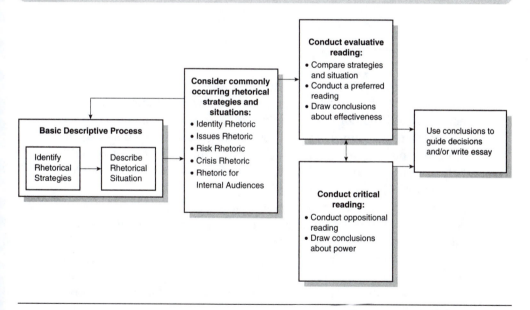

SOURCE: Adapted from Ford (1999).

Most people's lives are structured in large part around organizations. As students, you are part of a university, and usually part of one or more student groups. Outside of school, you may hold a job in an organization or be a member of a civic or religious group or a political party. You may play on a recreational sports team or be part of a book or cooking club. Each of these organizations influences how you structure your time, with whom you interact, how you spend your money, and how you formulate your personal values. Even organizations of which you are not a member have tremendous influence on your life. They influence national policy and public thinking on issues such as who has access to health care and at what price, what sorts of pollutants are released into air or water, what safety features are included in cars, and what principles and practices guide how U.S. organizations operate in other nations.

One of the most common, and often understudied, ways that organizations exert this influence is through the use of rhetoric. In this chapter, we build a foundation for our ongoing exploration of organizational rhetoric. We discuss what it means to study organizational rhetoric, explain why it is important to investigate this type of communication, and preview the two approaches we will take to organizational rhetoric.

❖ DEFINING RHETORIC

The term *rhetoric* often has negative connotations, as we hear people label some statement as "just rhetoric," or we hear them say, "The action doesn't match the rhetoric." In reality, though, rhetoric is a neutral term that simply refers to the strategic use of symbols to generate meaning. Understanding an early definition of rhetoric will help establish a foundation for how organizations use the ancient art of rhetoric.

One of the earliest and certainly most well-known definitions of rhetoric comes from Aristotle (trans. 1932), who argued that it was "the faculty for discovering in the particular case what are the available means of persuasion" (p. 7). For Aristotle, rhetoric was an ability to see what would be persuasive to a particular audience in a particular situation. For example, when you ask an instructor to allow you to enroll in a class that is already closed, you should have a sense of what sort of appeals will help your case, and what sort will hurt it. You might tell the professor how much the topic area interests you, or how important it will be to your future career. You will likely avoid telling her that you heard the class is really easy or that it is the only section that fits your 2-day-a-week schedule.

In his book *The Rhetoric,* Aristotle (trans. 1939) identifies the means of persuasion as appeals to personal character *(ethos)*, appeals to emotion *(pathos),* and the use of reasoning *(logos)*. Both Aristotle's definition of rhetoric as an ability to see what will be persuasive and his identification of the basic appeals are useful in the study of how organizations persuade.

For our purposes, rhetoric can be understood as *the strategic use of symbols to generate meaning.* To say that rhetoric is "strategic" is to emphasize that messages are created to accomplish a goal. This requires that a speaker or writer carefully consider the challenges in meeting the goal, as well as all of the potential resources available for doing so. A *symbol* is something that represents something else. Words and other symbols, such as nonverbal emblems or visual cues, come to be associated with particular objects or ideas because humans make that association. Symbols allow us to make sense of events and create a world in which we can construct meaning (or understand our world through language), and thereby accomplish tasks such as organizing.

The symbols used to describe the study of rhetoric are numerous, and sometimes confusing. The term *rhetoric* may refer to the practice or the product of message creation. We may say that a speaker used rhetoric to make his or her point, or we may ask to see the rhetoric a speaker or author produced—perhaps a videotape or transcript of her remarks. This product may also be referred to as *rhetorical discourse* or a *rhetorical artifact*. A person who creates rhetoric is known as a *rhetor.* The process of analyzing artifacts or discourse is called *rhetorical criticism,* and is guided by sets of questions or lenses known as *rhetorical methods.* Over the centuries, scholars have done enough rhetorical criticism to formulate some general principles governing how rhetoric works. These principles are referred to as *rhetorical theory.* There is a circular relationship between rhetorical theory and rhetorical criticism. Theory helps determine what critics look for when analyzing rhetoric, and the findings of the analysis modify and supplement what we know about rhetorical theory.

Although early rhetorical critics primarily studied single speeches from individuals in political positions, contemporary critics have a much broader conception of what constitutes a rhetorical artifact. Contemporary critics study films, music, Web sites, works of art, public memorials, and almost any other "text" that makes an argument. Organizational rhetoric is one rapidly growing area of interest to scholars. At its most obvious, we might say that organizational rhetoric is rhetoric produced by organizations, and that would be true. However, in order to understand the unique nature of organizational rhetoric, it is necessary to determine what is meant by an organization, and to recognize the basic ways in which organizational rhetoric differs from more traditional types of rhetoric.

❖ DEFINING ORGANIZATION

Since you no doubt belong to and receive messages from so many organizations, you may not stop to think about exactly what the term *organization* means. Whether organizations are for-profit, not-for-profit, government, business, or social entities, they have some characteristics in common. In 1939, Chester Barnard (1939/1969) argued that people form organizations because they lack the power to accomplish some of their goals independently. This makes sense when we consider some contemporary examples.

Recently, homeowners in an Austin, Texas, neighborhood were concerned that if Wal-Mart were allowed to build a store there, it would create additional traffic problems and have a negative impact on small business. If each neighbor had tried alone to challenge the development, he or she would have been fairly powerless against a major national chain. However, by joining their voices and creating an organization, residents were able to get the attention of city planners and have a voice in deciding how the area would be developed. Likewise, an engineer might have an idea that could revolutionize computer hardware, but she may lack the resources to develop, produce, market, and service the equipment. By forming or joining an organization, she increases the chances that she will accomplish her goal. Similarly, an individual athlete might love playing hockey, but he knows he can't have a game by himself, so he forms a team and joins a league (both organizations) in order to meet his goal.

Organizations can lend power to our individual voices, but what exactly does it mean to affiliate with an organization? One of the most well-known definitions of organization was developed by Barnard (1939/1969). He wrote that "a formal *organization* is a system of consciously coordinated activities or forces of two or more persons" (p. 73, emphasis added). This definition suggests three characteristics shared by all organizations: communication, willingness to cooperate, and common purpose. Each of these is important in understanding the role of rhetoric in organizations.

First, organizations cannot exist apart from communication. In fact, some scholars argue that communication is what creates an organization (e.g., Cooren, Taylor, & Van Every, 2006). If organizations are systems of "consciously coordinated activities," communication is essential if all of the interdependent parts and practices of any group are going to work together. Think of a factory producing athletic shoes. Communication is necessary to make sure that among thousands of other activities, shoes are designed; supplies arrive; workers are hired, trained, motivated, and paid; there is agreement about the level of quality needed in each shoe; and potential customers are persuaded to purchase the product. This conscious coordination results in what organizational scholars refer to as *structure*—the system of relationships that guides the actions of an organization.

For many groups, this structure is represented visually in an organizational chart that shows who the supervisors are, and to whom each subordinate reports. Structure is also evident in titles and status indicators (such as office size and location). Structure is created, reinforced, and sometimes challenged by communication (Poole & McPhee, 2005). Without communication, organizational members cannot build relationships or accomplish tasks—both elements that are key in the second characteristic of organizations.

The second characteristic is what Barnard (1939/1969) called "willingness to cooperate." He wrote, "Activities cannot be coordinated unless there is first the disposition to make a personal act a contribution to an impersonal system of acts, one in which the individual gives up personal control of what he does" (p. 84). This characteristic points out the voluntary nature of organizational membership. Individuals join organizations if they believe that membership will work to their advantage in achieving individual goals. Think about student organizations you may have considered joining. Maybe you declined to join a particular group because you found yourself thinking, "I am not going to get anything out of that." Individuals understand that although joining an organization may help them accomplish their goals, it also requires that they sacrifice some level of control to the group.

Organizations depend upon individuals being willing to participate, and therefore they create messages to show individuals that the
benefits of joining outweigh the costs. Recent U.S. Army advertising,
for example, attempts to show young people that the financial, educational, and personal advantages of military experience outweigh the
potential disadvantages of personal danger, time away from family
and friends, or loss of personal freedom.

Barnard (1939/1969) also identified "common purpose" as a key
element in organizations. Groups can function only if the members
agree about the goal to which they are dedicating their individual
efforts and for which they are sacrificing their individual control.
Communication is central in this element as well. Members must communicate with one another and the leadership in order to negotiate
understanding of the common purpose.

For example, consider a recreational hockey team. The members
of the team probably have a variety of individual reasons for
participating—some want to stay in shape, some want to improve
their skills, and some want to win games. The team will not function
effectively if they fail to agree on a common purpose in playing.
That purpose may be to win games, in which case the individual
goals of poorer players to improve their skills may not be met. Or
the purpose may be to have fun and get some exercise, in which case
the individual goals of highly competitive players may not be met.
Depending on which common goal the team embraces, some
members may lose their willingness to cooperate, and might join a
different organization.

Our discussion of the nature of organizations makes it clear that
rhetoric has an important role to play in persuading individuals to
cooperate and in negotiating common purposes, so we now need to
examine a definition of organizational rhetoric.

❖ DEFINING ORGANIZATIONAL RHETORIC

Though you may not have heard the term before, you are very familiar
with organizational rhetoric—you are bombarded by it every day.
When your university sends you a free mascot T-shirt to help build
school spirit, when you see television or print ads claiming that energy
companies are protecting the environment, or when a charitable organization asks for a donation by showing you the victims of a disaster,
you are the audience of organizational rhetoric.

Organizational rhetoric is the strategic use of symbols by organizations to influence the thoughts, feelings, and behaviors of audiences important to the operation of the organization. Three elements of this definition merit further explanation: the strategic nature, the goals, and the audiences of organizational rhetoric. First, organizational rhetoric is strategic because it is concerned with how messages are fashioned to meet specific goals. To be strategic is to carefully consider the impact of the selection and arrangement of symbols in the message.

In 2001, Philip Morris, known primarily as a producer of cigarettes, but also the parent company of brands like Kraft and Nabisco, announced that it was changing its name. In the press release announcing the name "Altria," representatives of the organization even explained the strategic nature of their rhetorical choices. They wrote,

> The significance of the name "Altria," Bible [the CEO] said, is derived from the Latin word "altus" which reflects the corporation's desire for its family of companies to always "reach higher" in striving to achieve greater financial strength and growth through operational excellence, consumer brand expertise and a growing understanding of corporate responsibility. (Altria Group, 2001)

Given that tobacco is often an unpopular product, Philip Morris likely wanted to put distance between people's perceptions of a tobacco company and their perceptions of other brands produced by the company. By strategically selecting a new name that makes no reference to tobacco, or to the well-known brand "Philip Morris," the organization sought to deflect negative attention from those opposed to tobacco production and marketing.

As this example illustrates, rhetoric doesn't happen by accident; it is the result of careful thought and planning on the part of CEOs, managers, human resources, public relations, and other communication professionals in organizations. The amount of time and money organizations spend crafting messages, or having others craft messages for them, is one indication of the strategic nature of this type of discourse.

Second, the goals of organizational rhetoric are to influence thoughts, feelings, and behaviors of audiences. When a major discount retailer runs ads to refute public criticism of its employment practices, it is encouraging us to think about the company differently. When a nonprofit organization gives us examples of people in need, it is attempting to influence our feelings. Thoughts and feelings influence how we behave. Thus, our changed thinking might lead us to shop at Wal-Mart, Target, or K-Mart, or our changed feelings might encourage us to donate to the American Red Cross or Salvation Army.

Finally, it is important to acknowledge the importance of audiences in the definition of organizational rhetoric. All rhetoric is strategically generated for one or more audiences. Organizations face many audiences, and often those audiences have multiple and potentially conflicting interests. Contemporary channels of communication such as the Internet, email, and 24-hour business reporting means that nearly all audiences have access to the messages designed for other audiences.

❖ UNDERSTANDING ORGANIZATIONAL RHETORIC

In order to more fully understand what we mean when we talk about organizational rhetoric, it is helpful to know how it emerged as a field of study and the two ways that scholars continue to study it.

In some respects, to study organizational rhetoric is to study both the oldest and one of the newest areas of communication. The study of communication was born with the study of rhetoric, and scholars have been examining the creation and reception of public messages for thousands of years. In 1965, Edwin Black refocused rhetorical scholars' attention on methods for analyzing messages, and over the next few decades critics developed a wide range of methods, or lenses, to analyze rhetoric.

In addition to building new tools to analyze discourse, rhetorical critics began to explore a much broader array of texts. Early critics primarily studied speeches and essays, but later critics turned their attention to messages produced by social movements, artists, and lyricists. As the pool of acceptable objects of study expanded, rhetorical critics began to look to the rhetoric produced by contemporary organizations. While rhetorical scholars were beginning to see organizations as sources of texts for analysis, organizational communication scholars were beginning to recognize the importance of focusing on symbol use in organizations. This converging of interests would set the stage for the emergence of organizational rhetoric as an independent area of study.

Early scholarship in organizational communication was heavily influenced by the social scientific movement in the study of communication.

A focus on improving productivity, often influenced by theorists in business, added to the idea that the scientific method could be used to create more effective communication in organizations. In the early 1980s, though, scholars began turning to more qualitative and interpretive methods. They began conducting interviews and focus groups, and looking at organizational documents in order to learn how individuals understood their experiences in organizations (Putnam & Pacanowsky, 1983).

A rhetorical approach to studying organizations emerged parallel to this movement. Although some earlier authors had embraced a rhetorical approach, conferences of organizational communication scholars in 1988 and 1989, and a special issue of the *Journal of Applied Communication Research* in 1990, made organized arguments for the value of using rhetorical concepts to understand organizations and laid out some basic principles (Meisenbach & McMillan, 2006).

In the years since then, scholars have studied a wide variety of organizational texts from perspectives informed by rhetorical theory and criticism. Some of these texts were items that we would traditionally consider rhetorical—for example, speeches or editorials by organizational leaders, newsletters, or advertisements addressing public policy issues. One example of this type of analysis is Hoffman and Cowan's (2008) analysis of organizational Web sites. These authors analyzed the Web sites of 50 organizations in order to investigate organizational perspectives on initiatives to address work/life balance among employees. Other authors have taken this approach in studying rhetoric addressing rhetorical crisis in order to determine what are effective and ineffective crisis messages for organizations (Benoit, 1995a; Hearit, 1995).

Other critics investigate texts that are more familiar to qualitative social scientists, such as notes from observations made in organizations, observations of physical décor, or transcripts of interviews or small-group meetings with organizational members. Murphy's (1998) analysis of how flight attendants resist the authority of the airlines is an interesting example of this approach to understanding organizations. Murphy, who was working as a flight attendant, observed interactions, interviewed other flight attendants, and looked at organizational documents to understand how power was exercised and resisted at the airline.

Studying both of these kinds of texts has the potential to generate a great deal of knowledge about organizations and the social system in which they exist. In this book, we focus primarily on traditional rhetorical texts, but the methods presented can help you analyze almost any message in an organization.

❖ CHARACTERISTICS OF ORGANIZATIONAL RHETORIC

If you have taken a class in public speaking, then you are probably familiar with the concepts of speaker, situation (or context), audience, and message, and understand their importance in crafting an effective speech. These terms are also important to those who study organizational rhetoric because for a long time the primary goal of rhetorical critics was to assess the persuasive impact of a message on an audience (Wichelns, 1925). At the time that Wichelns advanced his theory of criticism, this meant that, unlike literary critics who looked primarily at language choices and ideas in a work outside of its context, rhetorical critics needed to pay particular attention to such factors as speaker goals, audience composition, and context in addition to analyzing the message itself.

Although Wichelns's ideas remain relevant, contemporary scholars of organizational rhetoric find the elements of speaker, situation, audience, and message to be much more complex. Understanding these characteristics should help you understand some of the ways in which organizational rhetoric differs from what we consider "traditional" rhetoric.

Speaker

In the early days of rhetorical criticism, it was easy for a critic to identify the speaker—it was the man (usually) at the podium, or whose name appeared at the top of the text. However, because so little of today's organizational rhetoric is distributed in traditional spoken form, and because the actual spokesperson speaks for the entire organization rather than for him- or herself, it is much more difficult to isolate and investigate the "speaker." The rise of what Cheney and McMillan (1990) call "the corporate person" is one of the ways that organizational rhetoric differs from traditional rhetoric. McMillan (1987) wrote that every organization (for-profit and nonprofit) has "a persona not a flesh-and-blood entity, but an organizational image which has been *created* from the accumulated symbols by which the organization represents itself" (p. 37, italics in original).

Because it is influenced by so many people and developed from the accumulation of so many symbols, studying this persona is more complicated than studying a single speaker would be. When a spokesperson says, "State University is happy to announce our new football coach," who is the speaker? The whole university—including students, staff, and faculty? The athletic department? The president and her cabinet? Personnel in the University Advancement Office? McMillan's (1987) perspective on the organizational persona suggests that it is all of these groups, and at the same time not really any one of them. The announcement does not tell us who was involved in the decision, or who can be held responsible for the outcome. Understanding who is speaking, and for whom he or she is speaking, is an important element in analyzing organizational rhetoric.

Situation

Rhetorical critics have always paid careful attention to what Bitzer (1968) labeled the *rhetorical situation,* in order to determine the goals of rhetors and the obstacles faced in accomplishing them. This, too, is more complicated in organizational rhetoric. Contemporary organizations are what systems theorists refer to as *open systems,* meaning that they take information and events from the outside world and produce information, products, and services that have an impact on the larger community (Katz & Kahn, 1978). As a result, it is critical that organizations attend to what is happening around them, monitor their impact on the organizational environment, and respond appropriately. A detailed discussion of the rhetorical situation in organizational rhetoric is the focus of Chapter 3 of this book.

Audiences

Audiences are also much more complicated. With the expansion of technology and the concurrent shrinking of the world, the concept of audience now involves a complex tangle of interests, particularly because organizations need to consider so many diverse audiences when formulating messages.

Pharmaceutical companies provide an excellent example. Customers are clearly one audience. They are concerned about prices, safety, and availability of products, and perhaps the charitable or community contributions made by the organization. At the same time, stockholders are an audience. They are concerned with prices as well, but that concern is based on profit rather than on the need to purchase drugs. Employees are a third audience; the Food and Drug Administration, a fourth audience; Congress and the executive branch is a fifth audience; and the scientific community is a sixth audience. You can probably think of several additional audiences as well, and recognize that each of them will have different concerns and different opinions about how concerns should be addressed. A detailed discussion of audiences in organizational rhetoric is found in Chapter 3 of this book.

Message

Organizational rhetoric is still founded on the basic elements identified by Aristotle centuries ago, but the strategies and the forms in which those strategies occur are vastly more complicated and diverse. Years of research in rhetoric and in organizational communication have created a large body of ideas used to label and understand the strategies found in organizational rhetoric. In Aristotle's day, rhetoric appeared in one form—oral and in person. Today, organizations use Web pages, print, radio and television advertising, even blogs and virtual Web worlds in addition to newsletters, posters, speeches, and events.

Cheney and McMillan (1990) introduce a set of categories for classifying messages in organizations that can help identify types of organizational messages. They explain that all organizational messages could be placed somewhere on a series of five continua: formal to informal, impersonal to personal, public to private, universal to particular, and external to internal. Any message can be described by using a combination of these continua.

To say that rhetoric is *formal* means that its content is guided by organizational policy, and the sender is an official representative of the organization (Stohl & Redding, 1987). An email from the dean of students announcing a snow day would be formal in nature, but a conversation between that dean and her office manager would be informal. Most of the day-to-day interactions of individuals at work, while clearly interesting and clearly organizational communication, are not considered organizational rhetoric for the purposes of the beginning critic.

Impersonal messages are directed at a general audience rather than a specific individual. The exact identity of the source also may not be clear in an impersonal message. *Personal* messages are directed at, and adapted to, specific and identifiable individuals or groups. A television ad or Web pop-up window designed to create awareness of an organization is impersonal—it seeks a wide, nonspecific audience, and it is not made clear who actually crafted the message. A letter or instant message directly addressed to an individual or small group of individuals is personal. Such phrases as "To our employees" or "Today, the church announces" are clues that a piece of discourse can be called impersonal. You have probably noticed that some organizations make impersonal messages seem personal by individually addressing mass mailings or personalizing emails. This may make it even more difficult to determine if a message is more personal or more impersonal.

Universal messages are crafted to appear to express the thoughts and attitudes of all members of an organization, rather than the thoughts and attitudes of the leadership or of those creating the messages. Particular messages identify for whom they are speaking. Universality and impersonality are related characteristics. An impersonal message allows for a sense of universality, as in "The United States Navy announced . . ." This statement suggests that all members of the Navy support the policy being announced, when in fact, we can be quite sure that there is some level of dissent. Organizations may use similar statements to suggest the agreement of all, when in reality, many members of the organizations likely were not consulted on the issue. Although organizations are collections of individuals, they often appear to speak as if they have only one shared voice. The corporate voice may encourage audiences to think of, and perhaps act toward, organizations as singular entities rather than as collections of individuals.

A *public* message is one that is accessible to wide audiences and not intended to circulate to a prescribed group of people. For example, a mass mailing of a fundraising letter, a Web site that is not password protected, or an employee newsletter would be public messages. A memo designated for a few people would be a more private message.

Finally, Cheney and McMillan's 1990 work discussed the continuum of *external to internal* characteristic of messages. They argued that organizational rhetoric is primarily external—that it consists of messages directed at audiences outside the organization such as customers, legislators, and so forth, rather than at internal audiences such as employees. Recent work by both of these authors, however, makes it clear that their thinking about organizational rhetoric has expanded to demand more attention to rhetoric that is internal to the organization (e.g., Cheney, 2005; Cheney & Christensen, 2001a; Meisenbach & McMillan, 2006).

Documents designed to communicate the organization's ideals, principles, processes, or identity to its members are clearly rhetorical—the public audience is simply internal to the organization rather than external. In this book, we will consider such materials as training programs, employee newsletters in print or electronic form, events and strategic office décor as examples of internally directed organizational rhetoric.

Two examples demonstrate how these categories can help us classify messages. Following a prolonged controversy and many deaths and injuries in vehicle rollovers, the Ford Motor Company ran several newspaper advertisements emphasizing safety. These messages were formal in that they were phrased as being from the organization and were the result of strategic planning. They were impersonal because they were directed at the wide audience of newspaper readers rather than at specific individuals. They were universal since the company itself rather than a single individual was identified as the "speaker" in the discourse. They were public because they were targeted at a general audience, and since they were published in national newspapers there was no attempt to limit access to the information. Finally, in this case, the messages were external—directed at audiences outside the organization rather than at employees, though internal audiences would also have access.

Employee orientation materials in many large organizations can also be classified using these continua. They are formal because they conform to organizational standards. They are impersonal because they are directed at all new employees rather than tailored to individuals. They are universal because they represent the "organization's" perspectives on priorities and procedures. They are public within the organization because they are available to all employees rather than a select group. Clearly, in this case, they are directed at an internal audience, though they may also be seen by members of external audiences.

As you look at discourse produced in organizations, it may be difficult to place samples cleanly in these categories because there is no "yes" or "no," only a "more" or "less." The most important thing is that you are able to use the characteristics to make an argument for why the discourse you have selected should or should not be studied as an example of organizational rhetoric.

The methods introduced in this book can be used to analyze almost any type of message produced by and in organizations; however, beginning critics may find it easiest to start with messages that are on the formal, impersonal, public, and universal segments of the continua.

Although product advertising and marketing share many of the characteristics of organizational rhetoric, we exclude them from consideration in this text because they are highly specialized messages designed for the audience of consumers, while organizational rhetoric is defined in part by the existence of multiple audiences. In addition, a wide range of academic and popular literature already addresses the topics of advertising and marketing.

❖ REASONS FOR STUDYING ORGANIZATIONAL RHETORIC

Now that you have a clearer understanding of the development and focus of organizational rhetoric, it is important to explore why its study is worthy of an entire book, and perhaps an entire college course. It is vital to study organizational rhetoric because of the power that organizations exercise, and because they exercise much of that power through the strategic use of symbols. There are both philosophical and practical reasons to study this type of rhetoric. On a philosophical level, it is important to realize how much power organizations wield in contemporary culture, and to identify how that power is constructed and reinforced through the use of rhetoric. On a practical level, understanding how organizations use discourse may make us wiser consumers and citizens, and in turn, more ethical and effective producers of rhetoric for the organizations in which we work.

Organizations Are a Powerful Force in Society

In the days of Aristotle, individuals, rather than organizations, produced all of the rhetoric. As the world changed, individuals pooled their skills in guilds and associations. This required them to surrender their individual voices, but they gained some power by becoming part of a collective voice. As the world became industrialized, the balance shifted even further, and organizational voices became more powerful than individual voices (Cheney & McMillan, 1990). Many authors even argue that organizations—particularly corporate organizations—have come to have more influence over individuals than do governments. Organizational communication scholar Stanley Deetz (1992) is especially concerned with the influence of corporations. He writes, "Major national and international corporations have frequently, wittingly and unwittingly, replaced religious, familial, educational and community institutions in the production of meaning, personal identity, values, knowledge and reasoning" (p. 17). Deetz argues that organizations, particularly corporations, have gained power to such an extent that they can, in essence, tell individuals who they are (an IBMer, a State University Lion), what is true (that global warming is, or is not, scientifically supported), and what they should believe and value (that buying a new car is a patriotic act).

Perhaps even more thought-provoking to college students is Deetz's (1992) argument that the push for education to create workers for corporations has changed the very nature of education. Rather than teaching students to think critically and independently, he explains, the educational system now focuses on creating successful employees who will support organizational perspectives.

In addition to considering these larger social impacts, it is helpful to think of the daily power of organizations in individual lives. Cheney and McMillan (1990) conclude that organizations have become so influential that they have "become, in many cases the individual's voice, source of authority and resource for identity" (p. 97). We define ourselves in part by the organizations to which we belong, whether they are fraternities or sororities, professional organizations, labor unions, churches, or the organizations for which we work. We make arguments based on affiliation with organizations, by claiming expert knowledge and information, and we allow organizations to speak for us when we endorse a political party, a social movement, or a church group.

Organizations do much good in society. They produce products and services that people need to live happy and healthy lives, they provide jobs that give both income and fulfillment to workers, and they contribute to the social and cultural lives of their surrounding communities. However, despite the good that organizations do, and their central place in our culture, they may also abuse their power. Some produce products that endanger lives and refuse to take responsibility for their actions; some exploit or mistreat workers by paying substandard wages or maintaining unsafe working conditions. Some may endanger the physical environment, and some may mislead investors through dishonest business practices. Surely, entities with this level of power over individuals and society should be studied carefully. One way to understand the values, goals, motives, and practices of all organizations is to examine the rhetoric that they produce.

Organizations Produce a Great Deal of Rhetoric

You are confronted with a vast number of organizational messages every day. If you wake up to the radio, the station is probably using rhetoric to establish or reinforce its identity in your head before you even get out of bed. When you drive onto campus, you see the banners promoting the identity and excellence of your school. If you have a job, the bulletin board in the break room likely holds messages trying to influence how you feel about your work, as well as how you perform it. Organizations produce a massive amount of discourse in a wide variety of forms, all of which is intended to persuade audiences to think, feel, or behave in a particular way. There are philosophical and practical reasons why it would be foolish not to study a phenomenon that is so widespread.

As you may have concluded from the sheer number of messages swirling around you, organizations are the largest producers of rhetoric in contemporary society. By analyzing the messages used to influence audiences, critics can note the actions and strategies of organizations using power responsibly, and challenge the actions and strategies of those that use it irresponsibly.

❖ GOALS FOR STUDYING ORGANIZATIONAL RHETORIC

Because we understand why it is important to pay attention to the rhetoric of organizations, we can examine the goals we hope to accomplish in doing so. Most critics of organizational rhetoric will pursue one or more of four goals when analyzing an artifact: (1) determining whether or not the rhetoric should have been effective, or how it could be more effective; (2) understanding and judging what is revealed by an organization's presentation of itself, including what values the organization claims to uphold; (3) understanding and judging the general role and power of organizations in society; and (4) improving understanding of theory about organizational rhetoric.

When examining a single piece of rhetoric, critics may seek to learn whether or not it seems well-crafted to meet its persuasive goal—in other words, should it have been effective? For example, a critic might study the produce industry's attempts to restore faith in the health value of its product following the ecoli outbreak of 2008. By looking at multiple samples, they can draw a conclusion about the overall effectiveness of rhetorical choices across situations. In another example, major U.S. retailer Wal-Mart has faced much negative publicity in recent years. Critics might conduct an analysis of several samples of the company's responses to controversy in order to make a judgment about its rhetorical choices.

Critics might also want to know what a particular piece of rhetoric reveals about the ethics or culture of an organization. Analysis of the Web site of a company at which you are interviewing, for example, might help you decide whether or not you would be comfortable with the company's policies and practices. Studying organizational rhetoric can also enlighten critics about the organization more generally and allow them to make judgments about whether an organization operates in an ethical manner. Viewing a wide range of rhetoric from a single organization can also allow a critic to learn more about the identity, values, and priorities of an organization. For example, if you want to get a sense of what is truly important at your university, you might do a close comparison of the mission statement and goals with other rhetoric such as newsletters or specific Web sites that might reinforce or contradict the stated mission and goals.

Critics might also study organizational rhetoric in order to learn about a national or international culture. Organizations are a tremendous force in contemporary society, and studying the messages of multiple organizations may help reveal what sorts of influence they have as well as the implications of that influence.

Finally, all rhetorical criticism, whether organizational or not, should contribute to our understanding of rhetorical theory. In the case of organizational rhetoric, there is a chance to help build a relatively new but growing body of general principles that help explain the area of study. For example, Rowland and Jerome (2004) explore a model to explain how organizations defend themselves in the face of accusation, and Kuhn (1997) proposes a model of how organizations can best manage public issue campaigns.

❖ PRACTICAL OUTCOMES OF STUDYING ORGANIZATIONAL RHETORIC

Being able to answer each of these four questions can make you both a wiser consumer and a wiser creator of organizational rhetoric. Rhetorical analysis provides the tools you need to make an informed judgment about whether a business moving to your neighborhood will have the benefits it claims in the pamphlet its representative leaves on your porch. These same tools will also allow you to make wiser choices about which organizations you support with your business and which you avoid. Finally, you will be able to think critically about what kind of organization you want to work in, and analyze the ways in which you allow that organization to control some elements of your life.

Being able to analyze organizational rhetoric can also make you a more effective and ethical producer of such rhetoric. Knowing what strategies are most effective in particular situations and knowing how rhetoric can be used to exercise or resist power can help you when you need to create messages for an organization. Organizations spend billions of dollars each year to produce rhetoric designed to accomplish a variety of goals. For example, in recent years, many fast food chains have attempted to alter the perceptions of consumers that fast food is unhealthy, and create new identities that include fast food as a healthy option. In addition, large energy producers have initiated campaigns to make their identities more environmentally friendly, and any number of organizations have needed to create messages to restore faith in their products or services following some sort of crisis. Public relations and other communication professionals design and execute each piece of discourse created by these organizations. With training and practice in organizational rhetoric, you could be one of those professionals. Even if you don't want a career focused on developing messages for organizations, understanding rhetorical situations and strategies in organizations will make you a more effective employee in a range of areas, including organizational development, training, sales, and strategic planning.

❖ A PROCESS FOR ANALYZING ORGANIZATIONAL RHETORIC

With an understanding of the reasons for studying organizational rhetoric, it is important to have an overview of how a critic approaches a sample of organizational rhetoric. This process also serves as the structure of the first half of this book, as we take beginning critics through each of the steps in the process of analyzing organizational rhetoric.

No matter which of the above goals they want to accomplish, critics must be systematic in their approach to analyzing organizational rhetoric. To be *systematic* means to use a standard set of practices or steps to reach a conclusion. As critics become more experienced, some of the steps may be modified or their order changed, and some may be done almost by reflex. For beginning critics, however, it is important to recognize and carry out each of the steps in the system. Several authors have developed systems for analyzing rhetoric (e.g., Campbell & Burkholder, 1997; Rowland, 2008). Even more authors have used systems to conduct rhetorical criticism, and we will discuss samples of that work throughout the book. Figure 1.2 summarizes a process for analyzing organizational rhetoric.

All rhetorical critics begin with the same basic descriptive process: (1) Identify the rhetorical strategies in the sample, and (2) describe the elements of the rhetorical situation for which the rhetoric was created. The first step, identifying the rhetorical strategies, requires the critic to examine the artifact many times using a list of the basic elements that appear most often in samples of organizational rhetoric. These elements have been discovered by rhetorical theorists and critics over the course of centuries. In Chapter 2 of this text, we catalog and explain rhetorical strategies that appear frequently in organizational rhetoric.

Figure 1.2 Process for Analyzing Organizational Rhetoric

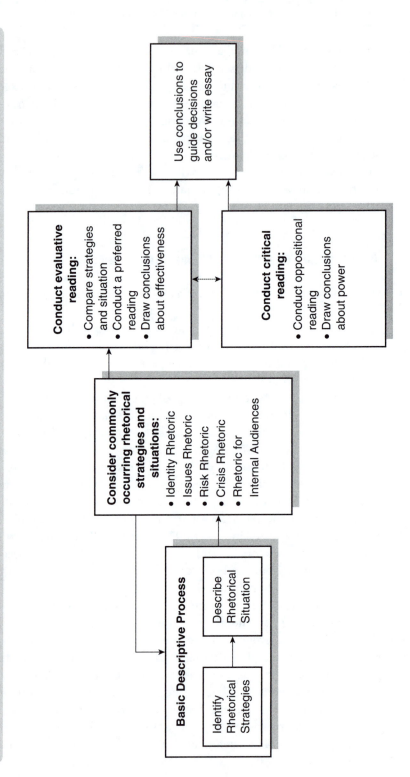

SOURCE: Adapted from Ford (1999).

The second step involves researching and describing the elements of the situation for which the rhetoric was created. Several scholars have provided theories to help explain rhetorical situations. We explain two approaches to describing the rhetorical situation in Chapter 3.

Once a critic has identified the rhetorical strategies and described the rhetorical situation, the third step is to consider whether the elements of the situation or patterns of strategies are the type that scholars have recognized as happening with frequency across a variety of organizations. If they are, the critic then reviews theory about those situations and strategies and uses that added knowledge to inform additional readings of the artifact. In Chapters 6 through 10, we introduce five sets of situational and strategic elements that appear with frequency in organizations: identity rhetoric, issue management rhetoric, risk management rhetoric, crisis management rhetoric, and rhetoric directed to internal audiences.

Fourth, using all he or she has learned in the first three steps, a critic must decide what type of question to ask about the rhetoric. All critics will approach their analysis from one of two larger perspectives. These perspectives are sets of assumptions about the purpose of rhetorical analysis and about how rhetoric works. In the case of organizational rhetoric, we identify two general approaches or ways to "read" texts—an evaluative approach and a critical approach.

The type of question being asked will determine whether the critic makes only an evaluative reading or also adds a critical reading of the rhetoric. Critics who want to determine how effectively a piece of rhetoric functions should proceed with an evaluative reading. An evaluative reading involves comparing the strategies with the elements of the situation to identify what the rhetor wanted to say, and how well he or she said it.

Critics who want to understand organizational positions or power in organizations will also complete an evaluative reading, but will follow that with a critical reading. A critical reading encourages the critic to ask questions about who has a voice in the organization's rhetoric, and about how much choice the audience has in understanding and influencing the organization. Neither the evaluative nor the critical reading can be completed without an understanding of both situations and basic rhetorical strategies. The theory behind the evaluative reading is discussed at the end of Chapter 3, and the theory behind the critical reading is discussed in Chapter 4. In Chapter 5, we present a more detailed discussion of the procedures for both types of analytical reading.

Finally, critics must apply the conclusions drawn from the evaluative and critical readings. For academic critics, the conclusions will result in a critical essay. For those tasked with creating organizational rhetoric, it may result in a list of strategies to remember in future situations; for practical critics, it may result in a decision about whether to support or work for a particular organization.

❖ CONCLUSION

This chapter sets the stage for our exploration of organizational rhetoric by defining our object of study. Organizational rhetoric is the strategic use of symbols by organizations to influence the thoughts, feelings, and behaviors of audiences important to the organization. Organizations are powerful and pervasive voices in contemporary society, and they exercise that power through the use of rhetoric. The chapters that follow explore ways to understand and analyze that power.

2

Identifying Rhetorical Strategies in Organizational Rhetoric

❖ ❖ ❖

Figure 2.1 Process for Analyzing Organizational Rhetoric (Rhetorical Strategies)

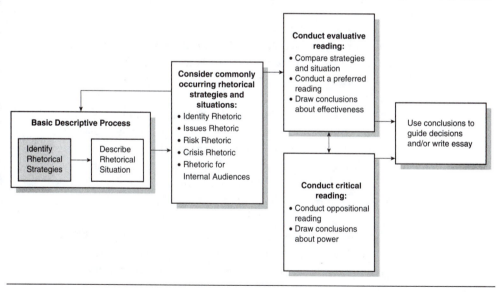

SOURCE: Adapted from Ford (1999).

Note the following message that appeared on a Web page for Cerner Corporation (2009), a health care information technology company in Kansas City, Missouri:

Spirit of Innovation: Since 1979, our three founders, Neal Patterson, Cliff Illig and Paul Gorup have focused on building a healthcare company that creates unmatched value for our clients.

Cerner has an entrepreneurial spirit. Our founders bet the company when we created the industry's first person-centric architecture—*Cerner Millennium.* Today, this multi-billion-dollar investment fuels the most comprehensive suite of clinical and healthcare management solutions in the world. (n.p.)

Consider for a moment how you react to this message. Does the idea of entrepreneurship (a value) or money (a need) appeal to you? How does language like "bet the company" or "first person-centric architecture" strike you? Would the fact that this text appears in the middle of a long home page for Cerner make a difference in how you pay attention to it? Does the statement that the company has invested billions of dollars in development (a claim) have an effect on you? In this chapter, we provide tools to help you identify rhetorical strategies like values, needs, claims, and language (and others) at work in any organizational text.

Use the series of Look Boxes incorporated throughout the chapter as a guide for conducting an analysis of organizational rhetoric. A summary worksheet of the look box activities is located at the end of the chapter (Worksheet for Identifying Rhetorical Strategies in Organizational Texts).

Critics begin slicing into a text by identifying the rhetorical strategies found in a piece of discourse. These strategies are the most basic elements commonly found in almost any sample of rhetoric, no matter what the rhetor's goals may be. A critic of organizational rhetoric must be able to identify the types of persuasive choices made by rhetors. Rowland (1999) explains that the goal of this descriptive analysis "is to see clearly what is being said and how the rhetoric is saying it" (p. 9). We see and hear so many messages each day that we often accept them at face value, but knowing how to see and name strategies will help us make more conscious choices about how we receive and act upon organizational rhetoric.

Whether your purpose is to decide if a particular piece of rhetoric meets its persuasive goal, or to determine how a piece of rhetoric reveals the use of power by an organization, learning to see the rhetorical strategies in a piece of discourse is the first step in becoming an informed consumer of rhetoric. Although people have been studying rhetoric for thousands of years, some of the oldest concepts still provide the best framework for understanding how messages work.

Rooted in the ideas of Aristotle, but refined and labeled by early Roman scholars of rhetoric, the *five canons of rhetoric* describe the five basic ingredients of any speech—the most traditional form of rhetoric. The five canons are as follows:

1. **Invention**—the development of ideas and support

2. **Organization**—the order in which ideas appear

3. **Style**—the use of language

4. **Memory**—how rhetoric is committed to memory

5. **Delivery**—the way that verbal and nonverbal actions contribute to the speech

Although the canon of memory is much less important than it was during the pinnacle of Greek and Roman culture (when far fewer people could write and using notes was a sign of weakness), the canons remain the foundation for analyzing organizational rhetoric.

Over the years, authors have built on the five canons of rhetoric and the ideas of Aristotle to develop systems for describing rhetorical strategies found in traditional rhetoric (Campbell, 1996; Campbell & Burkholder, 1997; Rowland, 2008). In the following section, we explain the fundamental rhetorical strategies found in most organizational rhetoric, and how you can use them to describe what you see when you examine an artifact. This list of strategies is based on classical theories of rhetoric, but also is informed by contemporary research in organizational communication and organizational rhetoric. These strategies are summarized in a worksheet at the end of this chapter.

❖ CANON OF INVENTION

The classical *canon of invention* refers to the creation and development of ideas in rhetoric. When critics analyze invention in a piece of organizational rhetoric, they identify the arguments made by the author and how they are supported and developed. Aristotle (trans. 1932) divided the types of arguments made from the evidence used to support them. He labeled the types of arguments artistic proofs and the evidence nonartistic proofs.

Artistic proofs are ideas generated by the rhetor himself or herself. They are actually "invented" by the rhetor for a particular piece of rhetoric. Aristotle divided artistic proofs into three types that still serve as the basis for contemporary discussion of proof in rhetoric. He said the rhetor created persuasion by building personal credibility (ethos), appealing to the emotions of the audience (pathos), or by making and supporting reasonable arguments (logos). In this section, we introduce the classical conception of each of these types of proof, and then discuss how they have been adapted to organizational rhetoric.

Ethos in Traditional Rhetoric

In discussing ethos, Aristotle (trans. 1932) contended that a speaker could persuade an audience by showing himself (rhetors were all men in ancient Greece) to be a good person. He wrote that

> the character of the speaker is a cause of persuasion when the speech is so uttered as to make him worthy of belief; for as a rule we trust men of probity more, and more quickly, about things in general, while on points outside the realm of exact knowledge, where opinion is divided, we trust them absolutely. (p. 8)

In other words, Aristotle argued that we always trust honest people more readily, and we rely on our judgment of honesty even more when the issue is one on which people disagree.

According to Aristotle (trans. 1932), a speaker with the persuasive power of ethos had three qualities—intelligence, character, and goodwill. Intelligence is fairly self-explanatory. An *intelligent* rhetor has made wise decisions based on knowledge and ability. The criterion of *character* compares the beliefs and actions of rhetors against the standards of the society in which they operate. *Goodwill* refers to whether or not rhetors demonstrate concern for their audiences.

Although Aristotle argued that ethos is generated in the speech itself, contemporary scholars also recognize the influence of reputation on credibility. Depending on the audience and the situation, rhetors have some level of inherent credibility that they can either build on or trade on in a particular situation. A speaker with a good reputation may be able to communicate negative ideas without getting a negative reaction. Modern conceptions of credibility also include the concept of *charisma*—the quality of being interpersonally attractive and enthusiastic.

Ethos in Organizational Rhetoric

As you learned in Chapter 1, identifying the "speaker" is much more difficult in organizational rhetoric than it is in traditional political rhetoric. Cheney and McMillan's (1990) idea of the *corporate person* also suggests that organizations would have corporate ethos. Just as people respond to organizational rhetoric as if it is coming from a single source, they also perceive organizations as if they have a shared character apart from the individual ethical judgments of owners and employees. You can probably name organizations that you perceive to have good character and some with more questionable character.

The complex nature of *organizational credibility* is explained in part by the theory of corporate social legitimacy (Hearit, 1995). In discussing how organizations respond to crisis, Hearit explains that organizations are accepted only if they demonstrate a balance between the costs and benefits to the communities in which they operate. This balance is labeled corporate social legitimacy. *Corporate social legitimacy* is accomplished when an organization persuades the community that it possesses two characteristics: competence and community. (Note: Corporate social legitimacy is closely related to the concept of *corporate social responsibility* [CSR]. For an emerging perspective on CSR, see McMillan, 2007.)

Competence is very similar to Aristotle's concept of intelligence. An organization must demonstrate that it can accomplish its goals—that it can produce a product or deliver a service that meets societal standards. When examining a piece of organizational rhetoric, a critic may find appeals to competence by identifying statements that claim that an organization's products or services are safe or effective, or that vouch for the financial stability of the company.

> **Look for** statements that claim that an organization's products or services are safe or effective, or that vouch for the financial stability of the company.

The second element of corporate social legitimacy is *community.* In order to be accepted, an organization must demonstrate that it operates as a responsible member of the larger community. This component is similar to the traditional rhetorical concepts of character and goodwill. Hearit (1995) explains that "a corporation's actions must be ethically defensible; that is, its acts must demonstrate responsibility, create trust, and be legal" (p. 3). A critic might identify appeals designed to create community by looking for claims about the charitable activities of the organization, or arguments that show that community members trust the organization. For example, in its rhetoric Target frequently reminds customers that when they use a Target credit card to make a purchase, the company donates a portion of the proceeds to a school of the customer's choice.

> **Look for** claims about the charitable activities of the organization or arguments that show that community members trust the organization.

Many organizations have found their corporate social legitimacy challenged in recent years. Public response to events at Enron Corporation provides excellent examples of violations of competence and community. Some people argued that Enron failed to operate competently by engaging in business practices that eventually led to the failure of the company. In addition, because executives and board members were able to sell stock while employees and other shareholders were left uninformed of looming problems, some argued that the organization demonstrated a lack of commitment to community. Enron's actions were perceived by many as irresponsible, untrustworthy, and illegal.

Although Hearit (1995) discusses corporate social legitimacy specifically in reference to rhetoric during crisis, the concept is useful for understanding how organizations can secure and maintain the social capital to operate in noncrisis situations as well. The contemporary notion of corporate social legitimacy helps tailor the traditional elements of credibility—intelligence, character, and goodwill—to the complex and unique idea of what it means for an organization to have credibility.

Pathos in Traditional Rhetoric

In addition to creating persuasion through personal credibility, Aristotle (trans. 1932) argued that a rhetor could sway an audience by putting them in a frame of mind that would make them more likely to accept the speaker's ideas. Aristotle indicated that this attitude was most effectively produced by arousing emotions in the audience. He wrote, "We give very different decisions under the sway of pain or joy, and liking or hatred" (p. 9). In other words, rhetors may accomplish their persuasive goals in part by using emotions to make audience members more receptive to the ideas being presented. Aristotle pursued his study of emotions as a persuasive force by cataloging a long list of feelings such as shame, anger, pity, and indignation, and explaining how those emotions are best created in the audience.

Aristotle's discussion of fear and shame, in particular, are reflected in the contemporary focus on emotional appeals as linked to needs and values (Rowland, 2008). Aristotle (trans. 1932) wrote that "fear may be defined as a pain or disturbance arising from a mental image of impending evil of a destructive or painful sort" (p. 107). He also explained that "shame will be aroused by such evils as are thought to bring disgrace to ourselves or those we care for" (p. 112). By calling audience attention to unmet needs, rhetors may create fear, and thus a desire to act. By linking their persuasive goals to commonly held societal values, rhetors may suggest that shame will result from failing to act on the message.

Contemporary conceptions of pathos often focus on how rhetors craft appeals that create and offer to satisfy needs, or that appeal to commonly held values. The effectiveness of appeals to needs and values is explained in part by *consistency theories.* These theories, often rooted in psychology, argue that human beings seek to maintain a state of logical and psychological balance (Festinger, 1962; Heider, 1946). By calling attention to unmet needs or showing a contradiction between values and behaviors, rhetors may create a sense of imbalance in their audience. Then they offer their audience a way to minimize the imbalance by altering a thought, feeling, or behavior.

Pathos in Organizational Rhetoric: Needs, Values, and Identification

Appeals to emotion are rhetorical strategies that often play an important role in organizational rhetoric. In this section, we examine more closely appeals to needs in organizational rhetoric, a specifically organizational approach to values as a source of persuasion, and the concept of identification as a source of emotion in organizational messages.

Needs

A number of psychologists, sociologists, and communication scholars have discussed the importance of needs in persuasion. Larson (2001) explains the significance of needs for humans: "[W]ithout them [particular needs being met] or some substitute, we feel frustrated, anxious, afraid, or even angry" (p. 136). Our needs have great power to move us. Organizational rhetors often use that power as they attempt to influence thoughts, feelings, and behaviors.

You are probably familiar with Maslow's (1943) *hierarchy of needs.* Maslow argued that humans have five types of needs that are arranged in order of priority. He placed physiological needs at the bottom of his hierarchy, making them the most basic. He followed them with safety, love and belonging, esteem, and self-actualization. By analyzing the needs most often appealed to by advertisers, advertising scholar Vance Packard (1964) found that humans were susceptible to the needs for emotional security, reassurance of worth, ego gratification, creative outlets, love objects, a sense of power, roots, and immortality. Yet another catalog of needs comes from Schutz (1958), who argued that humans communicate to meet one of three basic needs: affection, inclusion, and control.

No matter which list of needs you find most useful, they all function in the same way in rhetoric. Rhetors recognize that humans have needs, and they find ways to appeal to those needs in order to motivate some change in thought, feeling, or action. If, for example, an organization sends out a pamphlet asking employees to make payroll-deduction contributions to the United Way or some other charitable organization, the authors may suggest that every contribution is important—thus appealing to the need for reassurance of worth. If an employer needs workers to stay late, he or she may appeal to the need for inclusion or love and belonging by advocating that teammates stick together until the job is completed.

Appeals to needs are also found in rhetoric directed at external audiences. For example, when a company that poses possible environmental or social hazards wants to move into a neighborhood, public relations and other communication professionals at the company might argue that the organization will create jobs. Thus, the organization may offer many community members the opportunity to meet the basic physiological needs of food and shelter. In the midst of a controversy over the construction of new coal-fired power plants in Texas, one organization, Texans for Affordable and Reliable Power, used an appeal to safety and emotional security in an advertisement suggesting that failing to build new power plants would result in blackouts across the state. The organization then offered an option for avoiding the fear of blackouts: "[L]et's have the politicians and energy companies work together to build additional power generation and make sure Texas doesn't become another blackout casualty like some other states" (advertisement in *Austin American-Statesman*, February 22, 2007; see ad in Figure 2.2, p. 52).

When examining a piece of organizational rhetoric, critics can identify appeals to needs by looking for statements that identify an existing audience need or create a new need similar to those listed by Maslow (1943), Packard (1964), or Schutz (1958).

> **Look for** statements that identify an existing audience need or create a new need.

Values

As outlined above, Aristotle (trans. 1932) suggested that negative emotions result when we fear that we may be disgraced, or that others will view us negatively. One situation in which others might view us negatively is if we violate commonly held social values. *Values* are generally agreed-upon ideas of what is right or wrong or good and bad in a society. Some values you might think of immediately might be honesty, hard work, and respect for authority. In 1962, Steele and Redding assembled a list of 18 commonly held American values, including achievement and success, change and progress, equality of opportunity, external conformity, and patriotism. It is likely that American values have changed somewhat since the 1960s, but the idea that a society generally agrees about what is right or wrong, or good or bad, has not.

Value appeals in organizational rhetoric are often statements meant to demonstrate that the values of the organization align with the values of the audience or society in general. For example, in the wake of the September 11, 2001, attacks on the World Trade Center and the Pentagon, many businesses incorporated the value of patriotism into their advertising and other messages. Lowe's Home Improvement distributed free "Power of Pride" bumper stickers, and Chevrolet argued that purchasing a new vehicle would show faith and support for the United States. By demonstrating shared values in one or more areas, organizational rhetors attempt to build agreement in other areas.

Organizational communication scholars Bostdorff and Vibbert (1994) have paid particular attention to how values are used in organizational rhetoric. After studying many organizational messages, they concluded that organizations use a practice called *values advocacy* in much of their rhetoric. In discussing this type of appeal, we first explain what it can accomplish, and then we describe the four specific strategies discovered by Bostdorff and Vibbert.

Organizational rhetors advocate values to accomplish one of three goals (Bostdorff & Vibbert, 1994). First, appeals to values may be used to enhance the image of the organization. By referencing things that are viewed by the audience as good or right, organizational rhetors can create positive overall thoughts about the organization. For example, when we hear that a major corporation has donated a large amount of money to charity, we may feel more positively about the organization than we did before we knew about the contribution.

Second, appeals to values may be able to help minimize the impact of criticism of an organization. If a company's corporate social legitimacy is in question, rhetors may reference values upheld by the organization in order to distract audiences from the violation, or to demonstrate that the values of the organization are inconsistent with the accusations being made against them. For example, when Wal-Mart was sued for discrimination against women and minorities, a large number of messages on their Web site referred to values of equality and concern for employees.

Finally, Bostdorff and Vibbert (1994) assert that appeals to values may be used to help prepare audiences to accept future arguments about policy issues. If an organization can establish that particular values (like access to employment or economic growth) are important, then it may be easier to get the audience to accept future arguments about a policy or regulation. We will discuss these goals more fully as we talk about specific rhetorical situations throughout the book.

In their research, Bostdorff and Vibbert (1994) also identified four strategies that rhetors use to appeal to values: explicit appeals, linking organizational activities to values, discussing how the organization contributes to social causes, and using examples of individuals who uphold particular values.

First, organizations may make *explicit appeals* to values held in common by audience members. For example, Caterpillar Corporation bases its code of conduct, which functions for both internal and external audiences, on four commonly shared values: integrity, excellence, teamwork, and commitment (www.cat.com). These four value terms are used throughout the document, and could enhance the image of the organization and defuse possible questions about its business practices.

When using the second strategy of values advocacy, those creating rhetoric show how the organization's products and services *uphold shared values*. For example, a pharmaceutical company advertisement appealed to ideas that an audience would view positively when it stated, "Our goal at Pfizer is to discover and develop innovative medicines, help make them available to patients, share health information, and partner on public health programs" (Pfizer Inc., 2007).

Third, organizations may appeal to values by discussing their *participation in philanthropic or charitable activities*. One long-running Phillip Morris advertising campaign showed examples of employees delivering meals to older people, tutoring children, or providing assistance following natural disasters. Although these activities have nothing to do with the products of the organization, they may help to enhance its overall image.

Finally, communication professionals might show how the values of the organization align with the values of the audience by *praising individuals who enact those values*. For example, when University of Texas basketball coach Jody Conradt retired after more than 30 years and 900 wins, a State Farm Insurance Company advertisement stated, "Without her dedication, caring, and leadership, women's basketball would not be where it is today. Thank you, Jody, for making us proud to be a premier sponsor of women's athletics and a founding member of the Women's Basketball Hall of Fame" (advertisement in *Austin American-Statesman*, March 17, 2007). By citing virtues associated with the coach, State Farm implied that it shares and supports those virtues, thus encouraging audiences to view it more positively. The advertisement says nothing about insurance, only about values.

Value appeals take a wide variety of forms and serve key functions in organizational rhetoric. When analyzing a piece of rhetoric for values, critics should look for statements or images that appeal to ideas that are commonly viewed as good or right in society. It is also helpful to look for the four specific strategies outlined by Bostdorff and Vibbert (1994).

> **Look for** four specific strategies: appeals to shared values, examples of how organizational practices uphold shared values, discussion of charitable activities, and praise of individuals who embody shared values.

Identification

The concept of identification is related to both needs and values, and is an additional form of pathos often found in organizational rhetoric. Kenneth Burke (1937/1984) argued that human beings are inherently separated from one another because we can share our thoughts, feelings, and so forth to only a limited degree. He posited that we attempt to overcome that division by creating connections through language, and he called this process seeking *identification*. Burke asserted that humans create their individual identities in part by piecing together their affiliations with larger groups. He wrote, "The so-called 'I' is merely a unique combination of partially 'conflicting we's'," and "in America it is natural for a man to identify himself with the business corporation he serves" (p. 264).

The idea that people get their identities in part from the groups to which they belong is important to those who study rhetoric in organizations. Your current status as a student at a particular college or university is part of your identity, as is your membership in campus organizations or religious groups, or as an employee if you have a job. Concern with the overall welfare of an organization, the use of the term *we* to refer to the organization, and the use of organizational logos or buzzwords are all signs that someone is identified with an organization.

The human desire to identify is strong—think about how strongly people feel about the sports teams with which they identify, even though the fate of the team usually has no direct bearing on their lives. People purchase clothing, engage in heated arguments with family and friends, and often experience strong emotional reactions to their team's victory or defeat. In the 1950s, and again in the 1990s, the Green Bay Packer football team held a stock sale to raise money to support the team. Thousands of Packer fans purchased the stock, which had little to no monetary value; it simply allowed holders to attend the annual meeting and claim that they were a part of the organization.

Identification is an important concept for those who create or study organizational rhetoric. Although the act of identifying is performed by individuals, Burke (1937/1984) and Cheney (1983) point out that organizations, through the use of rhetoric, attempt to provide individuals with reasons to identify. It is in the best interest of an organization to build and maintain identification among members. Identification is important, not as an end in itself, but because of its persuasive power. People who are highly identified with an organization are more likely to make decisions that benefit that organization (Tompkins & Cheney, 1985).

Much of the internal rhetoric created by organizations—items like newsletters, training materials, and employee events—have as one of their goals creating and maintaining identification on the part of employees. Even people who are not employees may identify with an organization, so rhetors directing messages to external audiences also try to invite identification. Certainly stockholders want to feel a part of a company in which they have invested. Brand loyalty is also a sign of identification among external audiences—using the product or service has made the consumer feel a part of the organization, and they reinforce that sense of belonging by continuing to purchase the brand.

After examining a collection of organizational newsletters, Cheney (1983) identified strategies that organizational rhetors use to solicit identification from audience members. He based his analysis in Burke's (1937/1984) three basic approaches to creating identification. Burke argued that identification could be created through the use of the common ground technique, identification by antithesis, and the use of an assumed "we." After his study, Cheney added a fourth, the use of unifying symbols.

When using the *common ground technique,* rhetors demonstrate that they share things in common with the audience. Individuals are more likely to identify with an organization that aligns itself with goals, values, and ideals similar to their own. Cheney (1983) discovered six specific tactics that organizations use to create a sense of commonality with their employees; each of these is a rhetorical strategy that a critic might identify in a sample of organizational rhetoric. Cheney found that rhetors expressed concern for individuals in the organization, recognized the work of specific individuals, advocated shared values, promoted benefits and activities provided by the organization, quoted outsiders who had praised the organization, and provided testimonials by employees speaking positively about the organization.

Table 2.1 provides an example of each of these strategies from contemporary organizational rhetoric. Some elements of the common ground technique are similar to the strategies of values

Table 2.1 Samples of Common Ground Strategies

Common Ground Appeal	Example From Organizational Newsletter
Expression of concern for the individual	"To me, the Century Family means that we, as a company, in all circumstances, maintain true and genuine concern for employees . . . we take utmost care and responsibility when making decisions that affect them."
Recognition of individual contributions	"On Thursday, June 20 . . . our Emergency Room Staff was faced with SWGH's worst trauma yet. The Emergency Room staff took immediate action to stabilize the patient and transport safely to the nearest Trauma Center." (A list of staff names follows.)
Espousal of shared values	A newsletter included a graphic with the following terms on the opening page: "Unifying Principles: Fairness, Honesty and Integrity, Commitment to Excellence, Positive Attitude, Respect, Faith, Perseverance."
Advocacy of benefits and activities	"We are happy to announce the introduction of our new Pet Insurance provider—Veterinary Pet Insurance."
Praise by outsiders	"The ER staff also received direct compliments on a job well done by SAPD for having handled everything calmly and proficiently."
Testimonials by employees	In one newsletter, an employee tells the story of having her coworkers build a Habitat for Humanity home for her family.

SOURCE: Common Ground Appeal column from Cheney, 1983.

advocacy. The organization invites individuals to identify by demonstrating that it recognizes and appreciates the individuals who make up the organization, and that it shares values in common with those individuals.

When using a second strategy, *identification by antithesis*, rhetors create a sense of unity and belonging by showing that the organization and the audience share a common enemy. The "enemy" is sometimes another organization, but it may be an idea or a social problem as well. Cheney (1983) found that the enemies portrayed in newsletters were often the agencies that regulated the activities of the organization. Other common enemies might be competing organizations or protestors.

A third identification strategy invites audience members to identify with an organization by using the term *we* in a way that includes audience members as part of the organization. Cheney (1983) called this the *assumed or transcendent "we."* By using the term *we* in discourse, rhetors create the sense that everyone in the audience is important, and that all members share the views of the organization. This strategy is found frequently in policy statements from executives as well as in articles designed to create a sense of shared values and goals.

Finally, Cheney (1983) found that organizations use unifying symbols to invite identification from their members. We are all familiar with the distinctive symbols of contemporary organizations including the "brown" of UPS, the "swoosh" of Nike, and the symbols used by Coke and Pepsi. The use of unifying symbols in organizational rhetoric helps to reinforce the identity of the organization, and may even allow individuals to wear those symbols of their identification.

Cheney's (1983) work on organizational identification offers a helpful catalog of identification-related rhetorical strategies for a critic to look for in discourse. Although he focused on internally directed discourse, the strategies are also apparent in discourse designed for audiences outside of the organization.

Appeals to needs, values, and identification are all strategies that may create an emotional response in the audience, and thus move them to modify their thoughts, feelings, and ultimately behavior toward an organization. Critics should look carefully for examples of these rhetorical strategies in any sample of organizational rhetoric.

> **Look for** identification-related rhetorical strategies including common-ground appeals, identification by antithesis, the transcendent "we," and unifying symbols.

Logos in Traditional Rhetoric

The final form of artistic proof is *logos,* which refers to the use of arguments and reasoning. Aristotle (trans. 1932) devoted a great deal of his book, *Rhetoric,* to explaining how logical arguments are effectively built and supported. Contemporary discussions of argument and reasoning build on the work of Aristotle. We begin with a discussion of the basic principles of argument in rhetoric, and then discuss how these basics appear in organizational rhetoric.

Karl Wallace (1963) defined an *argument* as a claim supported by good reasons. All arguments have three parts: the *claim,* or the idea that the rhetor wants to prove true; the *evidence* or data that support the claim; and the *reasoning,* the logical leap that connects the evidence with the claim or that makes it possible for the evidence to prove the claim to be true.

A *claim* is the conclusion of any argument, traditional or organizational—it is the idea that the rhetor is asking the audience to accept. Claims may be about facts, values, or policies. Organizations make claims of fact when they claim that they have higher profits than their competitors. They make claims of value when they argue that their products or services are superior to those of others. Finally, organizational rhetors make claims of policy when they argue in favor of or against a particular piece of regulatory legislation that may affect how they do business. For example, rhetors for the automobile industry may argue against legislation calling for higher fuel-efficiency standards if they feel that the legislation will have a negative impact on profits, or that it will not help solve the problem of climate change.

If an audience is to find a claim persuasive, it must be supported. The second part of any argument is the *evidence* that provides this support. We discuss evidence later in this chapter. In order for an argument to be well-constructed, the evidence must be accurate, objective, qualified, and timely.

The final component of any argument is *reasoning,* or the logical connection between claim and evidence. It is often difficult to identify the logical leap in arguments because most of the arguments we hear and make leave the reasoning unstated. One goal of studying organizational rhetoric is to be able to recognize and critique the reasoning used in messages. In the following subsections, we explore basic concepts of reasoning and illustrate how they may function as strategies in organizational rhetoric.

Logos in Organizational Rhetoric: Inductive and Deductive Reasoning

Aristotle identified two types of reasoning—inductive and deductive. We use each of them every day, often without conscious thought. As critics of organizational rhetoric, though, it is important to be able to identify how rhetors use reasoning to accomplish their goals. Each argument presented in a sample of rhetoric is an example of a rhetorical strategy.

Inductive Reasoning

Inductive reasoning begins with specific instances accepted by the audience, and ends with a more general conclusion that had not been accepted by the audience before they saw or heard the argument. When an organization gives its audience examples of several charitable actions (donating money and supplies or participating in local projects), and then claims that it is good for the community, those creating rhetoric for the organization are asking the audience to reason inductively.

The above argument is a good example of the hidden nature of reasoning. The organization may state the evidence by listing the examples, using photos or video, or providing testimony from participants. They may also state the claim, concluding the rhetoric with a statement like, "We are proud to be good citizens of our community." They are unlikely, however, to explicitly state their reasoning. By pairing the claim and evidence as they do, they are appealing to an unstated idea that contributing money, supplies, and effort qualifies as being a good corporate citizen. When we accept their argument, we accept that unstated reasoning.

Any sample of organizational rhetoric may contain any or all of three types of inductive reasoning—reasoning by example, reasoning by analogy, and causal reasoning. The illustration above is an example of inductive *reasoning by example.* This type of reasoning is very common in traditional rhetoric, in organizational rhetoric, and even in everyday conversation. Whenever we generalize to a larger claim from a number of specific examples, we are using argument by example. In this case, the audience is asked to move from known examples provided by the organization to an unknown general conclusion that the organization is a responsible member of the community. The audience cannot be certain of the conclusion, but based on the examples and a belief that the future will resemble the past, they can infer the conclusion. Audience members may then use the argument to support later behavior on behalf of the organization.

Because we use inductive reasoning so often, and are so used to hearing it, we often use it inaccurately. By asking four questions, we can be certain that reasoning by example is valid. The first question to consider is whether enough examples have been considered to justify the conclusion. For example, does the organization present enough examples of its charitable activities to lead a reasonable person to the conclusion that it is a good citizen, or does it present only one or two examples over a period of many years? Drawing an inductive conclusion after examining too few examples is known as making a *hasty generalization,* and can result in poor conclusions.

The second question to consider is whether the examples being used are *representative* of the other examples that exist. Audience members cannot accurately make a generalization on a few examples that could be exceptions to the norm. For example, a critic should ask if there are more examples of negative community behavior that might outweigh the positive examples. Third, audiences and critics should consider whether the examples provided are *relevant* to the conclusion being drawn. For instance, examples of high profits or innovative design would not be relevant to a claim about community citizenship. Finally, in order to accurately draw a general conclusion from a series of examples, audience members must account for any *counterexamples*. If there are few examples that contradict the examples used to support the argument, can they be explained? Perhaps the organization failed to make a contribution to a community charity when the organization was having a particularly difficult year financially.

Reasoning by example is often extended into a second type of inductive reasoning, *reasoning by analogy*, when we move from the general conclusion (this company is a good citizen) to a specific conclusion that will often guide our behaviors (they are likely to donate to my preferred cause, so I will give them my business). In addition to asking the questions, we would ask about reasoning by example, we need to ask whether the specific example about which we are making a decision is *similar* to the examples we used to reach the general conclusion. For example, is your preferred cause similar to the other causes usually supported by the organization?

A third type of inductive reasoning, *causal reasoning*, is concerned with establishing a relationship between an apparent cause and an apparent effect. It is considered inductive reasoning because we move from a specific, known cause or effect, to an unknown effect or cause. For example, organizational executives might make an argument to stockholders that decreased profits have been caused by economic conditions rather than by executive error. In this case, the argument begins with the effect—executives and stockholders know that profits have decreased. The claim of the argument is about the cause—executives want stockholders to believe that the cause is economic. When evaluating reasoning from cause to effect or effect to cause, two questions are important: Is the alleged cause strong enough to have created the alleged effect, and is there some other possible cause that could have happened between the alleged cause and the alleged effect?

> **Look for** arguments built on examples. Identify and evaluate the claims and evidence supporting these arguments. Use the questions in this section on inductive reasoning as a guide.

Deductive Reasoning

A second method of reasoning works in the opposite direction: from a general, already accepted idea, to a conclusion about a specific instance. For example, many people accept the *general* idea that in order for a company to be considered responsible, it must treat employees fairly. Because they accept this general idea, when presented with the *specific* example of an organization that fails to treat employees fairly, they will conclude that the organization in question is not responsible.

Aristotle laid out this kind of reasoning in the form of a *categorical syllogism* with a major premise (all responsible organizations treat employees fairly), a minor premise (WorldWide Inc. does not treat employees fairly), and a conclusion (WorldWide Inc. is not a responsible organization). Another example of an organizational syllogism is, "What is good for my organization is good for me" (major premise); "This legislation is good for the organization" (minor premise); therefore, "This legislation is good for me" (conclusion). This conclusion may result in behavior designed to support the legislation, such as sending an email to an elected official to ask for support.

Rather than using a formal syllogism, which requires that all three parts be clearly stated in any argument, most rhetoric uses what is called an enthymeme. An *enthymeme* has come to be understood as a syllogism where one (or more) of the parts is left unstated. The audience then fills in the missing element based on knowledge that they share with the author (Delia, 1970). Just as it is sometimes difficult to identify the reasoning in an inductive argument, it is often difficult to recognize a syllogism because we are so used to filling in premises that we may not even realize they exist.

Tompkins and Cheney (1985) used the concept of enthymeme to help explain how organizations influence decisions made by members. They argued that as individuals become identified with an organization, they are likely to accept major premises offered by organizational leaders, and use those premises to help make decisions. Tompkins and Cheney called these organizational premises *decision premises*. For example, many people accept the idea that when they are at work, they should do things that will benefit the organization rather than themselves. This is a decision premise. When these employees are presented with a situation where, for example, working late would be good for the company (even if it isn't necessarily good for them), their acceptance of the major premise will lead them to agree to work late (the conclusion). These decision premises, or general principles that guide employee beliefs and actions, are introduced and reinforced in organizational rhetoric that appears in newsletters, on Web sites, in messages from organizational leaders, and even in some corporate décor like motivational posters.

Just as there are questions that help us evaluate inductive reasoning, there are two questions we need to consider when analyzing deductive reasoning. In philosophy or argumentation, these elements are known as truth and validity. For the sake of understanding arguments made by organizations, however, critics should simply ask if the information in the premises is information that the audience would accept as *accurate*. For example, would audience members agree that in order to be considered responsible organizations must treat employees fairly, or that what is good for an organization is good for members of that organization? Second, critics need to ask if the *parts of the argument fit together*—in other words, is there a connection between the items in the major premise and the minor premise and between both premises and the conclusion? For example, if the major premise is about treatment of employees, the minor premise and conclusion cannot be about charitable donations or environmental responsibility.

Look for arguments built on principles generally accepted by the audience. Evaluate those arguments based upon whether they are accurate and whether the parts of the argument fit well together.

It is important that critics carefully identify and analyze the rhetorical strategies of claims, evidence, and reasoning that appear in organizational rhetoric. Making arguments is a key way in which organizations seek to influence the thoughts, feelings, and behaviors of audiences.

Interdependence of Ethos, Pathos, and Logos

Although most discussions of the three modes of proof (credibility, emotion, and reasoning) tend to separate them into distinct categories, it is clear that they are often intertwined and interdependent. Appeals that build credibility may require the use of claims and evidence to establish that the organization does indeed enact competence and community. Appeals built on reasoning and argument will be more effective if the audience believes the speaker to be credible, and if the audience members' emotional state makes them receptive to the logical argument. Organizations may also appeal to commonly held values (pathos) in order to build credibility with audiences. Although it is important that you are able to identify elements of ethos, pathos, and logos in organizational rhetoric, it is also important to recognize that their uses will often overlap.

Evidence in Organizational Rhetoric

In addition to an extended discussion of the artistic proofs of ethos, pathos, and logos, Aristotle (trans. 1932) outlined the importance of nonartistic proofs. *Nonartistic proofs* are materials that already exist, and need only to be put to use by a rhetor. In Aristotle's time, these proofs included "witnesses, admissions under torture, written contracts, and the like" (p. 8). A more contemporary and less violent catalog of nonartistic proofs includes examples, statistics, and testimony.

Examples are individual instances of a phenomenon. As illustrated above, if a company wants to persuade an audience that it has corporate social legitimacy, the spokesperson might use several examples from charitable programs to support his argument. In a sense, *statistics* count examples. They are a numerical representation of a larger group of phenomena. A spokesperson might also use a statistic as proof that her organization has corporate social legitimacy. She might explain, for example, that 20% of yearly profit is donated to various charities. Rhetors generally use testimony by relaying the opinion of another person, either an expert or a layperson. To use testimony to address the scenario above, the spokesperson might quote a community member who benefited from the contributions of the organization.

No matter which type of evidence is used, a critic should always evaluate it against some basic standards. In order to be considered useful or reliable, evidence should be accurate, come from a qualified source, be reasonably objective, and be timely. *Accurate evidence* is gathered in a reliable manner. Accurate examples are relevant and typical of other examples. Accurate statistics are the result of sufficient sample size, as well as correct gathering and processing of data. *Qualified evidence* comes from sources with experience or expertise in the area being discussed. Information about the qualifications of sources should be included in the rhetoric. *Objective evidence* is information that is relatively neutral. *Timely evidence* has been gathered close to the date of the release of the discourse.

Although evidence is most clearly useful in supporting arguments that fall under the artistic proof of logos, it is also important to consider the role of evidence in supporting appeals to credibility and emotions. Organizational rhetors who wish to create an impression of corporate social legitimacy need to provide evidence for their claims. For example, financial planning companies may provide statistics to demonstrate how the investments of their clients have matured, thus supporting the idea of competence. In recent television advertisements, major pharmaceutical firms have used testimony from patients who have received free or reduced-price drugs to demonstrate that the companies are concerned for their communities. Recent rhetoric produced by energy companies has included examples of steps taken to reduce the environmental impact of energy production. Organizational rhetors may also rely on evidence to support claims about needs and values. Statistics, testimony, or examples may serve to illustrate that a need exists for individuals or a community, or to illustrate that an organization truly enacts a value that it claims to hold.

> **Look for** instances of testimony, statistics, and examples. Evaluate whether that evidence is accurate, comes from a qualified source, is reasonably objective, and is timely.

❖ CANON OF ORGANIZATION IN ORGANIZATIONAL RHETORIC

Obviously, invention is a complex and important element of persuasion, but the classical canon of organization is also important in understanding how organizational rhetoric works. *Organization* refers to where arguments are placed within a speech, Web site, newsletter, advertisement, or other sample of organizational discourse. You probably spent time in your introductory public speaking class learning about the organization of speeches. You know that all speeches should have an introduction, a body, and a conclusion. You may also recall that informative main points may be presented in order of time (chronological), physical order (spatial), or by subtopics (topical). Persuasive speeches are sometimes organized with the strongest argument first or last, or by cause and effect, or problem and solution. Because of the varied purposes and forms of organizational rhetoric, the structure of organizational artifacts is much more complex than the structure of most public speeches.

The primary question to consider when analyzing the arrangement in a piece of organizational rhetoric is, "What impact does the organization of the ideas have on the overall effectiveness or impression of the rhetoric?" Three specific questions can help account for how ideas are arranged in most organizational rhetoric.

First, critics should ask how the rhetoric gets the *attention* of the audience. Audiences are surrounded by vast amounts of information at all times—effective rhetoric must stand out from the enormous number of messages people receive each day. In speeches, attention-getting devices have been things like anecdotes, startling statistics, or vivid descriptions. Some of these traditional elements will still get audience attention in more contemporary organizational rhetoric; however, graphics, sound, and layout can also serve this purpose. When examining a selection of organizational rhetoric, critics need to ask what elements function to attract audience members to the rhetoric and encourage them to spend time reading, looking, or listening.

Second, critics should ask about the *order* in which the ideas appear in the rhetoric. In addition to determining how the rhetor initially attempts to connect with the audience, critics must also describe what the main arguments are, in what order they are presented, and the impact of that order on the rhetoric as a whole. When analyzing speeches or printed texts, it is sometimes easy to identify an organizational pattern because a speech or a text occurs in a predetermined order. Television or radio advertisements also flow in a predetermined order.

The task becomes more difficult with messages that are not inherently ordered—when looking at a Web site, for example, receivers work their way through the messages in no predetermined order. No matter which form of rhetoric critics are analyzing, it is helpful to identify the traditional organizational patterns and combinations of those patterns, if possible. Critics should try to determine if points are made in a chronological, topical, causal, or problem-solution pattern, or in a pattern that places strongest arguments first or last.

Third, critics should ask about how the rhetor *concludes* the discourse. Although much contemporary organizational rhetoric does not flow in a linear manner, it is still important to determine how the rhetor invites the audience to exit the discourse. In traditional rhetoric, a closing often includes a call to action for the audience. This often holds true for organizational rhetoric as well. Rhetors may ask the audience to visit another link, request more information, donate money, or sign a petition. Sometimes, however, organizational rhetoric may not have a specific call to action because it may be designed solely to create premises for future action. In either case, critics should be able to explain how the rhetoric concludes.

> **Look for** ways in which the creator of the rhetoric captures the audience's attention, orders the arguments, and concludes the message.

❖ CANON OF STYLE IN ORGANIZATIONAL RHETORIC

Style, traditionally referred to as elocution, is the third canon of rhetoric. It plays a key role in organizational rhetoric. *Style* refers to the aesthetic or artistic choices made by the rhetor in order to make the message more persuasive. In traditional rhetorical analysis, studies of style have been concerned with language devices such as metaphor, hyperbole, alliteration, and parallel structure. These language tools are still useful for organizational rhetors, but those analyzing contemporary rhetoric also pay attention to visual and aural elements of style. For example, organizational Web sites often use visual aesthetics such as color, graphics, still photographs, and video. They may also include audio effects such as music, sound effects, and the recorded voices of organizational executives.

In general, when studying a selection of organizational rhetoric, critics should consider any impact stylistic devices may have on the overall presentation of a piece of rhetoric. A few specific questions about the nature and functions of the stylistic choices can assist in the analysis of style. First, critics simply need to describe the devices present in the rhetoric. In this step, they can look for interesting word choices or word order, and graphics or music that attract attention. Second, they need to determine what purpose(s) the devices serve in the rhetoric. Devices may gain or hold attention, arouse emotion, provide evidence for claims, serve as a major or minor premise in an argument, or provide a guide to the structure of the rhetoric. Finally, critics need to assess the impact of the stylistic choices made by the organizational rhetor. They need to determine if the aesthetic choices reinforce the verbal message, contradict the verbal message, or perhaps distract from the verbal message.

Branding is an important and largely stylistic practice in organizational rhetoric. Brands are composed of visual and verbal elements that come to represent the identity of an organization. They may include elements such as a "name, letters, numbers, a symbol, a signature, a shape, a slogan, a colour [sic], a particular typeface" (Blackett, 2004). Critics of organizational rhetoric need to ask how the aesthetic elements of the brand are evident in the rhetoric of an organization. For example, the Nike swoosh is often the only obvious signal of what company a television advertisement is promoting. The recognizable nature of the brand plays an important stylistic role in the rhetoric.

> **Look for** interesting language choices, graphics, video, music, or elements of the organization's brand.

❖ CANON OF DELIVERY IN ORGANIZATIONAL RHETORIC

In classical rhetoric, the canon of delivery was concerned with how a speaker used his voice and body to present and support the ideas of the speech. In those times, face-to-face speeches were the only outlet available for sharing ideas with public audiences. Ever since mass distribution of writing was simplified by the invention of the printing press, the methods available for delivery of ideas have continued to expand. People who create rhetoric for contemporary organizations can choose to deliver their messages through a wide range of print, broadcast, and Internet outlets. When analyzing organizational rhetoric, it is important for a critic to consider how organizational rhetors disseminate their messages. A blog will reach a different audience and have a different tone than a press release, and both of these will operate differently from a message on Twitter. An in-person event will work differently from a group on Facebook. When considering the canon of delivery in organizational rhetoric, a critic should ask if the choice of outlet reinforces or contradicts the messages being sent.

> **Look for** ways the delivery method reinforces or contradicts messages developed with other strategies. Ask if the delivery method is well-suited to the audience.

❖ INTERDEPENDENCE OF INVENTION, ORGANIZATION, STYLE, AND DELIVERY IN ORGANIZATIONAL RHETORIC

Just as ethos, pathos, and logos overlap and work together, the canons of invention, organization, style, and delivery are also interdependent. Stylistic elements may serve as evidence for arguments, or they may help to signal the organization of a piece of discourse. The order of arguments (organization) is also tied to how the arguments function (invention) and perhaps to the appearance of the rhetoric (style). The choice of outlet for the messages (delivery) should be linked to questions of style. Critics should not be surprised or frustrated if they have difficulty placing every rhetorical strategy in the discourse clearly in a category. It is most important that critics are able to recognize and describe the basic strategies of organizational rhetoric. Whether taking an evaluative or critical approach to analyzing organizational rhetoric, all critics must begin by identifying the rhetorical strategies in the rhetoric being studied.

❖ CANON OF MEMORY IN ORGANIZATIONAL RHETORIC

As was mentioned earlier, one of the traditional canons, memory, is missing from our discussion. *Memory* is concerned with how traditional speakers committed speeches to memory when reading and writing was a much less common skill. Although it is important that you can name and explain all five canons, it is unlikely that the canon of memory will play a role in the organizational rhetoric that you analyze.

❖ SPECIAL SITUATIONS AND RHETORICAL STRATEGIES

In addition to these fundamental rhetorical strategies, some strategies or combinations of strategies are associated with organizational rhetoric designed to accomplish particular recurring goals. Once a critic has identified the rhetorical strategies in an artifact, and—as you will learn in the next chapter—described the situation in which the rhetoric was created, he or she can determine if it will be helpful to look at more specific strategies. In Chapters 6 through 10, we discuss the theories and strategies behind five commonly occurring types of organizational rhetoric.

❖ CONCLUSION

Being able to identify fundamental rhetorical strategies is an important step in any analysis of organizational rhetoric. In this chapter, we have discussed the canons of invention (the artistic proofs of ethos, pathos, and logos, as well as nonartistic proofs), organization, style, and delivery, and their application in organizational rhetoric. Table 2.2 is a guide for summarizing the differences and similarities among the traditional

Table 2.2   Rhetorical Strategies: Traditional Strategies in Contemporary Forms

Aristotle's Canons	Overarching Rhetorical Categories	Traditional Forms	Forms as Found in Organizational Rhetoric	
Invention	Ethos/ Credibility	Intelligence Character Goodwill	Corporate social legitimacy: competence, community	
	Pathos/ Emotion	Needs Values	Values advocacy	Explicit appeals
				Upholding of shared values
				Philanthropic activities
				Praise for individuals
			Identification	Common ground
				Antithesis
				Assumed "we"
				Unifying symbols
			Needs	
	Logos/ Argument	Claims Evidence Reasoning: inductive, deductive	Claims Evidence Reasoning: inductive, deductive	
			Organizational enthymeme	
Organization	Organizational patterns	Chronological Topical Spatial Problem-Solution	Traditional organizational patterns Visual placement of arguments Web site navigation	
Style	Style/ Aesthetic strategies	Metaphor Language devices	Visual elements Branding Language choices Music or other sound	

(Continued)

Table 2.2 *(Continued)*

Aristotle's Canons	Overarching Rhetorical Categories	Traditional Forms	Forms as Found in Organizational Rhetoric
Delivery	Verbal & nonverbal behavior	Gestures Movement Vocal quality	Media selection (TV, print, Internet, public meeting, etc.)
Memory	Memorization	Memory tricks	Not relevant in organizational rhetoric

canons and the canons as applied in organizational rhetoric. Table 2.2 may also be used for identifying the strategies used in any selection of organizational rhetoric (see last column).

At the end of the chapter is a Worksheet for Identifying Rhetorical Strategies in Organizational Texts. Use the worksheet and your knowledge of rhetorical strategies to describe the strategies found in the following samples of organizational rhetoric from the Texans for Affordable and Reliable Power (Figure 2.2, p. 53) and Texas Clean Sky Commission (Figure 2.3, p. 54).

WORKSHEET FOR IDENTIFYING RHETORICAL STRATEGIES IN ORGANIZATIONAL TEXTS

In order to describe the rhetorical strategies in the artifact that you have selected, please identify and give examples of statements in the rhetoric that fall into the following areas.

Ethos: Appeals to Organizational Credibility

Competence

Community

Pathos: Appeals to Emotions

Needs: Identify the need being created or appealed to

Values: Identify the value being appealed to

Values advocacy

Explicit appeals to values

Demonstration of how products or services uphold values

Discussion of philanthropic activities consistent with values

Praise of individuals who embody values

Identification

Common ground

Assumed "we"

By antithesis

Unifying symbols

Logos: Use of Claims and Evidence

Claims

Evidence

Statistics

Testimony

Examples

Reasoning

Inductive reasoning

By example

By analogy

Causal reasoning

Deductive reasoning

Strategies for Organizing Appeals

Introduction

Main body

Conclusion

Navigation (Web-based materials)

Stylistic Strategies

Language choices

Visual choices

Branding

Strategies for Delivering Appeals

What form is the rhetoric presented in (press release, newsletter, Web site, blog, event, etc.)?

Remember to consider whether the sample of rhetoric is similar to any of the types of rhetoric that occur with regularity in organizations (identity, issue, risk, crisis, or internal). If so, also consider the specific strategy questions posed at the end of the relevant chapters.

Figure 2.2   Advertisement From Texans for Affordable and Reliable Power, February 15, 2007

BLACKOUT 2009... WHO ARE YOU CALLING FIRST?...

Cartoons are funny.
Blackouts? Not so much.

Remember the blackouts in California? What about the ones in Ohio and New York? Who do you think they called when the lights went out? For now, let's have the politicians and the energy companies work together to build additional power generation and make sure Texas doesn't become another blackout casualty like some other states.

Texans for Affordable and Reliable Power (TARP) is an organization of elected officials, community leaders and Texas businesses who support the development of new, more efficient power sources for Texas, along with the overall reduction of pollution and the development of cleaner power-generating technology.

 TARP

www.TARPonline.org

Anita McCoy · 123 Commerce Street · Fairfield, TX 75840 · (903) 389-TARP

Figure 2.3 Advertisement From Texas Clean Sky Coalition, February 6, 2007

3

Rhetorical Situations in Organizations

❖ ❖ ❖

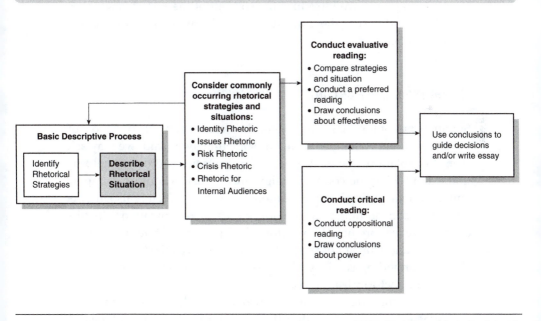

SOURCE: Adapted from Ford (1999).

On April 17, 2009, a fire broke out at North Star Foods, a meat processing plant in St. Charles, Minnesota. The fire spread quickly, and because there were potentially hazardous materials stored in the plant, the town of approximately 3,600 people had to be evacuated overnight. No one was seriously injured, but eventually the plant burned to the ground, and 250 employees found themselves out of work. The cost of rebuilding the plant was estimated to be between $60 and $70 million (Mann, 2009). Clearly, events like these demand that messages be sent by organizations. The city government needed to send messages to facilitate the evacuation; the American Red Cross needed to send messages about its role in the evacuation; and North Star Foods needed to send messages about the results of the fire, the cause of the fire, and the future of the company. Analyzing how situations like this and others unfold is a key element in understanding how rhetoric functions for organizations.

All communication is situated in a context. Events or conversations that occur prior to an instance of communication have an impact on what is said, how it is said, and the meaning that is assigned to it. In Chapter 2, we provided you with a system used to describe the basic elements you will find in samples of organizational rhetoric. Here in Chapter 3, we introduce the concept of the *rhetorical situation* to help you describe the contexts in which organizational rhetoric comes into being.

❖ THE IMPORTANCE OF CONTEXT IN RHETORIC

Situation or context has long been a key component of the study of communication. When people tell us something was said, we may ask them to explain the context in which it was said in order to help us understand what the comment might mean. Just as context is important in understanding communication in everyday life, it is also important in understanding how rhetoric works in organizations. In this chapter, we explore how two rhetorical scholars talk about the idea of situations, and look at how context is unique in organizations. We conclude by providing some specific instruction on how to research and analyze the rhetorical situation.

Because rhetoric is strategic—created to address issues or solve problems—it is important that those studying rhetoric understand the contexts in which messages are created. Probably the best-known perspective on context and rhetoric is that of Lloyd Bitzer (1968), who coined the term "the rhetorical situation."

❖ TWO PERSPECTIVES ON RHETORICAL SITUATIONS

Bitzer first introduced the concept of the rhetorical situation in 1968, and his work has been key in how rhetorical critics analyze and understand the circumstances in which rhetoric is created and received. In 1971, Richard Vatz challenged Bitzer's perspective, and suggested a new way of understanding rhetorical situations. Each of these perspectives, though different philosophically, offers important insights for those who study or create organizational rhetoric. We first review Bitzer's take on the rhetorical situation, and then explore Vatz's challenge.

Bitzer's Perspective: Situations Call for Rhetoric

Bitzer's (1968) primary argument was that situations call rhetoric into being. In other words, situations exist in the physical and social world, and rhetoric is required to address them. He also argued that the situation itself determines what an appropriate and effective response will look like. It is the duty of the person creating the rhetoric to determine what kind of response will be able to resolve the situation.

In order to understand this perspective, it is helpful to look at how Bitzer (1968) defined the rhetorical situation. He wrote,

> Rhetorical situation may be defined as a complex of persons, events, objects and relations presenting an actual or potential exigence which can be completely or partially removed if discourse, introduced into the situation, can so constrain human decision or action as to bring about the significant modification of the exigence. (p. 6)

This definition is easier to understand if explored one idea at a time.

Bitzer (1968) began by specifying that situations are composed of "persons, events, objects and relations." All of these things combine to create what he calls an *exigence*, or "an imperfection marked by urgency" (p. 6). This part of the definition is perhaps easiest to understand when illustrated with an example. When Hurricane Katrina struck the Gulf Coast in August of 2005, a large number of people were left without shelter, food, or clothing. This was clearly an imperfect situation marked by a sense of urgency because of the sheer amount of need and the number of people who were displaced. People (both those affected and those trying to help), events (the storm itself, storm preparation, and early recovery efforts), objects (buildings, equipment, and food), and relations (political issues, socioeconomic issues, and issues of race and ethnicity) combined to create a situation that required rhetoric in order to be resolved. In short, Hurricane Katrina created an exigence. In reality, Hurricane Katrina created a large number of exigencies, and the response itself created other long-term organizational exigencies for government and charitable agencies.

Bitzer (1968) also argued that in order for a situation to be considered rhetorical, rhetoric must be able to solve or at least modify the problem present in the situation. In other words, a situation isn't rhetorical if messages can't somehow modify the situation. For example, a hurricane cannot be considered a rhetorical situation in and of itself because no matter how many messages are created, symbols cannot modify a force of nature. On the other hand, many of the situations *surrounding* a hurricane are rhetorical. Symbols play a critical role in persuading people in the path of the storm to evacuate, and in securing physical and financial help following the hurricane's landfall. From Bitzer's point of view, if rhetoric can't make a difference in the situation, the situation should not be considered rhetorical.

Although he explicitly used the term exigence in the above definition, Bitzer (1968) only implied the other two constituents that he argued make up any rhetorical situation—audience and constraints. Bitzer was very specific about the meaning of the term *audience* in a rhetorical situation. Because the purpose of rhetoric in a situation is to create change in the exigence, the audience has to be capable of responding to the rhetoric in a way that can create that change.

In the situation unfolding immediately prior to Hurricane Katrina, any individuals who lacked the financial, mental, or emotional resources to evacuate could not be considered members of the rhetorical audience of evacuation messages. They were not capable of acting in a way that could modify the exigence. In the aftermath of the storm, many appeals were made to American citizens to help provide financial assistance for disaster recovery.

Anyone who was open to the idea that this was a noble cause, and who had the financial means to donate, could be considered a part of that rhetorical audience.

The final constituent addressed by Bitzer (1968) was *constraints*. He explained that they are "made up of persons, events, objects, and relations which are parts of the situation because they have the power to constrain decision and action needed to modify the exigence" (p. 8). Constraints are things that might "get in the way" of the rhetoric overcoming the exigence. Bitzer indicated that constraints may include "beliefs, attitudes, documents, facts, traditions, images, interests, [and] motives" (p. 8). For an organization, constraints might include customers' past experiences with, prior rhetoric issued by, or previous media coverage of the organization.

For example, over the years many residents of the Gulf Coast have evacuated for hurricanes only to come home and discover that the time and expense had been unnecessary. These prior experiences became constraints because they made it more difficult for authorities to persuade people that this hurricane was going to be different. After the storm, those trying to raise money for the recovery effort faced the constraint of so many competing messages aimed at people inclined to help out charitable causes. The elements of exigence, audience, and constraints will be discussed further later in this chapter, as we discuss the forms they take in explicitly organizational rhetorical situations.

Using Bitzer's Perspective in Organizations

Bitzer's (1968) perspective on the rhetorical situation has important implications for organizational rhetoric. It suggests that organizations operate in an environment that presents them with an ongoing parade of situations marked by an opportunity to address an imperfection or take advantage of positive circumstances, an audience capable of being persuaded and making change, and barriers or assets to the resolution of the situation. If they wish to be successful, organizational rhetors must monitor the situation around them in order to recognize situations that invite a response. They also need to be aware of who their rhetorical audiences are, and what beliefs, attitudes, and previous knowledge and experiences those audience members bring to the discourse. Critics of organizational rhetoric can also learn from Bitzer's perspective. If, as Bitzer suggested, situations dictate what kind of rhetoric should be successful, a critic can evaluate the constituents of the rhetorical situation and examine the rhetoric itself to make a judgment about how well the discourse met the demands of the situation.

Vatz's Perspective: Rhetoric Creates Situations

Richard Vatz (1973) challenged Bitzer's (1968) basic assumption that situations call rhetoric into being, arguing instead that rhetoric gives meaning to situations. Vatz wrote, "No situation can have a nature independent of the perception of its interpreter or independent of the rhetoric with which he chooses to characterize it" (p. 145). In other words, events have no objective meanings in themselves for Vatz; rather, they come to have meaning only when they are filtered through the perceptions of an observer and the rhetoric that the observer uses to share his or her perceptions. For Vatz, meaning is not located in the events that make up what Bitzer calls a situation; instead, meaning is created through how rhetoric selects and names events as situations.

Vatz (1973) viewed this creation of meaning as a two-step process composed of (1) selection and (2) naming. In the first step, a rhetor chooses which elements to emphasize from all of the possible choices that are perceived by the rhetor. Rather than viewing events as discrete objects, Vatz argued that we are faced with a stream of ongoing elements that can be punctuated in a variety of ways. We select elements out of that stream to label as "events." By selecting particular elements, rhetors call attention to some elements in the stream while distracting, or at least omitting, attention to others.

By selecting a series of injuries or accidents related to a particular product, for example, or by selecting a series of community contributions, a rhetor calls attention to particular events while diverting attention from other possible events. Theorist Kenneth Burke (1966) argued that language reflects, selects, and deflects reality—a position with which Vatz would likely have agreed, and one that helps explain his perspective on the rhetorical situation.

The second step in this meaning-making process is to name or label the elements that have been selected. Vatz (1973) viewed this as a creative or interpretative process. From this perspective, there is no single possible meaning for a series of events; rather, the rhetor selects a meaning and then shares that meaning with an audience. Vatz wrote, "To the audience, events become meaningful only through their linguistic depiction" (p. 157). For example, once the series of injuries or accidents mentioned above had been selected, the rhetor assigned an interpretation or meaning to that group of events—it could have been labeled "a crisis," "a series of unfortunate accidents," "negligence," or "sabotage" depending on the interpretation of the rhetor. The community contributions could have been called "good-will," "restitution," or "philanthropy" depending upon interpretations. Meaning is created for the audience through which events are selected and how they are named.

When several people were killed after taking poisoned Tylenol pain medication in the 1980s, public relations professionals and others creating organizational rhetoric focused attention on the actions of the saboteur who placed poison in the capsules. The rhetors then labeled the situation "a crime." Other rhetors could have called attention to the lack of safety precautions on the packages (features that were added by the industry after the Tylenol case) and labeled the situation "negligence." By selecting particular elements and naming those elements in a strategic way, rhetors are able to influence the meaning inferred by the audience (Benoit & Lindsey, 1987).

From this perspective, the rhetor has the power and the responsibility to determine which elements an audience should attend to, and what those elements should mean. In short, the rhetor constructs the rhetorical situation from available clues. In another article on the debate over the rhetorical situation, Consigny (1974) pointed out that rhetors cannot, however, make events mean anything they want them to. The meaning has to be reasonable to the audience. For example, it is unlikely that a rhetor could find a way to make an audience view a chemical spill as a "triumph" for the organization.

Using Vatz's Perspective in Organizations

From Vatz's (1973) perspective, organizations have slightly more rhetorical power than they do from Bitzer's (1968) perspective. If, as Vatz suggested, the environment is a stream of facts or events that are not given meaning until they are communicated, organizations can influence which facts are emphasized and what those facts mean for their audiences. Organizations can define events in their environments. A very simple example of this can be found in the terms used to describe some organizational actions. In the current economy, employees are no longer "fired" or even "laid off"; they are "downsized" or "separated." Some companies use the term *rightsizing*, which strives for an even less negative connotation. Airlines use the term *service recovery* to refer to the process of getting crews and passengers on jets, and jets in the sky, after a crash or other major problem. Each of these terms places a slightly different interpretation on the same event.

Vatz's (1973) perspective offers a more proactive approach to considering how events and messages interact. If rhetors select and name events in order to create meaning, it becomes critical that organizations carefully monitor their environments in order to be able to identify those elements that should be selected and labeled in particular ways to create effective and ethical organizational rhetoric. This means that organizational rhetors cannot wait to respond until the media or other groups select and label events. By acting early, organizations can shape perceptions of upcoming events. For critics of organizational rhetoric, Vatz's perspective offers an additional area of inquiry. A critic can move toward understanding the motives of organizational rhetors by examining how they select and label elements.

❖ THE RHETORICAL SITUATION IN ORGANIZATIONAL RHETORIC

Whether you agree with Bitzer's (1968) assumption that situations call for rhetoric, or Vatz's (1973) assumption that rhetoric calls situations into being, both perspectives are important in understanding organizational rhetoric. Both authors share the assumption that the environment and events in it cannot be separated from a consideration of the rhetoric that is created. Bitzer's constituents of exigence, audience, and constraints are particularly useful for describing situations, whether you believe they exist prior to the rhetoric or that they are created by the rhetoric. Bitzer's work provides a basic framework for understanding organizational rhetorical situations. The work of scholars in organizational communication, organizational rhetoric, and public relations helps adapt Bitzer's concepts specifically to the needs of those studying organizational rhetoric.

Organizational Exigencies

Bitzer (1968) defined exigence as "an imperfection marked by urgency," but the term *imperfection* may tempt us to think of rhetorical situations as only negative. The phrase "opportunity marked by urgency" better incorporates the range of reasons why organizations may create rhetoric. Certainly organizations do respond to problems through the use of rhetoric—profit projections go unmet, accidents and natural disasters happen, and employees sometimes need to be laid off. But organizations also use rhetoric to address positive situations—nonprofit groups win awards, corporations participate in charitable giving, donations or profits increase.

A concept developed by Elsbach, Sutton, and Principe (1998) and extended here can help illustrate the ways in which both potentially negative and potentially positive organizational rhetorical situations can be understood and described. In introducing a study of how hospitals strategically used billing practices to influence people's perceptions of the organizations, Elsbach et al. argued that two sets of variables can be used to describe situations that need to be addressed by organizations. They explained that all events can be described on a continuum between anticipated and unanticipated, and on a continuum between potentially positive and potentially negative. Together, these two sets of variables can help describe almost any rhetorical situation presented to an organization.

All of the organizational rhetoric discussed in this book addresses one or more of the four types of situations emerging from the intersection of these variables. Table 3.1 identifies how the variables interact and provides a sample of each type of situation.

Anticipated or Unanticipated Exigencies

All exigencies facing organizations can be described as somewhere between fully anticipated and fully unanticipated. For example,

Table 3.1   Rhetorical Situations in Organizations

	Potentially Enhancing	**Potentially Threatening**
Anticipated	Expected and more likely to make the organization "look good" Example: Drug manufacturer receives approval for new product.	Expected and more likely to make the organization "look bad" Example: Banking company must lay off employees for financial reasons.
Unanticipated	Unexpected and more likely to make the organization "look good" Example: Organization is surprised to win award for customer service.	Unexpected and more likely to make the organization "look bad" Example: Nonprofit organization discovers that a volunteer has stolen money from it.

organizations have some advanced information about whether their quarterly earnings will increase or decrease. In addition, they may be able to anticipate the opening of a new plant or the retirement of a key executive. Other types of exigencies cannot be anticipated ahead of time. A natural disaster may suddenly impair the ability of a business to serve its customers or make a profit. Likewise, an organization usually cannot anticipate that an employee will steal or commit sabotage.

Some events in organizational rhetoric are unique—they are anticipated and unanticipated at the same time. As we will discuss in Chapter 9, this is especially true in crisis management rhetoric. For example, even though your campus leadership cannot anticipate when, depending on your location, a fire, tornado, flood, hurricane, or earthquake might occur, they likely have a plan to deal with communication in the event that one or all of those possibilities occur. Similarly, universities don't know ahead of time that a nominated faculty member will win a prestigious research prize. If they know about the nomination, however, they can prepare rhetoric just in case, so that they can use the professor's accomplishments to promote the university.

Bitzer (1968) required that exigencies be marked by urgency, and it is clear that many organizational challenges and opportunities are. The timing of messages can be critical, either in order to solve a problem or to take advantage of a positive event before it moves out of public attention.

Potentially Positive or Potentially Negative Exigencies

All exigencies facing organizations can also be described as having the potential to enhance or threaten perceptions of the organization. For example, if an organization is releasing an innovative new product with the potential to save lives or has made significant contributions to community programs, communication professionals have an opportunity to produce messages that will help enhance positive perceptions of the organization. On the other side are events that have the potential to cause audiences to have negative thoughts or feelings, or to exhibit negative behaviors toward the organization. For example, if an organization has caused environmental harm or injured or contributed to the death of someone, audiences may begin to view it negatively.

Some events, depending on the rhetoric created by the organization, could work both ways. For example, an organization that uses rhetoric to handle a potential crisis (threatening event) in an especially positive way, may actually be perceived more positively after the crisis than it had been before. Seeger and Ulmer (2002) studied the responses of two companies to fires that had the potential to destroy the organizations. They discovered that the organizations' overall images were actually enhanced because their leaders responded with a commitment to the stakeholders, a commitment to rebuild, and a recognition that organizational renewal could be a by-product of the situation.

By thinking about all organizational exigencies as somewhere between anticipated and unanticipated, and as somewhere between potentially enhancing the organization's reputation and potentially threatening it, we have a foundation from which to describe any rhetorical exigence. In Chapters 6 through 10, we will use these characteristics to discuss some specific types of rhetorical exigencies that appear with regularity in organizations.

Audiences in Organizational Rhetoric

As noted above, Bitzer (1968) maintained that in order for an audience to be considered rhetorical, its members need to be able to be persuaded, and they must have the resources to create the change being sought. It is helpful to think about these criteria as we consider audiences for organizational rhetoric. Scholars in public relations have offered important tools for understanding and describing audiences of organizational messages.

Esman (1972) introduced the concept of *organizational linkages*—connections or publics that play a vital role in the survival of an organization. Esman argued that all organizations have enabling linkages, functional linkages, normative linkages, and diffused linkages, each of which has interests in the organization and its activities. In his study of the fatal chemical leak at Union Carbide's Bhopal, India, plant, Ice (1991) talked about these groups as "publics." We discuss these four groups as organizational "audiences" because their interests in the organization clearly make them targets of organizational messages.

Enabling audiences are composed of those people who allow the organization to operate. This category would include individuals who are part of legislative bodies and regulatory groups and, depending on the organization, stockholders. Without the proper laws, permits, and capital, organizations cannot produce products or provide services. Colleges and universities have a number of enabling audiences. State schools are accountable to their legislatures, perhaps to coordinating boards or boards of regents, and ultimately, to taxpayers.

Private colleges and universities answer to trustees or boards of directors, and sometimes to the leadership of a religious denomination. Nearly all schools are accountable to accrediting organizations, and to athletic organizations. Colleges and universities need to consider these groups as they monitor their environments and craft messages.

Functional audiences are composed of individuals or groups that help the organization function on a day-to-day basis. This includes employees, customers, and suppliers. On a college or university campus, the functional audiences include students, staff, and faculty. The university cannot operate without members of this audience. Students are needed to take classes and secure funding, staff are needed to do thousands of things across campus each day, and faculty are needed to teach classes and conduct research. Functional audiences are often targets for messages from the organization. Just think about how much rhetoric you receive from your university each semester.

Normative audiences are composed of individuals in organizations that face similar challenges. This group includes those that are members of the same professional organization or trade group, or are organizational peers. Most universities have a number of normative audiences. They may include the administration at other institutions in what is called their "mission class" (schools of similar size and educational goals), other schools in their state system or private consortium, or others in their athletic conference. These organizations are audiences for the schools' rhetoric because they share similar interests, and because they may learn how to handle a situation by observing how similar institutions do so. In addition, decisions made by one school may affect other schools in the normative audience (such as a school deciding to switch athletic conferences or change its name). Normative audiences are often secondary, but they frequently receive rhetoric created by organizations.

Finally, *diffused* audiences are removed further from the organization, yet still have an interest and potential influence. Diffused audiences may include individuals in the surrounding community, in interest groups concerned with human rights or environmental protection, voters, and representatives of the media. For colleges and universities, diffused audiences certainly include people living in the surrounding geographical area, and perhaps alumni.

It is sometimes difficult to classify groups into only one of these categories. In the above example, we called the alumni a diffused audience. Alumni could also be considered an enabling audience if they have enough monetary influence to impede funding of the institution. They might be a functional audience if they are involved in a day-to-day way on a particular campus. It is less important that you are able to place every single individual or group into one of these four categories. What is more important is the ability to identify all of the possible audiences of rhetoric in the organization in question.

Describing and understanding the audiences of organizational rhetoric is difficult because you not only have to consider these four large categories of audiences and the sub-audiences beneath, but you also have to determine if the audiences are likely to be sympathetic, neutral, or antagonistic. Sympathetic audiences are predisposed to agree with the rhetor, while antagonistic audiences are more likely to reject the message.

In addition, each of the four types of audiences has potentially conflicting interests, needs, and expectations of the organization, and all are potential receivers of messages designed for other audiences. For example, stockholders, rather than employees and customers, are the target audience of earnings statements and annual reports. However, employees and customers usually have access to that information as well. Actions that stockholders perceive as good business may be perceived as exploitation by employees or activists, and as price inflation by customers. In Chapters 6 through 10, we will consider the composition and interests of audiences in a variety of rhetorical situations that occur frequently in organizations.

Constraints and Assets in Organizational Rhetoric

The final constituent of the rhetorical situation as discussed by Bitzer (1968) is constraints. Whether you believe that constraints have an objective existence in the situation (like Bitzer), or that they are selected and labeled by the rhetor (like Vatz), they are a key component in understanding any situation. Bitzer said, "Every rhetorical situation contains a set of constraints made up of persons, events, objects, and relations which are part of the situation because they have the power to constrain decision and action needed to modify the exigence" (p. 8). He included "beliefs, attitudes, documents, facts, traditions, images, interests . . . and motives" in his description of constraints (p. 8). He also suggested that not only do these potential limitations exist in the situation, but the rhetor also can add constraints in the construction and delivery of the response. Much like his use of the term *imperfection,* Bitzer's use of the term *constraints* suggests that the rhetors only have challenges and have nothing working in their favor. It is important to also recognize that "beliefs, attitudes, documents, facts, traditions, images, interests . . . and motives" also make the rhetor's job easier in some situations. Rowland (2008) used the term *advantages* to describe factors that might work in the rhetor's favor. In fact, due to the multiple audiences and complex nature of rhetorical situations in organizations, some elements may even serve as potential limitations and potential assets at the same time.

In simple terms, a constraint is anything that may have an impact on the likelihood that the rhetor's message will be able to address the situation in the desired way. Rowland (2008) introduced the concept of *rhetorical barriers* that helps clarify the idea of constraints and adds specificity to the types of barriers that may occur in rhetorical situations. Rowland defined a rhetorical barrier as "an attitude, belief or other problem that a rhetor must overcome in order to persuade an audience to accept a given position" (p. 42). He argued that a barrier may be related to the audience, the situation, the occasion, or the reputation of the rhetor.

Both Bitzer (1968) and Rowland (2008) wrote about rhetoric in general, so it is important to recognize how these concepts might play out in rhetorical situations in organizations. There are a number of constraints that are likely to recur in organizations because of their nature as public entities. All organizations need to be aware of potential limitations that fall under the categories of reputation and legal issues. Both of these types of constraints are influenced by past occurrences and rhetoric.

Like any rhetor, organizations enter situations with a preexisting reputation that may make persuasion easier or more challenging. Because of the public nature of organizations, and the amount of media coverage large organizations often receive, this factor is multiplied. Unlike in a typical political speech, it is not the reputation of the spokesperson that is under scrutiny. Rather, the reputation of the organization as a whole influences how rhetoric is received.

Audiences, whether enabling, functional, normative, or diffused, often have both firsthand and mediated experiences with organizations. This means that audiences may have developed beliefs and attitudes about the reputation of a particular organization that can either make it easier or more difficult for the rhetor to persuade the audience. For example, most Americans are familiar with major retailers such as Target or Wal-Mart, and have formed opinions about the quality of their products and services, their philanthropic efforts, and their status as community citizens. These attitudes and beliefs influence how audiences receive any rhetoric created by these organizations on any topic. These preexisting ideas have the potential to make the audience more receptive or less receptive to new messages.

Organizations also face legal constraints that may not weigh as heavily on an individual speaker. Liability issues in particular may limit the rhetorical options open to someone creating messages on behalf of an organization. Organizational rhetors may need to avoid language that suggests a legally binding promise or that takes responsibility for some action in a manner that could be considered a legal admission of guilt.

Some combinations of exigencies, audiences, and constraints happen with frequency across a wide range of organizations. In Chapters 6 through 10 of this book, we will focus on five rhetorical situations that scholars have noticed occur on a fairly regular basis in organizations: situations calling for identity, issue, risk, crisis, and internal rhetoric. As you continue through the process of analyzing organizational rhetoric, you will want to consider the basic elements of rhetorical situation discussed in this chapter and those that may be specific to the situation and artifact that you are analyzing.

❖ RESEARCHING THE RHETORICAL SITUATION

We know that isolating and analyzing the components of exigence, audience, and constraints is a good way to gain an understanding of any rhetorical situation, whether you believe situations call for rhetoric, or that rhetoric names situations. Research from published sources and original empirical research may both be important in creating a picture of the rhetorical situation.

Using Published Sources

For students and critics of organizational rhetoric, research in published sources is the primary tool for gathering information about the rhetorical situation. This subsection outlines some useful sources, and provides questions to ask as you analyze the information you have discovered. In gathering information about a rhetorical situation, you should certainly visit the Web site of the organization that is involved. Organizational Web sites generally include a vast amount of information about organizational history, community contributions, and ethics policies. In addition, many organizations provide public access to their press release archives through their Web sites. All of these materials may inform your understanding of the situation.

When using organizational Web sites, however, remember that they are themselves organizational rhetoric—they are strategically designed to influence the thoughts, feelings, and behaviors of audiences important to the organization. You will need to think critically about the messages that you discover before you decide how you should use them to help reconstruct the rhetorical situation.

Newspapers, news magazines, business magazines, and trade publications are also good sources of information. They can provide background on particular organizations, and they also contain information on the social, legal, regulatory, and economic environments in which organizations operate. These sources can be searched through a variety of general and business-specific databases. Many are also indexed in LexisNexis.

When using published sources to analyze the rhetorical situation, there are a number of steps and questions to help you make the most of the information you have discovered. Not surprisingly, they center on issues of exigence, audience, and constraints. Begin by identifying the events in the situation. Ask yourself what sorts of things are discussed, and about the social, legal, regulatory, and economic environment in which the organization operates. Try to determine what potential meanings an organization might give an event, and pay attention to the meanings others seem to impose on those events. Determine if the events can be considered exigencies and be able to make an argument for why or why not.

Next, identify the potential audiences of this discourse. Ask yourself who can be persuaded and who has the power to change the situation. Consider whether enabling, functional, normative, or diffused audiences are involved, and what the beliefs, attitudes, values, or interests of those audience members might be. Finally, consider the potential constraints (both challenges and assets) that might be present in the situation.

Conducting Primary Research

A second method of research involves gathering and interpreting data firsthand from representatives of the organization and from potential audiences of the organization's messages. This may include the use of empirical research methods such as interviews, focus groups, participant observation, and survey research. All of these types of research are useful in understanding a rhetorical situation in an organization, particularly for those who want to create discourse. When creating rhetoric, it is first important to understand how the leadership in the organization perceives the exigence, the audience, and the constraints present in the environment.

The best way to gather this information is by conducting an interview with a representative or representatives of the organization. The interview questions should focus on the rhetorical goals and challenges of the organization, and on how the organization would like to be viewed by its most important audiences.

A creator of organizational rhetoric will also want to conduct primary research on the target audience of the rhetoric. Additional interviews and focus groups can gather detailed information about the beliefs, attitudes, values, and perceptions of a smaller group of individuals toward the organization. Survey research allows access to the same sort of information, though often less detailed, from a larger body of potential audience members. Interview and focus group research is often very helpful in determining what sorts of questions should be included in survey research. This kind of research gathers information about all three constituents of the rhetorical situation—exigence, audience, and constraints.

❖ CONCLUSION

Understanding why and how rhetoric comes into being is a critical first step in evaluating and critiquing discourse, and in learning to become a producer of more effective organizational discourse. The critic must be able to identify and analyze the elements of the situation in order to analyze the discourse created by the organization. The creator of organizational rhetoric must be able to recognize and analyze the elements of the rhetorical situation in order to craft discourse that can respond to or shape it. As we introduced in Chapter 1, all critics begin their analysis of organizational rhetoric with a description of the strategies in the rhetoric and the elements of the rhetorical situation. Chapters 2 and 3 have provided you with the background needed to begin an evaluative reading of a rhetorical artifact. Use your knowledge of the rhetorical situation to analyze the events described in the following case study. After you have finished studying the situation, you may want to revisit the advertisements reproduced at the end of Chapter 2.

❖ **CASE STUDY: A SHOWDOWN OVER POWER IN TEXAS**

In late 2006, the stage was set for a battle over electrical power production in the state of Texas (Fowler, 2006). Earlier in the year, TXU Power, a utility company based in Texas, had announced that it planned to build up to 11 new coal-fired power plants in the state. The situation was complicated by the governor's decision to "fast-track" the approval process for the plants in order to meet the goal of increasing energy production in the state (Vertuno, 2007). Governor Perry ordered that the process be completed in 6 months rather than the usual 18 months (Ratcliffe, Babineck, & Raskin, 2007).

Energy production was a concern of many diverse individuals and groups in Texas during the winter of 2006–2007. Concerns about the energy supply in the United States were present in the public mind at this time due to blackouts on the East Coast in July of 2006 and almost constant talk about the possibilities of blackouts in California during the summer months (Chan, 2007; Harden, 2006). Texans were also aware of the increased prices they were paying for energy—both for gasoline to fuel their cars and for energy to heat and cool their homes. Much of the electricity produced in Texas is created through the use of natural gas, which is a more expensive way to generate power (Steffy, 2007).

The environmental impact of energy production was also frequently in the news. In fact, as this particular situation unfolded, former Vice President Al Gore was an Academy Award nominee for his documentary on the dangers of climate change (Vertuno, 2007). Coal fired power plants have had a particularly poor reputation among environmental groups because of the amount of pollution they produce as well as the way in which coal is mined (Sierra Club, n.d.). Concerns about energy—supply, price, or environmental impact—were present in the minds of many Texans during late 2006 and early 2007.

Once TXU announced its plans, and a hearing date was set, some existing organizations spoke out for or against the plants, and other organizations formed for the purpose of either supporting or opposing the plants. Municipalities, environmental groups, and other private businesses joined forces in interesting ways to attempt to influence the proposal to build new plants. The group in favor of permitting TXU to proceed was composed of mayors of communities where plants would be located, and of businesses and manufacturers who had an interest in less-expensive power. This group argued that the positive economic impact on local communities and the state made it necessary to allow the plants to be built. The group opposed to the plants included large cities that already had air quality concerns, environmental groups, and organizations that currently supplied electricity to Texas customers (Fowler, 2006).

As individuals and groups on both sides formed coalitions, they selected names for themselves. Among the groups in support were Texans for Affordable and Reliable Power (TARP) and Texas Business for Clean, Affordable, Reliable Energy (Price, 2007). The groups opposed included Texas Clean Air Cities Coalition, Texas Business for Clean Air, Clean Air Watch, and Texas Clean Sky Coalition (Fowler, 2006; Ratcliffe & Babineck, 2007).

These groups, TXU itself, and other interested parties were responsible for a flurry of rhetoric aimed at a variety of audiences. The rhetoric took the form of press releases; radio, television, and newspaper advertisements; lobbying of state officials; banners being towed by aircraft; an anti-coal rally at the state capitol in Austin; and many messages designed for organizational Web sites (Plohetski & George, 2007; Ratcliffe & Babineck, 2007; Vertuno, 2007). The *Houston Chronicle* estimated that between TXU efforts to influence the process and the efforts of parties such as those listed above, "more than $7 million combined is expected to be spent on lobbying, lawyers and advertising before a final decision is made on whether the state should permit construction of the plants" (Ratcliffe et al., 2007).

The advertisements found at the end of Chapter 2 (Figures 2.2 and 2.3) are just two examples of the messages produced by parties on both sides of the issue. A series that argued "coal is filthy" ran as full-page and smaller advertisements in six major Texas newspapers on February 4 and 5, 2007. The advertisement indicated that it was paid for by the Texas Clean Sky Coalition, and included links to environmental organizations. After the ads ran, it was discovered that the Texas Clean Sky Coalition was financed in large part by Chesapeake Energy Corporation, which is the third-largest producer of natural gas (a more expensive, but cleaner alternative to coal) in the United States. The environmental organizations whose links appeared on the ads claimed that they were unaware of the ads before they ran, and that they were not associated with the Texas Clean Sky Coalition. Ratcliffe and Babineck (2007) quoted the state director of one of the organizations as saying that "he was happy to see 'another loud voice' opposing the proposed coal plants, but he was afraid 'readers might infer' that his organization was part of the group placing the ads."

The other selection of rhetoric is from TARP, or Texans for Affordable and Reliable Power. TARP was composed of small-town officials who believed that the plants would improve their local economies. The TARP chair told the *Houston Chronicle* that "he and others spent $100,000 setting up the group but TXU has agreed to pay additional expenses" (Ratcliffe et al., 2007).

Ultimately, all of this forming of coalitions and lobbying in favor of or against the new power plants became somewhat irrelevant because TXU was acquired by Kohlberg Kravis Roberts & Co., Texas Pacific Group, Goldman Sachs, and other investors in October of 2007 (Energy Future Holdings, 2008). The new owners proposed to abandon nearly all plans to build the coal-fired plants and announced several environmental initiatives as part of the acquisition deal (Koenig, 2007). Despite this change in plans, this rhetorical situation and the resulting messages (reproduced at the end of Chapter 2) illustrate the pervasive and complex nature of organizational rhetoric. As you consider the rhetorical situation, use the Worksheet for Describing the Rhetorical Situation in Organizations to guide your analysis.

Case Study References

Chan, S. (2007, January 18). Regulators say Con Ed failures led to blackout. *New York Times.* Retrieved June 19, 2009, from http://query.nytimes.com/gst/fullpage.html?res=9C07EED91130F93BA25752C0A9619C8B63

Energy Future Holdings. (2008, January 8). *John F. Young becomes first CEO of Energy Future Holdings.* Retrieved February 19, 2008, from http://www.energyfutureholdings.com/news/newsrel

Fowler, T. (2006, December 15). Battle lines are drawn in coal fight. *Houston Chronicle,* p. 19.

Harden, B. (2006, July 26). Deadly heat continues in Calif.; Slight cooling trend this week may ease blackout concerns. *Washington Post,* p. A04.

Koenig, D. (2007, February 26). TXU board OKs buyout offer. *Houston Chronicle,* p. A1.

Plohetski, T., & George, P. (2007, February 12). Hundreds protest plans for coal plants. *Austin American-Statesman.*

Price, A. (2007, February 17). TXU aims to line up support for plants. *Austin American-Statesman.*

Ratcliffe, R. G., & Babineck, M. (2007, February 6). Newly formed group launches "coal is filthy" ads against TXU. *Houston Chronicle.*

Ratcliffe, R. G., Babineck, M., & Raskin, A. (2007, February 11). Big money fueling fight over proposed coal plants; TXU faces tough battle against an odd alliance for 11 new facilities. *Houston Chronicle,* p. A1.

Sierra Club. (n.d.). *The dirty truth about coal.* Retrieved February 19, 2008, from http://www.sierraclub.org/coal/dirtytruth/

Steffy, L. (2007, March 4). System encourages coal-fired power plants. *Houston Chronicle.* Retrieved June 19, 2009, from http://www.chron.com/disp/story.mpl/business/steffy/4599206.html

Vertuno, J. (2007, February 12). Timeout urged on coal plants plan; Rally draws protestors seeking conservation, other energy sources. *Houston Chronicle.*

WORKSHEET FOR DESCRIBING RHETORICAL SITUATIONS IN ORGANIZATIONS

In order to systematically describe the rhetorical situation, please answer the following questions based on information that has been provided in a case or that you have gathered through research.

Exigencies: What elements in the situation appear to be challenges or opportunities for the organization? Is there an imperfection or opportunity? Was it anticipated or unanticipated? Is it marked by urgency? What are some options for how organizational rhetors might frame the elements?

Audiences: What types of audiences seem to be the most appropriate target in the situation—enabling, functional, normative, or diffused? What are the characteristics or interests of members of these audiences?

Constraints and Assets: What things might make it more difficult or easier for the organization to answer the exigencies? Are there preexisting beliefs, attitudes or values, or past rhetoric or experiences that will affect how the message is interpreted by audiences?

Recurring Situations: Is the rhetorical situation similar to any of the types of situations that occur with regularity in organizations (identity, issue, risk, crisis, or internal)? If so, also consider the specific elements of situations discussed in the relevant chapters.

4

Critical Approaches to Organizational Rhetoric

❖　❖　❖

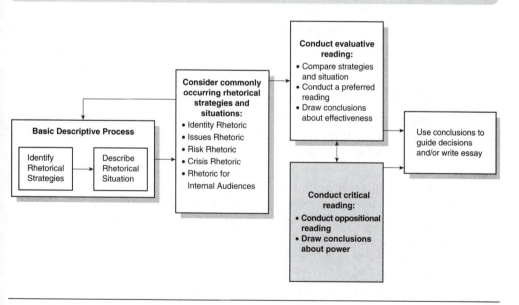

SOURCE: Adapted from Ford (1999).

The corporate voice, not surprisingly, is the loudest in the land.

—Schiller, 1989, p. 4

It might well be argued that nothing at once fair, coherent, and brief can be written on this topic.

—Alvesson & Deetz, 2003, p. 191

I n Chapters 1 through 3, we have focused upon analyzing organizational rhetoric from an evaluative perspective: a set of key questions for gaining an understanding of the language choices used by an organization in a particular artifact. In contrast, a second key approach to gaining an understanding of an organization's rhetorical choices is the critical approach. Up to this point, the word *critical* has been used primarily in the sense of *critique*. Now we add a second sense of the term: Critical approaches to organizational rhetoric center on questions of power and resistance to power. The answers to the questions of power and resistance help us analyze whether an organization is acting fairly and ethically, with a particular focus upon the organization's choices about *voice* and *choice* as they are demonstrated in its messages.

The quotations above help us on the path toward understanding critical approaches to organizational rhetoric. First, we need tools to help us critique the loudest voices in the land because organizations influence so many aspects of our lives, and second, the perspectives that emerge from critical theory are some of the most difficult for understanding the study of communication processes. However, the tentative answers to the questions posed by critical approaches to organizational rhetoric have important consequences in our lives.

The central questions in the critical approach to understanding human behavior in organizations focus on power. The concept of power and that of its close companion, control, have generated extensive study in philosophy and social science fields for centuries. Power and control's related companion, resistance, has been studied more specifically since the mid-20th century. Useful for this chapter is Conrad and Poole's (2005) discussion of power because of its succinct connections among power, control, and resistance: "Power is in the eye of the beholder. . . . Power is not possessed by a person. It is granted to that person by others" (p. 257). What is contested when we study organizational rhetoric is the organization's right to control some type of resource (e.g., money, time, service or product, ability to promote a position, and so forth) to the extent we can judge from its messages.

Clearly there is a wide range in a person's ability to grant power to another. If someone holds a gun to your head, you are likely to rather easily grant power to the person who threatens you. However, you have a wider range of choice in whether to grant power to a large oil company based upon its argument that huge profits are appropriate in a recession because that company invests those revenues in large-scale research projects. You also have a wider range of choice when you decide whether to support a nonprofit organization based upon its use of funds raised. In other words, you are more likely to feel that you can resist or accept the oil company's or the nonprofit's arguments. For example, you could withhold contributions based on the nonprofit organization's arguments, or you could buy gas from another oil company.

Thus, the questions that are the primary focus for critical theorists include the following: Who has power and in what circumstances? Who are the less powerful? How did these power relationships emerge in such a way, and why and how do these relationships continue in the way(s) that they do? What are the consequences for the humans involved? These are the questions most often asked by critical philosophers, critical sociologists, and critical anthropologists.

From a communication perspective, or the perspective that features messages of various kinds, the questions become the following: Who has the right or uses the right to speak in decisions? When an organizational representative speaks, who is responsible (Meisenbach & McMillan, 2006, p. 101)? Whose voices are left out of the decisions described in this book—those decisions that affect the organization, its members, and the communities of which the organization is a part? How do organizational voices interact to maintain the status quo in society and organizations? What rhetorical strategies do those in power (i.e., organizations) use to influence the likelihood of their desired outcomes? What are the consequences of what is said and by whom for the department, organization, and communities of which the organization and its members are a part? The critical approach to organizational rhetoric helps us critique wide-ranging problems; below are two examples.

First, the rights of workers, particularly in manufacturing settings, continue to be an ongoing issue between unions and corporations. For example, in 1994, workers at Staley Corporation unsuccessfully tried to protest rotating 12-hour shifts, gain increased salaries and education benefits, and gain lifelong health insurance benefits. In her critical rhetorical analysis, Cloud (2005) described the rhetorical strategies used by the workers to try to force Staley's management to act upon their demands, as ranging from a warrior stance (i.e., going on the offensive) to ultimately a victim stance (i.e., suffering attacks). She concluded that their rhetorical strategies were ineffective without "material strategies"—i.e., the ability to shut down Staley's production line—to back them up.

Second, in 2006, an estimated 47 million people in the United States did not have health insurance (DeNavas-Walt, Proctor, & Smith, 2007). This might have included you because many college students are too old to be carried on their parents' insurance, and yet do not have the cash to afford a policy. It included many families who live at a socioeconomic level only slightly higher than the poverty level. That means that they did not qualify for Medicaid, but they also did not have the money to pay for health insurance. The costs of food, housing, clothing, and transportation needed to come first. Bills that would establish universal health insurance have been defeated multiple times since the first U.S. proposal in 1913, partially due to the combined corporate voices of the medical profession, pharmaceutical companies, and insurance companies, among others. These well-funded, well-organized organizations representing hundreds of companies have been extremely successful in helping to maintain the current health care system with its expensive access (Center for Public Integrity, 1995a, 1995b, 1995c; West, Heith, & Goodwin, 1996). Ford (1999) concluded that the American Medical Association's rhetorical strategies, in concert with other trade organizations' strategies, helped to defeat the 1993 proposal to provide all Americans with health insurance. The plan's defeat meant that many Americans with low and middle incomes had little access to health care other than through the emergency room, the most expensive type of health care available.

This chapter explores how organizational communication scholars have applied principles of critical theory to understand how power is created and maintained in organizations. Specifically, we will discuss a perspective that questions how organizations use rhetorical strategies in order to establish and maintain their power in society. In order to understand this perspective, we first introduce a brief history of the critical approach in organizational communication. Then we discuss the key concepts in the critical approach to organization studies and organizational rhetoric.

❖ HISTORICAL OVERVIEW

The critical approach to organizational communication (including organizational rhetoric) grew out of two primary concerns. First, in the late 1970s and early1980s, interpretive approaches (in contrast to quantitative approaches) to studies of organizational behavior primarily focused on describing how meanings were created in organizations. While these were useful questions, scholars (e.g., Mumby, 1997) questioned why differences in power among organizational members were not considered in these interpretive studies. In other words, critical scholars asked, when one person has more power than another, does that difference in power influence whether an idea comes to have one meaning rather than another? How do employees resist such control?

A second key concern in critical research challenged the managerial bias of traditional organizational research (Mumby & Putnam, 1992). This means that critical scholars challenged the assumption of many organizational researchers that research findings should help managers control organizational behaviors. Critical scholars asked how research findings could help everyone, in all organizational positions, participate more fully in what happened in the organization.

The critical approach also emerged from an application of various critical philosophies to organization studies.[1] For example, organizational communication scholar Stan Deetz (e.g., 1982) has applied the work of the French critical philosopher Foucault, among others, to the study of organizational dynamics. The critical philosophies applied were those of 19th- and 20th-century philosophers who were writing in response to the strong Western European and Russian military influences, and the capitalist influence of the United States, prior to, during, and following the two world wars. Gramsci (1971), for example, was writing in response to his imprisonment by Mussolini prior to World War II. The organizational communication scholar Dennis Mumby (e.g., 1997) often applies Gramsci's concept of hegemony (to be discussed later) in the development of his ideas.

At about the same time that critical approaches to organizational communication were emerging, a critical theory movement in rhetoric also was emerging (e.g., Aune, 1983; McKerrow, 1989; Wander, 1983). Rhetorical scholars (e.g., Conrad, 1983, 1988) were beginning to examine those same processes of power construction in organizations using rhetorical methods.

Regardless of rhetorician or social scientist stance, a critical philosopher's overarching goal is to discuss ways in which state power could be resisted by individuals; thus their emphasis either was on power/domination or on resistance. As this work has evolved over the last 20 years in organization studies, a newer critical perspective has emerged: These more recent theorists argue that power and resistance are usefully understood as intertwined ideas, meaning that power and resistance function together (in other words, as a dialectic; e.g., Ashcraft, 2005; Mumby, 1997). In addition, scholarship focusing on the roles of gender, race, class, and work/life balance has emerged from this critical tradition (for examples, see Ashcraft, 2005; Ashcraft & Allen, 2003; Clair, 1993; Cloud, 2005; Kirby & Krone, 2002).

❖ KEY IDEAS IN CRITICAL APPROACHES TO ORGANIZATION STUDIES AND ORGANIZATIONAL RHETORIC

Several concepts support the majority of critical approaches to organizational communication, rhetorical theory, and organizational rhetoric. First, critical approaches to organizational communication assume that "messages can never be neutral" (German, 1995, p. 280). Working from the idea that one message can be interpreted in many ways by the various people involved, the critical theorist examines how organizations try to impose or fix meanings to advance the organization's interests. These organizational interests are often privileged at the expense of other, less powerful interests (Mumby, 2004). For example, in 1996, Nike responded to accusations of using sweatshop labor by trying to establish that using sweatshop labor was a legitimate business strategy in the arena in which it was operating (McHale, Zompetti, & Moffit, 2007). Therefore, Nike argued (or implied enthymematically), it had not violated societal expectations about how it should treat its employees and was thus a "good" organization.

A second basic concept upon which critical theory rests is that all organizational members, leaders, and followers must make choices. You might respond, "Well of course organizations make choices. So what?" A critical theorist does not just assume that choices are/were made; the critical theorist *foregrounds* the idea that there exists an "'ability to act otherwise' within all humans, although that ability may range from very constrained to very extensive" (Mumby, 2004, p. 242).

A rhetorical critic working from a critical organizational perspective asks how an organization presents those choices to its constituents in its messages and then examines the consequences of those choices.

More specifically, stakeholder theorists (Freeman, Harrison, & Wicks, 2007; Lewis, 2007) argue that organizations have multiple groups of people who have various "stakes," and whose needs must be met in a variety of ways for the organization to thrive. (For an alternative perspective featuring *stakeseekers,* see Heath & Palenchar, 2009.) Stakeholders include groups such as employees, stockholders, customers, suppliers, vendors, the media, and so forth. The choices of so many constituents present a tangle (and invariably conflicts) for organizational message designers that must be addressed (J. McMillan, personal communication, September, 2008). The critical organizational rhetoric scholar seeks to unravel those tangles by examining the organization's messages.

For example, an organization may be considering minimally following environmental protection laws in order to increase profits for stockholders, but that decision is likely to continue to contribute to pollution in an organization's physical community. When these conflicts of interest arise, critical rhetorical scholars specifically ask how those decisions are constructed and presented through an organization's messages. When those decisions are made and presented to the various groups, organizational rhetoric scholars examine the types of messages used to promote the organization's decisions.

In a related basic concept, critical approaches to organizational rhetoric also focus upon the voices of the various players involved. First, not all voices have equal access for presenting their interests. As we implied above, when organizational decisions are made, some stakeholders will see benefits and others will pay a price. Often those who pay a price are those stakeholders who have less power to influence the organization's decision makers. In essence, those stakeholders' voices are minimized or marginalized. Sometimes it is not obvious at first glance exactly whose voices are minimized, marginalized, or left out. It takes careful analysis on the critic's part to consider whose concerns are being overlooked, left out, or silenced. In other words, one of the critic's roles is to help give "the voiceless a voice" (Deetz, 1992, p. 4; see also Alvesson & Deetz, 2003).

For example, in most universities and colleges, students have a voice in how student fees are distributed to support various student organizations on campus. Often the groups responsible for these decisions are part of student government. In contrast, students often have little voice in decisions about which faculty members are hired. In those cases, student voices are marginalized.

Other questions of voice involve groups of individual organizations (nonprofits or corporations) that are presented as if they had one voice. Here are two examples. First, PhRMA, the Pharmaceutical Researchers and Manufacturers of America, is actually an interest group whose members include over 60 large pharmaceutical companies (PhRMA, 2007). By advocating specific positions as a group under PhRMA's identity, individual pharmaceutical companies may lobby for less-popular positions among their customer bases or within their industry with less risk to their individual identities or brands.

While these organizations certainly have the right to organize themselves in this way, the individual organizational members are shielded somewhat from direct consumer response to less-popular positions. Any particular member organization in question could disassociate itself from PhRMA's messages, reducing negative consequences to itself. In another example, it is less identity-threatening for the Recording Industry Association of America to issue confrontational advertisements asking people to stop illegally downloading music than for Sony to run the same advertisement. Responsibility for a message becomes diffused, leading the critical scholar to ask whose interests are being served with a particular message.

The Alliance for Managed Competition served a similar function for five individual insurance companies (Aetna Life and Casualty Corporation, Cigna Corporation, Metropolitan Life Insurance, Prudential Life Insurance, and Travelers Life Insurance) during the 1993–1994 health care reform debate (Schwartz, 1993). These "big 5" insurance companies actually supported the concept of universal coverage (health insurance for all U.S. citizens), as proposed in the Health Security Act, but that support was in conflict with the many smaller health insurance companies who would have been threatened by a universal health insurance plan. It is particularly important to examine the voices of, and the interests represented by, organizations whose identity is masked (Wander, 1983).

The following propositions form the foundation for critical approaches to organizational communication: (1) Messages are not neutral, (2) organizational members (leaders and followers) are choice makers, (3) organizational members' voices have a range of influence, and (4) an organization's voice is not always clearly identifiable. Key concepts of the critical approach to organizational rhetoric emerge from these foundations: power and the "discourse of suspicion," ideology, and hegemony. We discuss these key concepts next. In addition, we will discuss a critical bent to the concepts of organizational voice and publics.

Discourse of Suspicion and the Construction of Power

Since critical organizational theorists assume that messages are not neutral, that not all voices have an equal range of influence, and organizational voices are not always clearly identifiable, they work from the position that organizational stakeholders are in an ongoing struggle involving power (especially in terms of domination) and resistance to that power. Critical theorists are working to uncover sources of hidden or taken-for-granted power so that those whose freedom is more limited (usually employees, customers, or community members) than that of others (usually organizations as a whole and organizational leaders) can have more influence (voice) in what happens in their lives. More specifically, from the work of many critical theorists emerges a "discourse of suspicion" (Mumby, 2004, p. 237); in other words, critical theorists are suspicious of what organizations are up to. Mumby explains that this discourse of suspicion is a perspective for revealing the relationships among discourse (messages), ideology (discussed below), and deep-structure relations of power, particularly in the context of organizations. Thus, we might say that critical theorists believe there is more going on in messages than may appear on the surface.

Assuming this suspicious posture may feel somewhat depressing at times because it tends to emphasize the constraints within which we work, volunteer, or function as members of society. However, Deetz (1992) argues that this perspective actually reveals a measure of hope: From the process of revealing the sources of power and resistance (critique), organizational stakeholders (and others in society) can make changes in what is said and done in ways that may make the consequences of organizational actions less harmful to stakeholders, communities, and society as a whole.

German (1995) argues, "If we understand the implicit assumptions that frame our communication about such social priorities, then we can make more informed choices" (p. 281). At least the results may "make us aware of competing positions and interpretations" (Hauser, 1998, p. 100). For example, pharmaceutical companies argue that their patents for medicines they invent should last as long as possible before generically equivalent drugs can be created and sold. They assert that they need a longer-term patent in order to generate the profits to fund new pharmaceutical research. However, the prices of generically equivalent drugs are much lower than the original drugs, and therefore are more affordable to the average consumer. As a society, we have to examine the needs of the pharmaceutical companies to make a profit in order to stay in business and create new drugs (e.g., cancer drugs, AIDS drugs, etc.), as well as the needs of consumers to afford the drugs prescribed for their conditions.

The construction of *power* also is a central concept in critical approaches to organizational communication and organizational rhetoric. Specifically, critical approaches to organizational communication examine the ways in which power is constructed through communicative/rhetorical practices, or talk (messages). If you studied perspectives on power in a political science course, you likely would examine power in terms of raw force (e.g., military strength), arbitrary decision making (e.g., a monarchy), and monetary influence (e.g., contributions to campaigns), among others. In a business course, you likely would examine power in terms of control of raw materials or other types of resources (e.g., knowledge management), leadership, and management of bureaucracy (e.g., implementation of rules and regulations), and so forth. In a sociology course, you likely would examine power in terms of social characteristics, such as class, race, and gender. While all of these perspectives are certainly useful, they provide incomplete explanations for how organizations advocate for their interests.

From a critical organizational communication perspective, "what counts as power involves struggles over meaning" (Mumby, 2001, p. 593). In other words, the "stuff" of which organizational power is made is more than observable behavior and decision making, the control of resources, or social characteristics, although those issues certainly are present. Instead, power is understood as the ways in which basic forms of perception and social reality get constructed through language choices and communication processes (Mumby, 2004). Negotiating, forming perceptions, creating images, shaping stakeholder beliefs, and managing stakeholder consent to organizational values, all of which are grounded in carefully crafted rhetoric, are all examples of key strategies by which organizations create a meaning system that favors their interests over those of other stakeholders (Conrad, 1983; Mumby, 2001, 2004).

A critical organizational rhetoric perspective also draws attention to the balance of power among organizations and individuals in the public dialogue, and access to processes of message production. Critical organizational rhetoric scholars aim to challenge the domination of the organizational voice in our society by examining public messages (those messages designed for the organization's nonemployees; German, 1995). As we discussed earlier, in contrast to individuals, generally large organizations (including corporate, nonprofit, and governmental organizations) wield much more influence on society because they have the financial resources to access media outlets that most individuals do not have. While the Internet offers individuals access to broad audiences in ways not possible in the past, individuals still do not have the same access to more expensive media that larger organizations do. Thus, critical theory specifically asks us to "consider 'who' is really speaking when the organization makes a public announcement or participates in a social debate, as well as whose interests are being served as it does so" (Meisenbach & McMillan, 2006, p. 123). When the "organization" speaks, questions of authorship, intent, audience, and responsibility for what is said, as well as of the message's consequences, must be raised (German, 1995).

In addition, the critical perspective asks us to consider the consequences of organizations' and individuals' unequal capacity to control how messages are produced, distributed, and consumed (Leitch & Neilson, 2001). Most individuals and smaller organizations do not have the capital, the time, or other resources that large corporations do to design and distribute messages to mass audiences. Individual access to the Internet has changed that to some extent, but access to network television for message distribution, for example, normally is beyond the scope of most individuals and smaller organizations.

Critical organizational rhetoric scholars also specifically consider issues of power and voice of organizational members (usually employees), particularly those who have less status in an organization (Cheney & Christensen, 2001b). In contrast to early 1900s management approaches that featured ways to coerce employees to do their work, many of today's organizational members must be persuaded, not coerced, to work within the organization's parameters and advance the organization's goals (Bisel, Ford, & Keyton, 2007; Cloud, 2005; Tompkins & Cheney, 1985). Such persuasive messages, as well as who has the voice to influence design and distribution of those messages, are key issues for critical organizational rhetoric scholars who examine rhetoric primarily designed for an organization's employees and potential employees (e.g., Hoffman & Cowan, 2008).

In summary, the critical theorist approaches organizational messages suspiciously, asking "what is this organization up to"; works to untangle the construction of power in a particular situation; and raises the question of unequal voices or whose interests are being served by a message or set of messages.

Ideology

Closely related to the construct of power is the construct of ideology. From Foss's (2004) perspective, *ideology* is a "pattern of beliefs that determines a group's interpretations of some aspects of the world" (p. 239). Marx used the term *ideology* to refer to the ruling ideas of the ruling class (Wander, 1983). Critical scholars question how and whether the ruling ideas of the powerful should guide the creation of meaning by those who are ruled. For example, should advertisers, religious organizations, or government determine what "family" means, or should that be determined by family members?

Mumby (2001) argues that in the context of organizational communication studies, ideology concerns the ways in which the identities of organization members are constructed through the ways we talk and write at work. It is through such symbol use that power relations are produced, maintained, or transformed. As Mumby (1987) explains more specifically, "Ideology provides the underlying logic which guides and constrains discourse, while at the same time discourse is the means by which ideology is continually produced and reproduced" (p. 302). In other words, the way we talk—literally, the words we choose to use—impact how those people we work with understand what we and they can do at work (e.g., what projects we take on, what benefits we take advantage of, etc.), as well as how we and they do our work (e.g., how late we work at night, whether we work in teams, etc.).

Kirby and Krone (2002) describe a process of ideological enactment in an organization that constrains the choices its employees make. Employees of an auditing organization are allowed to take paternity leave at the birth of a child; however, few male employees actually take paternity leave in this organization. Why do fathers in this organization feel that they cannot take this leave? A variety of unwritten rules are played out in conversations among coworkers that influence fathers' decisions to not take advantage of the policy. These rules help the organization's leadership ensure that the work gets done, without regard to the sacrifices of the individual employees. Let's examine how this process occurred in this organization.

Ideologically, the policy itself confirmed that the organization's leaders are in power because the leaders are the ones who "allow" an employee to take leave. But going beyond this clear example of power, the issue was that few take advantage of the leave available, despite the policy that allows it. This must mean that there was something keeping the fathers from requesting leave.

An unwritten component of the organization's ideology was revealed in that the organization's work must still be completed in the absence of the employee. It was left up to the team members to get this work done without additional support (e.g., temporary help, bonuses for coworkers who take on extra work). This further established that the organization's leaders have the power to say who has to complete the work, but it also began to limit the team members' options. The managers never outright said, "You are not allowed to take paternity leave." Instead, communicative interactions among team members created pressure (like peer pressure) that prevented fathers from taking leave. In other words, the fathers were made to feel so uncomfortable about asking for leave that they *chose* not to ask for it.

Specifically, coworkers discouraged each other from actually taking paternity leave by what they said to each other. The work left by the person on leave still had to be covered by another member of the work team, and the remaining team members were reluctant to take on loads beyond their own duties. So, by making negative comments among themselves about leave taken by other coworkers (e.g., "He gets to take time off every week for his kid's baseball game"), team members discouraged fathers from taking paternity leave. In addition, managers did not outright encourage fathers to take the leave anyway. These combined messages made choosing not to take the leave appear to be legitimate. This discouragement by team members, and lack of encouragement on the leaders' parts, reproduced the unwritten rule that the organization's work must be done at the expense of personal priorities.

Where was the organizational rhetoric in this situation? In this case, the key is in what was *not* in written messages. For example, had the organization wanted to demonstrate that it actually did support fathers taking leave time (versus merely stating in its benefits statement that the policy was available), the organization might have included a procedure in its document about how to request the time off. More importantly, a procedure for managers could have been included that describes how to equitably redistribute workloads, or how to hire temporary help, so that individual employees did not have to pressure their colleagues to take on additional work by default. Even more visible to employees might have been stories (or at least blurbs) about the births of employees' children published in organizational newsletters. Because such rhetorical messages were missing, the company's influence over fathers' individual behavior was hidden.

Another example more specifically illustrates how organizations' ideologies were at work to subtly limit the understanding of their employee audiences. Hoffman and Cowan (2008) analyzed 50 company Web pages concerning work/life balance. The rhetoric of these organizations attempted to define for employees the meaning of "life" outside of work, and encouraged employees to view organizational objectives on a par with personal interests. Most importantly, the organizations used their own definitions of what was work, what was "life," and what constitutes a work/life balance. These organizations did not open a space for individuals to define for themselves what work/life balance meant to them individually.

These examples illustrate that ideologies are keys to understanding the ways in which power is enacted by organizations through rhetorical strategies when outright coercion (threat of firing, physical coercion) is not used (see also Tompkins & Cheney, 1985). In essence, this research focuses on "describing the practices and routines by which alternatives are disregarded or rendered invisible" (Deetz, 1992, p. 59).

Sociologist Anthony Giddens (1979) outlined a set of questions that we can ask to examine hidden practices like we have discussed above. He called these questions *ideological aspects of symbolic orders* (messages) (see also McKerrow, 1989). Giddens argued that three principal ideological forms (ways things are said) are used to strategically conceal sectional interest (in this case, an organization's interests). In the first ideological form, we would ask the following: How are sectional (organizational) interests represented as universal interests? For example, a manager's views traditionally are accepted without question as representing a department's situation, rather than employees' views of a department's situation (Alvesson & Deetz, 2003). Yet we know that some organizations have learned that certain decisions need to be made by those who have the most contact with customers, such as customer service representatives or sales agents.

In the second ideological form, we would ask the following: How are contradictions denied or transmuted? In other words, are contradictions in what is said either not acknowledged, or is our attention drawn away from what is going on in the message? For example, in the development of Medicare Part D (prescription drug coverage for seniors), it was not always clear to the general public that the addition of Medicare prescription coverage for those over 65 or who are disabled would cover costs only in certain ranges of annual cost (Pear, 2006). Medicare would cover prescription costs up to $2,250 per year, and then stop covering until an individual's prescription costs reached $5,100 per year. It took extensive press coverage to reveal this "donut hole" in coverage so that Medicare recipients could understand that they would still be responsible for over $1,000 in prescription costs per year. (Many prescriptions for people over the age of 65 can run as high as $100 per month for one prescription.) This contradiction in terms, "Medicare Part D will cover prescription costs for seniors," when it only covers to specific limits, was transmuted, or downplayed, by those who wrote the bill.

In Giddens's third ideological form, we would ask, What is occurring in the present that is naturalized—that is, made to seem unchangeable, when it really is changeable? By making the meaning-making process less transparent or obvious, organizational decisions are no longer seen as choices but as natural, self-evident, and "required" actions (Alvesson & Deetz, 2003). As humans, we often construct structures that seem to take on an objective, "natural" existence, independent from the fact that we are the ones who constructed them (Mumby, 2001). For example, at one time bureaucratic structures in organizations (rule-driven, chain-of-command ways to organize) had been as accepted as the best, and often the only way, to organize. These methods of structuring organizations seemed "natural." Yet organizations today are learning to organize with more flexible structures, such as web-like structures, or distributed or virtual organizations, that allow these organizations to more easily adapt to environmental changes.

In summary, the goal of ideological critique in organizational rhetoric is to reveal how power is hidden in messages. When we evaluate rhetoric critically (in this critical theory sense), we want to call into question the circumstances that appear to exist by common sense. These commonsense understandings may privilege organizational interests and goals over other individual or societal interests and goals, thereby creating conditions that may be harmful or oppressive to those who have less power (in our case, employees; Mumby, 1993). In other words, we may find that organizational rhetoric masks actions that may not be in the best interest of all groups of organizational stakeholders.

Hegemony and Whose Meaning "Wins"

The third key concept in critical approaches to organizational communication is hegemony. *Hegemony* involves the "struggle over systems of meaning and the processes by which social reality is framed" (Mumby, 1997, p. 364). Clearly the concept of hegemony is related to the concept of ideology as discussed above. Whereas ideological critique asks us to use a particular set of questions to examine whose interests are served by a message, hegemony focuses more specifically on the relationship between power and resistance. More specifically, hegemony may be distinguished from ideology by its emphasis on the process of struggle to determine whose meaning "wins."

For example, for over 100 years, physicians have sought to define the scope of medical practice in ways that limit the scopes of practice for other health care providers such as nurses, chiropractors, physical therapists, pharmacists, and so forth (Friedson, 1970/1998; Starr, 1982). This limitation is accomplished through policy development (regulations), as well as through messages in the media. However, as health care costs have skyrocketed, these other health care providers have demonstrated through research that allied health care professionals provide certain types of care equally well (using protocols approved by physicians), and more cost-effectively than physicians do. Thus, the legal scope of practice of nonphysician providers, such as physician assistants and nurse practitioners (usually nurses with master's degrees), has expanded over the years. While physicians clearly still wield considerable hegemonic power in the health care system, balances to such power have emerged. This competition, so to speak, over who should be allowed to do which type of work takes place through rhetoric directed at various audiences.

These contests over whose system(s) of meaning would prevail were initially described essentially as two-sided: one side the dominator, the other the repressed. Specifically, the question of hegemony originally asked the critic to examine how the repressed side participates in its own repression. A common example is when women argue that men should control an organization's hierarchy. The concept of hegemony has morphed into at least two different forms over time, but both perspectives seek to account for more than the two "voices" of the dominant and the oppressed. First, Condit (1994) argued that critiques of hegemonic struggles over policy acceptance are actually better described as a *critique of concord*. She explains,

> Social concord is the active or passive acceptance of a given social policy or political framework as the best that can be negotiated under the given conditions. . . . Concord is neither harmonious nor inevitably fair or equitable, it is simply the best that can be done under the circumstances. (p. 10)

A critique of such concord seeks to understand how multiple voices influenced the acceptance (or rejection) of particular policies. By seeking to account for the ways in which the individual organizations incorporated other organizations' interests into their own messages, an argument can be made for how a different public policy results from that which any single organization would have advocated. The process of hegemony from Condit's (1994) perspective, then, is more complex than earlier descriptions of it.

The second perspective on hegemony that more recent theories have taken also tries to account for more than two broad voices of domination and resistance (McKerrow, 1989). This form, advocated by Ashcraft (2005), Mumby (1997), and others, seeks to explain how the same "discursive space" reveals aspects of both domination and resistance. In other words, "even overt consent may constitute a form of resistance" (Ashcraft, 2005, p. 69). Thus, both newer explanations of hegemony recognize that the process of forming consent is more complicated than once thought (Fleming & Spicer, 2008).

Corporate Voice

The idea of corporate voice is not limited to critical theory approaches to understanding organizations or organizational rhetoric. It is also not limited to corporate organizations; nonprofit and governmental organizations also use corporate voice. *Corporate voice* is used to refer to the generally faceless, nonspecific source of organizational messages. These types of messages are rarely attributed to the CEO, public relations professional, or other organizational member who designed the message. The concept of corporate voice was one of the defining characteristics of organizational rhetoric from its earliest theoretical descriptions (e.g., Cheney, 1983; Cheney, 1991; Cheney & McMillan, 1990). However, the concept of corporate voice is key to understanding how organizations rhetorically position themselves to achieve their goals, whether that is building an image, influencing a policy, or responding to a crisis, among other goals.

The idea of corporate voice emerges from the legal concept that an organization is due the same protections as a person. This concept of organization-as-person was established by the U.S. Supreme Court in 1886 (*Santa Clara County v. Southern Pacific*, 1886; Cheney & McMillan, 1990). As Cheney (1991) explains, "The organization became in effect a *natural* person" (p. 5; emphasis in original). Today, that voice is the "loudest in the land" (Schiller, 1989, p. 4)—louder than religious institutions as a group or the government as a whole, for example, and much louder than any one individual.

Corporate voice is that disembodied "we," often used in statements by those representing the organization, regardless of whether it is for-profit, nonprofit, or governmental. Examples include, "The American Red Cross said today . . .," or "Wal-Mart explained . . ." While CEOs or other spokespersons often speak on behalf of an organization, it usually is assumed in American culture that the individual is not speaking on behalf of her- or himself, but rather is saying what the organization would say. The corporate "we" often appears in the passive voice, which gives it an air of being from an impersonal, collective source (Cheney & McMillan, 1990).

As Cheney (1991) notes, "Organizational messages take on a relatively placeless, nameless, omniscient quality, even when a corporate identity is assumed and declared" (p. 5). Thus, the critical organizational rhetoric scholar would ask "who is really speaking when the organization makes a public announcement or participates in a social debate, as well as whose interests are being served as it does so" (Meisenbach & McMillan, 2006, p. 123). In other words, the critical scholar of organizational rhetoric wants to reveal the often unstated purpose behind the organization's statements. Sometimes that purpose serves both the organization and selected stakeholder groups, including the community; sometimes the purpose serves only the organization.

"The" Public

As argued in Chapter 1, the concept of audiences or publics is a key component in understanding rhetoric overall and organizational rhetoric specifically. However, in the context of critical approaches to organizational rhetoric, the concept of the public takes on a slightly different twist. Understanding a critical perspective on the concept of publics or audiences in organizational rhetoric begins with the description that we used in Chapter 1: those audiences that are important to the operation of the organization. Those audiences have multiple and often conflicting interests. Audiences important to an organization will vary, but may include customers, stockholders, employees, volunteers, regulatory agencies, and the communities of which the organization is a part.

This definition follows a traditional, managerially focused idea of audience or public. In other words, these audiences or publics are defined by the organization, from the organization's perspective. By this definition, these audiences are considered a rather permanent collection of individuals with an enduring set of attitudes, demographics, and geographic locations (Vasquez & Taylor, 2001). Hauser (1998) stated that a poll would describe a public as a fixed meaning "in the frozen frame of a statistic" (p. 91). These publics are also generally considered passive, waiting for organizations to communicate with them, rather than "individuals actively involved in the ongoing construction of their own identities, strategies or goals" (Leitch & Neilson, 2001, p. 128). Thus, publics that are not defined as important to the organization are marginalized, or left out of conversations or actions that may have consequences for them because the organization feels it knows what is best for them (Karlberg, 1996).

Critical descriptions of publics assume a much more fluid, active definition that specifically acknowledges publics as groups of individuals. Vasquez and Taylor (2001) describe this view of publics as "a situationally developing social entity that emerges through spontaneous argument, discussion, and collective opposition to some issue or problematic situation" (p. 142). In other words, a public or audience per se may not exist until a group of people come together to agree or disagree with an organization's actions. For example, in 2007–2008, there were publics that emerged to support the building of two coal electricity plants in western Kansas, as well as publics that emerged to resist the building of the plants. Neither of those "publics" existed until the proposal to develop such coal-powered electricity plants was presented to Kansas governmental decision makers, but as people reacted to the proposal both negatively and positively, the publics emerged.

The critical perspective on audiences assumes that individuals within these groups participate as members of many publics or audiences that vary over time and circumstances. Consider how you may be a member of your college department, an employee of an organization, a member of a religious organization, and a volunteer for Big Brothers/Big Sisters of America. That means you are a member of at least four publics or audiences. Your membership in the religious organization (as well as other factors) may have influenced which college you decided to attend. So, your memberships in various publics may influence your memberships or actions in other publics, thus making your participation in a particular organization difficult to project as a statistic.

From a critical theory perspective, then, an organization's audiences or publics may be (1) defined by an organization or (2) defined by the publics themselves. If they are defined by an organization, then that organization may acknowledge that such publics are changing groups that may or may not acquiesce to the organization's messages. Leitch and Neilson (2001) explain, "There is no guarantee that such publics will be content with their status as organizational artifacts or will accept the meanings that organizations have imposed upon them" (p. 137). If a public is defined by the public itself, then this public-centered perspective may "expose the links as well as the disconnects between organization and public values, underscoring the importance for practitioners to provide meaningful contributions to the public-organization dialogue, creating, negotiating, and codefining meaning with publics" (Edwards, 2006, p. 836).

This perspective creates space for the idea that members of various publics participate in a conversation with an organization, rather than an organization working with just those publics it defines as linking with its interests (Leitch & Neilson, 2001). Creating space for a wide variety of voices to participate is a key goal of critical theory.

❖ SUMMARY OF KEY CONCEPTS IN CRITICAL THEORY/PERSPECTIVES

As has been shown, critical perspectives in organizational rhetoric draw our attention to several key issues:

- Power, particularly in relation to three concerns: (1) who has the right to speak in and for organizational decisions, (2) how organizations wield rhetorical influence to maintain the status quo in society, and (3) how an organization's publics might gain a voice in dialogues about organizational action;

- Choice, first in relation to the idea that all humans, but especially those in organizational leadership positions, have "the ability to act otherwise" (Mumby, 2004, p. 242);

- Voice, with two particular emphases: (1) analyzing the disembodied voice of the organization (corporate voice), and (2) creating space for voices beyond the corporate voice to be heard and acted upon in organizational decision making (McMillan, 2007); and

- The consequentiality of messages, in particular that organizational messages are not neutral; the message choices that organizations make have consequences for their members, as well as the society and communities of which it is a part.

(See Table 4.1 on p. 101 for a summary of characteristics of critical organizational rhetoric.) The combined ideas of power, choice, voice, and the consequentiality of messages lead us to a place where action is required of us. Such action may be our individual decisions about how we interact with an organization as a customer, an employee, or a community member. Such action may be our decisions about how we run an organization, if we become leaders. For now, such action concerns the questions we use to critique the rhetorical decisions made by organizations to build their identities; manage their impressions; or manage issues that affect them in terms of regulation, crisis, or risk. More importantly from the critical perspective, the answers to the questions of power and resistance help us analyze an organization's symbolic actions in terms of whether it is acting fairly and ethically. Our particular focus as critical organizational rhetoricians is on the organization's choices made about *voice* and *choice* as those are demonstrated in its messages.

❖ MAKING CHOICES: ETHICS AND ORGANIZATIONAL RHETORIC

Ethical choices among rhetorical actions are made based on sets of values. Conrad (1993b) defined values as "abstract and not-empirically verifiable beliefs" (p. 2). Examples of values (discussed in Chapter 2) include honesty and fair play. Values also are the basis of laws, such as truth-in-advertising laws. However, many decisions cannot be made merely upon the basis of a law. Particularly where there is no specific rule or law to follow in making a choice, ethics plays a role in decision making. As Fitzpatrick (2006) states, "Law is what people *must* do, while ethics is about what people *should* do. . . . Ethics begins where the law ends. Law is about compliance with set rules and procedures, while ethics involves more discretionary decision making" (p. 2).

There are many sources of criteria for making ethical decisions. Religious texts, such as the Bible, the Quran, and the Torah, provide sources of guiding principles for many people. For hundreds of years, philosophers such as Confucius, Aristotle, Kant, and Mills, among many others, have sought to establish sets of guiding principles for ethical decision making. Examples of such classic principles include the Golden Rule (i.e., "Do unto others as you would have them do unto you") and "The needs of the many outweigh the needs of the few." All of these are useful sources of guidance for those trying to make ethical decisions. However, as in most contexts, they are difficult to apply in the organizational context. Conrad (1993a) argues, "Organizational decision makers often are 'caught' between complex decision situations and varied and incongruent sets of values" (p. 11). He calls the interrelationships among values, ethics, and organizational decision making the "ethical nexus," to illustrate the complexity of such problems as "inherently problematic" (1993b, p. 2).

The purpose of this section is not to summarize the various ethical frameworks offered in countless philosophy and business textbooks. Rather, it is to highlight the assumptions advocated by critical theorists in judging rhetorical choices made by organizations, and to discuss the broad set of values themselves. These assumptions may be grouped into two broad categories of *voice* and *choice*.

A key assumption upon which values advocated by critical theorists rely is that organizations need to incorporate and act upon a broader range of voices in organizational decisions. Deetz (2003) explains, "The question is not whether but *whose* and *what* values get represented. Top executives do not lack values and do not hesitate using them implicitly in decision making. Competing values, however, do not have an opportunity to enter into the decision process" (p. 608, emphasis added; see also Conrad, 1993a). More specifically, Meisenbach and McMillan (2006) argue, "From a critical perspective, it may be less important whether organizations are allowed to 'speak' than whether they welcome other rhetors to the table" (p. 124).

As discussed earlier, a related key assumption upon which values advocated by critical theorists rely is that organizations must make choices. Early models of stakeholder theory assume that some organizational stakeholders will see benefits from those choices, and other stakeholders will pay a price (e.g., Freeman, 1984). In this perspective, stakeholders are identified by their power to influence the firm, the legitimacy of the stakeholder's relationship with the firm, and the urgency of the stakeholder's relationship with the firm (Mitchell, Agle,

& Wood, 1997). The primary stakeholder who benefits from these choices often has been the shareholder or financier of the organization. This perspective, based upon organizational survival as the prime goal, "drives organizational rhetoric toward a celebration of the organization itself . . . a stance now so familiar that citizens often forget that it represents a *choice*" (Cheney & McMillan, 1990, p. 105, emphasis in original). Often those who pay a larger price are those stakeholders who have less power to influence the organization's decision makers. In essence, consistent with the first assumption, those stakeholders' voices with less influence are minimized or marginalized. Sometimes it is not obvious whose voices are minimized or marginalized, so it takes careful analysis on the critic's part to consider whose concerns are being overlooked, left out, or silenced.

A stakeholder perspective emerging as this book is being written reframes stakeholder theory (Freeman et al., 2007; Lewis, 2007). This perspective recognizes that "alliances, or competitive relationships, among stakeholders of a given organization . . . give rise to a more complex stakeholder picture than the portrait of a manager assessing stakes and stakeholders and allocating resources accordingly" (Lewis, 2007, p. 193). This newer model of stakeholder theory far more inclusively recognizes the voices of groups that organizations need to include in their decision making. While still more managerially focused than most critical theorists likely would support, Freeman et al. advocate for far more recognition of, and participation by, a variety of organizational audiences than past models did. At minimum, the model now recognizes the various communities in which organizations are enmeshed as a set of the primary stakeholders for organizations. The authors also advocate for managers to consider what is best for *all stakeholders*, rather than just what is best for shareholders (when dealing with corporate organizations), advisory boards (when dealing with nonprofit organizations, such as museums), or legislative oversight groups (when dealing with governmental agencies), when managers make choices among organizational actions, including rhetorical choices.

Based upon these concepts of more inclusive voice and choice, the following values emerge from various critical theorists for making ethical decisions:

- *Open discussion* in order to provide "the fundamental opportunity for truth. If the message functions to constrict audience participation, then it lacks truth, since it exploits unexamined social values" (German, 1995, p. 292);

- Free discussion based upon *goodwill, argumentation, and dialogue,* rather than decisions based upon authority, tradition, ideology, or exclusion of participants (Alvesson & Deetz, 2003, p. 202; McMillan, 2007); and

- Exploration of statements on a basis of *comprehensibility* (clarity), *sincerity, truthfulness, and legitimacy* (Alvesson & Deetz, p. 203; see also Haas, 2001).

Cheney (1992) phrases these values in a more straightforward set of questions that we as critics can use to evaluate organizational messages:

- How do an organization's messages reflect its interests?
- What are the implications of a particular organization's rhetoric for individual audience members?
- What assumptions are made about the organization, its members, other stakeholders, and society in general?
- How are images employed by a corporate rhetor?
- What do those images *say* about the organization and other groups?
- Whose interests are represented by corporate messages? (p. 180)

The answers to these questions, as we examine any set of organizational texts, lead us to explore the set of values listed above, and move us toward evaluating the inclusion of various publics in organizational messages.

❖ CONCLUSION

In conclusion, critical theoretical approaches to organizational rhetoric are challenging to understand and use for evaluating organizational choices, as they are reflected in texts. (See Table 4.1 for a summary of key constructs in critical organizational rhetoric.) It is challenging for organizations to incorporate diverse perspectives, needs, and values into the choices they make. However, as Mumby (2004) reminds us, "Organizations are real structures that have real consequences for real people. Yes, that reality is socially constructed, but I think we must be careful not to forget the material consequences of that social construction process" (p. 252). Critical perspectives on organizational rhetoric provide organizational critics with tools to recognize, value, and examine whether multiple voices are reflected in organizational decision making.

Table 4.1   Characteristics of Critical Approaches to Organizational Rhetoric

Characteristic	Characteristic as it emerges in critical approaches to organizational rhetoric
Basic goal:	"Unmask organizational domination": Reveal whose social values are being endorsed by the rhetoric
Method:	Ideology critique, cultural criticism, feminist criticism (among others)
Hope:	Reformation of social order to enhance more equitable choices
Metaphor of social relations:	Political (i.e., organizations and their stakeholders attempt to advance their interests in particular ways)
Metaphor of organization:	Polity (i.e., organizations as political arenas)
Problems addressed:	Domination by those in power; consent and resistance of those not in power
Concern with communication:	Systematic distortion, misrecognition
Organizational benefits as a result of this approach:	Participation, expanded knowledge among many stakeholders
Mood:	Suspicious
Social fear:	Authority

SOURCE: Adapted from *Prototypical Discursive Features of Critical Theory Discourse* (Alvesson & Deetz, 2003, p. 198).

❖ NOTE

1. Examples of philosophical approaches that have been applied in organization studies include Foucault (1972; see Deetz, 1992), Giddens (1979; see Mumby, 1987), Gramsci (1971; see Condit, 1994), and Marx (1978; see Cloud, 2005), among others.

5

Evaluating and Critiquing Organizational Rhetoric

❖   ❖   ❖

Figure 5.1   Process for Analyzing Organizational Rhetoric (Readings)

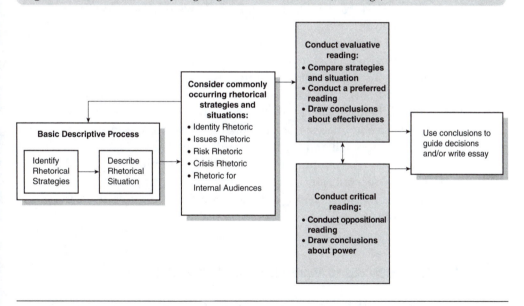

SOURCE: Adapted from Ford (1999).

People are interested in organizational rhetoric for a variety of reasons—some want to know how to create more effective organizational messages, while others want to better understand the role of organizations in culture. As we established in Chapter 1, these interests will generally fall under one of four goals: (1) determining whether or not the rhetoric should have been effective, or how it could be more effective; (2) understanding and judging what is revealed by an organization's presentation of itself, including what values the organization upholds; (3) understanding and judging the general role and power of organizations in society; or (4) adding to our general understanding of theory surrounding organizational rhetoric. Previous chapters have provided the theory and tools needed to conduct descriptive and critical readings of organizational rhetoric. In this chapter, we expand on the process used to conduct each type of reading.

Once you have determined your goal as a critic, you can select an analytical tool best suited to accomplish that goal. Methods, or lenses, for analyzing rhetoric have been a subject of great debate among rhetorical scholars over the last 100 years (Black, 1965; Campbell, 1974; Wichelns, 1925), and have been the subject of numerous textbooks (Foss, 2004; Hart & Daughton, 2005; Rowland, 2008). We focus our discussion on two general approaches to "reading" organizational rhetoric, rather than on specific methods. However, for those already familiar with rhetorical methods, any of the specific methods of rhetorical criticism (neo-Aristotelian, genre, cluster, pentad, metaphor and narrative, for example) can be very useful within at least one of the approaches. In this section, we present two basic approaches to the analysis of organizational rhetoric—an evaluative reading approach and a critical reading approach. We begin by explaining why it is important that a critic is familiar with both approaches. We continue by discussing the origins and goals of each approach, and then present the general procedures used in carrying it out.

❖ TWO APPROACHES TO ANALYZING ORGANIZATIONAL RHETORIC

Having the ability to use both approaches to organizational rhetoric enables a critic to answer a wide variety of questions. Neither of the approaches by itself can meet all four of the goals of analyzing organizational rhetoric outlined above, so a good critic needs to be able to use both. In general, evaluative methods are useful for critics who want to understand if a piece of rhetoric is likely to meet the goals of its creators. Rhetors who work in public relations, communication, or human resource departments of organizations, and who are responsible for organizational publications and promotions, will rely heavily on evaluative approaches.

The critical approach asks different, yet equally important questions and seeks different types of answers. This approach is useful for those who are interested in how organizations exercise power in society—whether it be power over local community decisions (whether or not to build a new plant in a particular neighborhood), in state and national decisions (whether communication companies should have immunity for electronic eavesdropping), or international decisions (what the role of global organizations in the economies of their host countries should be). At some point, every critic will need to answer questions about effectiveness and questions about power, and an understanding of the two approaches provides a full set of lenses with which a critic can view the rhetorical world.

Whether a critic plans to conduct only an evaluative reading or intends to also conduct a critical reading, he or she must always begin with the basic process of identifying the strategies in the rhetoric and describing the rhetorical situation. In addition, although we discuss the evaluative reading and the critical reading as two distinct procedures, it is important to remember that all critics must begin with the evaluative reading.

An Evaluative Approach

The goal of the evaluative approach is fairly clear from the name. A critic working from this approach seeks to evaluate the rhetoric's ability to meet its goal, and perhaps describe the characteristics of messages that would have more effectively met that goal. Critics determine effectiveness by comparing the rhetorical strategies that they found in the artifact with what they have learned about the rhetorical situation.

Origins and Goals of the Evaluative Approach

The evaluative approach is best suited to addressing two of the four goals of analyzing organizational rhetoric. First, the evaluative approach allows the critic to judge whether a piece of rhetoric should be successful and make suggestions about how the rhetoric could be more effective. Second, it can make contributions to theory about organizational rhetoric. The other goals of analysis, understanding the motives and interests of individual organizations, and the role of organizations in society, are not goals that can be met with the evaluative approach.

The evaluative approach is rooted in two fairly traditional approaches to rhetorical criticism—neo-Aristotelian criticism and genre criticism. *Neo-Aristotelian criticism* is of course named for Aristotle. Early critics used classic rhetorical concepts (modes of proof, canons of rhetoric) to analyze how well a rhetor selected from what Aristotle (trans. 1932) called the "available means of persuasion" (Black, 1965; Hill, 1972; Rowland, 2008; Wichelns, 1925).

Genre criticism was developed by authors who argued that some rhetorical situations occur repeatedly, and that by studying repeating situations and the speeches used to address them, a critic could uncover shared characteristics (Campbell & Jamieson, 1978). In one example of a traditional genre study, Campbell and Jamieson (1990) reviewed a variety of presidential addresses to uncover similarities in the situation, content, and style of the speeches. Genre was an important development in rhetorical criticism because it allowed critics to use preexisting lists of common rhetorical strategies to analyze rhetoric in particular recurring situations.

Although the categories of organizational rhetoric treated in the first five chapters of this text do not fit the tight requirements of genre as established by Campbell and Jamieson (1978) or Rowland (1991), their similarities make a genre-like approach useful for understanding both situations and strategies. Neo-Aristotelian and genre criticism are distinct approaches to rhetorical criticism, but they share several common assumptions and practices that together constitute an evaluative approach to analyzing organizational rhetoric. Critics using the evaluative approach have, for example, studied how the Tylenol company responded to deaths due to poisoned product in the 1980s (Benoit, 1995a, 1995b; Benoit & Lindsey, 1987). They have also explored how organizations can effectively manage issues (Kuhn, 1997) and whether there are common characteristics that can be discovered across cases of organizations addressing wrongdoing (Rowland & Jerome, 2004).

Procedures of the Evaluative Approach

Evaluative Reading

Compare the rhetorical situation and strategies.

Conduct a preferred reading.

Draw conclusions about how well the rhetoric met the demands of the situation and consider how it might have been more effective.

After describing all of the rhetorical strategies present in the artifact and identifying the elements of the rhetorical situation, the critic is ready for the first evaluative step—comparing the demands of the situation with the rhetorical strategies selected by the organizational rhetor. A critic who prefers Bitzer's (1968) approach to the rhetorical situation would begin by focusing on the exigence, the audience, and the constraints in the situation, and looking to see if there are strategies in the rhetoric that address those elements. For example, if your analysis of a rhetorical situation revealed an exigence that few people knew about the success of a particular organization, then you would want to look for examples of strategies in the rhetoric that help to address or overcome that constraint. As you examine the sample rhetoric, you might find that the rhetor's use of statistics about the reliability or growth of the organization seemed to address that rhetorical problem.

A critic who agrees with Vatz's (1973) approach might begin by looking at the situation to determine what choices the rhetor faced in selecting which elements to address, and determining how to frame those events. Then, the critic would examine the rhetorical strategies to see the choices the rhetor made from all of the possibilities, and how he or she assigned meaning. For example, following an explosion at a chemical-processing company in Wisconsin, the situation was such that the rhetors for the company could choose from organizational error, individual error, and weather conditions in describing what happened during the explosion and who was responsible. The critic, then, would try to understand the rhetor's choices, and how those choices were evident in the resulting rhetoric.

To facilitate the comparison of the elements of the situation to the strategies in the rhetoric, you may want to create a chart that allows you to list elements of the situation (including citations from your research) alongside strategies from the rhetoric (including direct quotation, paraphrase, or description). The appendix for this book includes a Worksheet for Conducting an Evaluative Reading.

The second step in the evaluative reading is to conduct a "preferred" reading (McKerrow, 1989). When doing a *preferred reading*, you use your knowledge of the rhetorical strategies and the rhetorical situation to make an argument about what you think the rhetor wanted the audience to think, feel, or believe after receiving the rhetoric. In the case of organizational rhetoric, the preferred reading of a newsletter article about an employee who routinely works on Saturdays might be that the author intends to praise a good employee in order to help other employees feel valued by the organization.

The third step in an evaluative reading is to *draw conclusions* about effectiveness. Your preferred reading allowed you to make an argument about what the rhetor likely wanted to accomplish, and your comparison of the situation and strategies allows you to make an argument about whether the strategies were well selected to meet that goal. You must decide if there were enough of the right types of strategies used to effectively address the constraints, take advantage of the assets, and resolve or at least minimize the exigence. Evaluative judgments must then be supported by references concerning the situation and by direct quotation, paraphrase, or description of the strategies in the rhetoric.

It is important to note that rhetorical criticism does not allow us to determine whether a piece of rhetoric actually was effective in the sense that it changed people's thoughts or behaviors. To make that kind of argument, we would need to use a social-scientific research methodology. It does, however, allow us to make an argument that says, "Based on what we know about the situation, and what we know about the strategies, the rhetoric should/should not have been successful."

The second half of the third step in an evaluative analysis goes a bit beyond the idea of drawing conclusions as laid out in neo-Aristotelian and genre criticism. To complete this part of the analysis, a critic needs to not only determine whether the rhetoric accomplished its goals, but also to make suggestions about which rhetorical strategies might have been more effective. These suggestions are made by comparing the demands of the rhetorical situation with a set of hypothetical strategies created in the mind of the critic. Then, the critic chooses which strategies would be most effective. This last step is a practical one—it allows critics to transfer their skills to the creation of organizational rhetoric.

An evaluative reading allows a critic to make arguments about what the rhetor wanted to accomplish and how well he or she was able to do so. It is an important tool for those who want to understand what successful messages look like, and for those who want to create them. As useful as an evaluative reading is, however, it cannot answer all of the questions a critic might want to ask about organizational rhetoric.

A Critical Approach

As explained in Chapter 4, a critical perspective on organizational rhetoric focuses on what the rhetoric reveals about how organizations create and use power. Critics coming from this perspective seek to understand how ideologies—ways of believing that influence how groups view the world—are used to gain and maintain power in a society.

Origins and Goals of the Critical Approach

This approach works from the assumption that symbols are never neutral—that instead they create or resist power in almost all situations. A critical approach is important because organizations are in a position to wield great power. Cheney and Dionisopoulos (1989) attributed this potential for power to organizations' "(a) access to great resources, (b), the concentration of information control among a relatively small number of organizations and institutions in our society, and (c) the 'one-way' nature of most (although not all) corporate communications" (p. 149). A second assumption is that a critic can understand the construction of power by looking at the rhetoric created by an organization (Mumby, 1987).

Taking a critical approach to organizational rhetoric allows critics to meet two of the four goals of studying organizational rhetoric. Depending on how much and what type of rhetoric they analyze, this approach can help critics learn about how power operates in a particular organization, in organizations in general, or in society. Critics using this approach may also contribute to the body of theory that currently explains organizational rhetoric. They cannot, however, use this approach to judge the effectiveness of the rhetoric, or to make suggestions for how the rhetoric could be more effective. Those goals are best met by the evaluative approach. Critics using the critical approach have studied how organizations present images of work to employees in potentially idealistic ways (Young & Foot, 2006), how organizations use messages about work/life balance to create a narrow definition of what counts as "life" outside of work (Hoffman & Cowan, 2008), and how organizations use messages about fitness to exert increased control over employees' choices (Zoller, 2003). This approach is particularly useful for those who want to understand what an organization values, and whether an organization ethically pursues its goals.

Procedures for the Critical Approach

Critical Reading

Conduct an oppositional reading.

Draw conclusions about power.

As McKerrow (1989) argued, although an ideological or critical approach to rhetoric is not so much a prescribed method as it is a practice, it is nonetheless important for beginning critics to have some systematic approach when considering organizational rhetoric. Unlike the evaluative approach that asks for a single reading that makes a seemingly neat comparison of situation and rhetorical strategies, a critical reading requires additional steps. Critical theorists discuss two ways that texts can be "read" or interpreted (McKerrow, 1989). These are often referred to as preferred readings and oppositional readings. You completed a preferred reading in the second step of the evaluative reading. In the critical approach, the preferred reading sets the stage for an *oppositional reading* that allows the critic to uncover the potential power implications in the rhetoric.

The first step in the critical reading, then, is to complete an oppositional reading. This type of reading looks more deeply for the power implications present in the preferred reading. The critic conducting an oppositional reading is looking for assumptions that may be taken for granted in the rhetoric, or for interpretations of the symbols not seen or intended by the organizational rhetor. In the newsletter example above, the oppositional reading might include questions about how the employee is compensated for extra work; how he or she has been persuaded to work on Saturday; or whether by praising the employee, the organization is actually seeking to encourage others to work during what many consider to be personal time.

Because learning to conduct an oppositional reading is challenging, the following section includes a number of questions that a beginning critic can use as a guide. In keeping with the overview of critical theory and practice outlined in chapter 4, the questions revolve around issues of choice and voice.

Questions of choice are an important starting point in a critical method. They ask a critic to consider both the choices made by a rhetor in presenting information and arguments, and the choices the rhetor leaves open to audiences of the message. A critic will ask some or all of the following questions when working on an oppositional reading:

- Is the information presented in a way that is comprehensive and truthful (Alvesson & Deetz, 2003)? Does the information allow audiences to make fully informed decisions?

- What is left unsaid in the rhetoric? What information is omitted, and what topics are not addressed (Cheney & Dionisopoulos, 1989)?

- Are apparent contradictions explained away in a manner that prevents audiences from understanding or questioning them (Giddens, 1979)?

- Are there assumptions about power and shared values that are taken for granted in the discourse (McKerrow, 1989)? Is the rhetorically constructed nature of power hidden in such a way that organizational arrangements are no longer seen as choices but as natural and self-evident or as just "the way things are" (Alvesson & Deetz, 2003)?

Questions of voice are also important in understanding how power is constructed and maintained in organizations, and can help a critic make an oppositional reading. Cheney and Dionisopoulos (1989) maintain that "organizations . . . should represent interests in such a way that both persuades and allows for others to persuade" (p. 148). Daugherty (2001) summarized a similar perspective by stating, "If there is to be an overall truth, then it must be one that is produced by all parties in the dialogue" (p. 408). Who has the authority to speak, for whom, and about what, are all questions of voice. The following list of questions can guide a critic's analysis of voice in a sample of organizational rhetoric:

- Who is "speaking" in the rhetoric? Whose interests are represented in the discourse, and whose are ignored, diminished, or obscured?

- How clearly can you identify the source of the rhetoric (Cheney & Dionisopoulos, 1989; Cheney & McMillan, 1990)? What additional parties are represented by the perspective of the authoring organization?

- Are the ideas or values of a few powerful parties presented as if they are the ideas or values of the whole (Giddens, 1979)?

- Also drawing on Giddens (1979), are contradictions denied, or treated in such a way as to minimize their importance and deprive audiences of the opportunity to explore and challenge those contradictions, and voice their objections?

- Does the discourse invite participation from other interested parties (Foss, 2004)? Does it offer opportunities for audiences to locate additional information, to provide feedback, or to ask questions? (German [1995] has argued that messages that constrict audience participation may exploit unexamined social values.)

The rhetorical strategies common to organizational messages play an important role in conducting an oppositional reading. Instead of asking whether the correct strategies were selected (as an evaluative critic would), a critic using the critical approach asks how particular strategies serve to influence issues of choice and voice. Foss (2004) calls this process "discovering the rhetorical mechanisms used to advocate for and defend" an ideology or point of view (p. 245).

In thinking about the relationship between rhetorical strategies and power, a critic may consider several ideas. First, do the particular values advocated by a rhetor privilege the interests of one group or ignore those of another? (An emphasis on the value of profit, for example, may obscure the fact that some parties might value quality of life more highly. Second, do the claims made and evidence provided expose some information while hiding other information that may be equally important, or are arguments based on assumptions that might not be shared by all audience members? In other words, is information presented in ways that are so complex that audience members cannot make an informed judgment?

Third, does the organization's presentation of itself through corporate social legitimacy strategies represent an idealized view or a view that both critics and supporters could recognize as accurate? For example, would the people who live next door to a production facility agree that the organization's donations to charity are enough evidence that they show concern for the community?

Fourth, do the language choices frame ideas in particular ways? In other words, are particular topics and ideas expressed with language designed to privilege emotion over reason, or reason over emotion, or that suggest preexisting ideas about whether something is good or bad?

The questions framed here represent the basic questions of emotional appeals, claims and evidence, credibility, and style, but a critic can ask similar questions about any of the more specific rhetorical strategies outlined in Chapter 2. Critics who are more familiar with traditional rhetorical methods may also use methods including pentad, cluster, narrative, and metaphor to inform their oppositional readings. By asking key questions about choice and voice, a critic can expose both the domination (exercise of power) and the freedom (points at which power can be resisted) that operate in a selection of rhetoric (McKerrow, 1989).

The final step in the critical approach to analyzing organizational rhetoric is to draw conclusions about how power is constructed, maintained, or challenged in the discourse. This step includes describing the ideology or worldview of the organization. A critic explains what the oppositional reading revealed about the values and practices of the organization that might have been invisible to someone doing only the evaluative reading. In our newsletter example, a critical theorist would compare the preferred reading that concluded that the organization wanted to praise good employees to the oppositional reading that concluded that the organization wanted to encourage people to work on personal time, and conclude that rhetors for the organization may have been trying to obscure their true motives by presenting the information as they did.

More general conclusions emerging from the critical reading might also concern the implications of organizational practices for audiences and society. The appendix for this book includes a Worksheet for Conducting a Critical Reading.

❖ CONCLUSION

A well-rounded critic of organizational rhetoric will be able to use both the evaluative and critical approaches to analyze organizational messages. Each approach allows critics to ask different questions and explore diverse, but equally important ideas. The evaluative approach asks a critic to determine how well the basic rhetorical strategies were selected and assembled to meet the demands of the rhetorical situation. This approach can help to determine if a piece of rhetoric should have been successful in accomplishing its goal. It is also a key for someone who wants to be able to create rhetoric. The ability to describe a rhetorical situation and to recognize and employ the strategies of organizational rhetoric is central to creating effective messages. Critical approaches are concerned with how power is revealed or concealed in organizational rhetoric. They are useful for understanding the motives of an organization, for making arguments about the role of organizational power in society or individual lives, or in evaluating the ethics of organizational decisions.

Despite their clear utility, these two approaches often exist in tension with one another, since one seems more suited to the practical world, and the other to the philosophical world. However, being able to use both approaches offers several advantages. As a member of an organization, you want to be able to recognize and create effective messages. The evaluative approach offers the best tools for this goal. At the same time, you want to create ethical messages, and you should be concerned with how organizational rhetoric wields power in various parts of your life. The critical approach provides the tool to answer these questions. Being able to use both approaches can make you a wiser employee, a wiser consumer, and a wiser citizen.

This understanding of how to conduct evaluative and critical readings will be useful as you move through the next five chapters of this text. In each of the remaining chapters, you will learn about a category of rhetoric, the situation it addresses, and the strategies it most often employs. You will also have the opportunity to think about how that type of rhetoric works to exercise power or allow for resistance.

To practice conducting these two types of readings, revisit the rhetoric debating new power plants in Texas (found at the end of Chapter 2) and the summary of the rhetorical situation (found at the end of Chapter 3). Use the Worksheet for Conducting an Evaluative Reading and the Worksheet for Conducting a Critical Reading to draw conclusions about the rhetorical artifacts.

WORKSHEET FOR CONDUCTING AN EVALUATIVE READING

Remember that before moving to this step, you should complete the basic descriptive process by identifying rhetorical strategies and describing the rhetorical situation.

Step I. Compare Rhetorical Strategies With Demands of the Rhetorical Situation

Situational Elements: From Worksheet for Analyzing Rhetorical Situation	*Rhetorical Strategies:* From Worksheet for Identifying Rhetorical Strategies
Exigence:	Identify strategies that seem to address the exigence.
Audiences:	Identify strategies that seem specifically tailored for a particular audience or audiences.
Constraints:	Identify strategies that seem specifically designed to address particular constraints.
	Identify strategies that appear in the rhetoric but don't seem to match specific elements of the situation.

Step II. Conduct a Preferred Reading

Answer the following question: Given what you know about the rhetorical strategies and rhetorical situations, what did the rhetor want the audience to think, feel, or believe after viewing or hearing the rhetoric?

Step III. Draw a Conclusion About Effectiveness

Your preferred reading allowed you to make an argument about what the rhetor likely wanted to accomplish. Now, use the comparison you made in Step I to make an argument about how well the strategies were selected to match the demands of the situation. Be able to support your evaluation with information about the rhetorical situation (including source citations) and with examples from the rhetoric (by quoting directly or paraphrasing from the rhetoric).

After the Analysis

Once you have completed your evaluative reading, you may apply your findings by writing an essay, discussing your conclusions with others, formulating general ideas about what is effective in organizational rhetoric, or using the ideas to make decisions about the organization. You may also want to take your analysis one step further by conducting a critical reading (Worksheet for Conducting a Critical Reading; see p. 117).

WORKSHEET FOR CONDUCTING A CRITICAL READING

Remember that before moving to this step, you should complete the basic descriptive process of identifying strategies and describing the rhetorical situation, and should have completed the preferred reading (Worksheet for Conducting an Evaluative Reading; see p. 115).

Step I. Conduct an Oppositional Reading

Use the following chart to consider questions of choice and voice, and how rhetorical strategies provide support for your answers.

Questions of Choice and Voice:	Strategies That "Advocate or Defend" the Organization's View (Foss, 2004):
Choice: Is information presented in a way that allows audiences to make informed decisions? (Alvesson & Deetz, 2003)	
Choice: Are there any apparent contradictions that are ignored or de-emphasized, thus limiting the information available to audiences? (Giddens, 1979)	
Choice: Are there assumptions about power or shared values that are taken for granted? (McKerrow, 1989)	
Choice: What is left unsaid in the rhetoric? What information is omitted, and what topics are not addressed? (Cheney & Dionisopoulos, 1989)	
Voice: Who is "speaking"? Which groups' interests are revealed? Which are concealed? Can you clearly identify the rhetor? (Cheney & McMillan, 1990)	
Voice: Are the ideas or values of a few power parties presented as the ideas or values of the whole? (Giddens, 1979)	

(Continued)

(Continued)

Questions of Choice and Voice:	Strategies That "Advocate or Defend" the Organization's View (Foss, 2004):
Voice: Are there any apparent contradictions that are dismissed or reframed such that the voices of those identifying them are muted? (Giddens, 1979)	
Voice: Does the discourse invite participation from all interested parties? (German, 1995)	

Step II. Draw Conclusion About Power

Formulate conclusions about how power is constructed or maintained in the rhetoric. Answer some or all of the following questions as you consider what you found in Step I. The first two help you to describe in part the ideology or world-view of the organization.

1. What things seem to be most important to the organization? What things seem to be least important?

2. Which groups of people seem to "matter" to the organization? Who seems less important?

3. What possible implications for society grow out of this ideology? For example, does the ideology expand or limit opportunities for diverse groups of people? Does it reflect a tendency to focus narrowly on organizational interests, or to take a broader view?

After the Analysis

Once you have completed your critical reading, you may apply your findings by writing an essay, discussing your conclusions with others, formulating general ideas about the role of rhetoric in constructing or challenging organizational power, or using the ideas to make decisions about the power you give organizations in your own life.

6

Identity Creation and Maintenance Rhetoric

❖ ❖ ❖

Figure 6.1   Process for Analyzing Organizational Rhetoric (Identity Rhetoric)

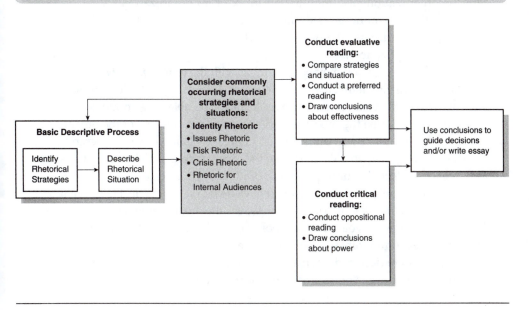

SOURCE: Adapted from Ford (1999).

Many college students have pages on Facebook, MySpace, or other social networking sites. Although individuals are clearly not organizations, these Web pages are excellent examples of efforts to create and maintain a positive identity. When you assemble your page on Facebook, you make many decisions about how to represent yourself. You select photos to reveal or conceal things about yourself. You decide which "flair" you want on your bulletin boards, consider what impressions are created by your status line, and determine which popular culture trends should appear in your lists of favorite things.

By designing and maintaining your page, you create an identity for yourself in the minds of those who visit the site. Some people create identities that suggest they are "party guys or gals" while others may portray identities that are "artistic" or "eclectic" or "intelligent." Employers have reportedly begun checking the social-networking sites of applicants to see their online identities. Creating an identity that can be viewed negatively by a future employer may cost a college student a job. Identity creation and maintenance are important because they help build personal and professional relationships.

Organizations use a similar process in presenting themselves to audiences, and in addressing events that could enhance the identity of the organization. You might even think of an organization's Web site and other promotional materials as a corporate Facebook page. In this chapter, we discuss rhetoric designed to create and enhance the identity of organizations.

Even though you may be unfamiliar with the term *organizational identity*, you are very familiar with the concept. If I asked you to describe specific discount retail stores, you would likely be able to give me several words to describe the products, services, and "personality" of the organization. You might also attach an emotional evaluation to your description—saying that you like or dislike the organization, or claiming that it is "good" or "bad." Your response is a product of your personal experiences with the organization and what you have heard on the media. However, it also results from the hundreds of messages the organization has designed to influence what you think and how you feel about it. Television advertisements, community service activities, and even in-store signs and shopping bags are designed to create an identity for the organization. Almost anything you see in or about an organization can be considered rhetorical.

❖ THE FOUNDATION FOR IDENTITY RHETORIC: ORGANIZATIONAL IDENTITY

Even though you are bombarded with hundreds of identities each day, it is important to consider how the term *organizational identity* has been defined by communication scholars. Kuhn (1997) argues that identity is "the central, enduring character projected by an organization, as perceived and interpreted by others" (p. 199). Aust (2004) writes, "Organizational identity (OI) refers to those core, distinctive, and enduring features unique to an institution" (p. 516). Both of these definitions rely on ideas introduced by Albert and Whetten (1985). They argued that an organization's identity is based on three elements: the central character of the organization, the claimed distinctiveness of the organization from other organizations, and a consistency of these elements over time.

By "central character of the organization," the authors mean those practices, values, and so forth that are at the core of "who the organization is." This may include the products the organization produces or sells, the services that it provides, its status as a family-owned company, or its affiliation with a larger organization. The idea of claimed distinctiveness is fairly self-explanatory. An organization's identity is composed in part by what makes it different from other, similar organizations. For example, FedEx, DHL, and UPS all deliver packages, but they each must demonstrate their distinctiveness from their competitors if they wish to have clear, strong identities. You can likely describe some of the distinctive elements of these organizations, including colors, logos, and slogans. The third characteristic, consistency over time, simply refers to the fact that an organization's identity needs to be consistent. The importance of this element is demonstrated by the money and effort organizations spend when they make an identity change such as selecting a new name, merging with another company, or launching a new logo or color scheme.

Kuhn's (1997) definition of identity as "the central, enduring character projected by an organization, as perceived and interpreted by others" (p. 199) is more "rhetorical" than other definitions because it is concerned with how audiences perceive the organization, not just with how the organization sees or presents itself. Organizational identity is sometimes understood as how the organization wishes to be seen, and sometimes as how the organization is actually perceived by audiences. Because we take a communication-based perspective on this process, we argue that it must be studied as both the messages offered by the organization and how those messages are processed by audiences. There is an ongoing tension between how the organization sees itself and how it is perceived based on the messages it conveys. In short, identity messages attempt to persuade audience members about who an organization is, what it does, and what it stands for.

Scholars of public relations and organizational rhetoric have used several terms to describe the basic concept of identity. There is little agreement about many of the details, but you may hear terms such as *image, impression,* and *reputation* used to define the same essential concept that we refer to as identity (e.g., Argenti, 1998; Heath, 1997). Although there are some benefits to all choices of terminology and some important potential distinctions among the ideas, we narrow our terminology and our discussion to the concept of identity. This concept best accounts for the messages created by the organization to represent how it views itself as well as how those messages are received by audience members.

It is important, however, to distinguish between the concepts of identity and identification. As explained in Chapter 2, *identification* refers to the way in which individuals connect themselves to an organization (Burke, 1937/1984; Cheney, 1983). Organizational identity is different from organizational identification, though the concepts are linked. A distinct and attractive identity may encourage audience members to identify with an organization.

With an understanding of the theoretical underpinnings of organizational identity, we can examine the elements of rhetorical situations in which it is necessary. Some situations call for an organization to establish or fundamentally alter an identity, while others may simply require the organization to enhance its existing identity or protect itself from challenges.

❖ IDENTITY BUILDING RHETORIC

The Rhetorical Situation for Identity Building

Some situations that call for identity rhetoric are potentially positive, while others have more negative potential. Situations that can enhance or challenge positive perceptions of the organization may be both anticipated and unanticipated. There are many specific situations that can threaten perceptions of an organization. We explore three of those situations—issues controversies, risk controversies, and crisis response—in detail later in this text. In this chapter, we focus on identity rhetoric designed to create, maintain, and defend the organization's identity in

more day-to-day circumstances. The nature of rhetorical situations calling for identity rhetoric becomes clearer with a discussion of exigencies, audiences, and constraints.

Exigencies

Because of the rhetorical situation in which contemporary organizations operate, building a strong, positive, and distinct identity is
challenging. The first exigence is that with so much of the economy
relying on service, and on the production of similar products, organizations have to set themselves apart from others based on some other
element. For example, cellular telephone companies all offer essentially
the same services, but in order to attract customers, each company
needs to set itself apart from the others. Companies may do this by giving their services unique names or by demonstrating better service or
lower prices than their competitors.

The second challenge or exigence in the rhetorical situation is the
sheer number of organizational messages audiences receive each day.
We hear radio advertisements; see television ads, Web sites, and pop-
up ads; and read magazines, newspapers, and billboards. In addition,
organizations are the subject of many news items in a variety of
media. With the huge number of messages produced and received
each day, organizations must find a way to be heard (Cheney &
Christensen, 2001a).

Audiences

It is important that all types of audiences be able to identify a
positive and distinct identity for an organization. First, enabling
audiences such as regulatory agencies may make different decisions
about requests from an organization depending on what ideas about
that organization most easily come to mind. Second, functional audiences such as customers and employees will react differently to organizations with distinctive and positive identities. Most of us would
prefer to support or work for an organization that is viewed positively by others.

Third, normative audiences will also have some level of interest in
identity rhetoric because organizations in the same class need to distinguish themselves from one another. Finally, diffused audiences,
or those who are interested but more removed from the organization,
are also important. Members of diffused audiences may influence the

environment in which organizations operate by supporting or opposing organizational actions in the community. How these audiences perceive the identity of the organization may influence whether they are supportive or oppositional.

Constraints and Assets

Finally, it is important to consider constraints or limitations that may have an impact on identity-creation rhetoric. Prior organizational actions may constrain the sorts of messages a rhetor can produce to create organizational identity. If an organization is perceived negatively in one or more areas by audiences, it will be difficult to craft messages to overcome those negative perceptions unless there are specific improvements that can be used as evidence. In addition, prior efforts at identity creation may pose limitations. Because one element of an identity is consistency over time, organizations that attempt to modify their identities too frequently, or make drastic changes to the identity, might not succeed in creating clear, distinctive, and positive views of themselves. Prior actions and rhetoric may also serve as positive constraints, or assets. Actions or rhetoric that placed the organization in a positive light may make the rhetor's job easier by forging a foundation of shared values and good works on which to build. With this understanding of the goals, audiences, and potential limitations facing those creating identity rhetoric, we can explore three key strategies found in this type of rhetoric.

Rhetorical Strategies for Identity Building

There are several rhetorical strategies that can help to build a positive and distinct identity for organizations. Each strategy is based on one or more basic rhetorical strategies. We will discuss three key identity strategies: association, differentiation, and branding.

Association

One way in which organizations build identities is by associating or connecting themselves with things that are viewed positively by their audience. The rhetorical strategy of values advocacy is key to the strategy of association. Bostdorff and Vibbert (1994) identified four ways in which organizations demonstrate that they share values with audience members: (1) They may make explicit appeals to social values, (2) show how their products or services match societal goals,

(3) discuss participation in philanthropic activities, and (4) praise individuals who exemplify values. Any of these approaches can serve as an association strategy to build a positive identity for an organization.

For example, shortly after the September 11, 2001, terrorist attacks, Ralph Lauren ran an advertisement featuring a picture of him in a sweater with an American flag on the front. Copy on the facing page informed readers that a portion of the purchase price would be donated to a charity to help victims of 9/11. This advertisement used an explicit appeal to the value of patriotism and promoted the organization's charitable activities. Either the shared value of patriotism or the evidence that the organization was donating money, or both, likely helped to create a positive identity for the organization in the minds of audience members.

Differentiation

The strategy of differentiation is the opposite of the strategy of association. Since one of the goals of identity-creation rhetoric is to create a distinct impression of the organization, some messages need to demonstrate what is unique about the organization. For example, cellular telephone companies all offer cellular service, long-distance calling, voice mail, and Internet access. In order to stand out from the crowd, organizations must show how their services are unique. Some offer a special calling plan for calling your friends, others may use a particular celebrity to promote their product, and still others claim that their service drops fewer calls.

No matter which specific appeal is used, the overall goal is to distinguish, or differentiate, the organization from similar organizations competing for customers. The current ads featuring characters named "Mac" and "PC" are a good example of differentiation. By using humor to enumerate the ways in which Mac computers are different from (and, according to the ads, superior to) PCs, rhetors are able to draw attention to differences that help create a positive and distinct identity for Apple's Mac as a computer that is easier to use for creative purposes.

In addition to differentiating themselves from the competition, organizations also establish identity by placing symbolic distance between themselves and things that are viewed unfavorably by the public. For example, you are probably familiar with television advertisements that create distance between organizations that produce alcoholic beverages and underage drinking or drinking and driving. This rhetoric is based on the assumption that society objects to illegal or dangerous drinking, and allows the organizations to draw a distinction between the use of their products as intended, and its use by irresponsible consumers. The ads help create a positive identity for the organization by demonstrating that the company shares community values, and that it is taking action to uphold those values.

Branding

In addition to building identity by creating positive associations and distancing themselves from negative perceptions, organizations use stylistic strategies—often referred to as the visual and verbal elements of branding—to create positive and distinct impressions of themselves. Although some authors argue that brand and identity are synonymous (see Adamson, 2006), we discuss branding as the verbal and visual strategies used to call forth identity in the minds of the audience. When audience members see or hear the verbal or visual elements of the brand, such as a logo, characteristic colors, or a slogan, they should immediately recall the distinct, positive identity of the organization.

Although the concept of branding originated for use on products, it has evolved into a much broader and more pervasive concept. In the distant past, local production and limited transportation meant that most people had little choice about what to purchase—they simply bought whatever was available. As both communication and transportation became easier, the consumer was presented with a seemingly never-ending list of choices. For example, try naming all of the different kinds of laundry detergent or toothpaste. This wide range of choice meant that producers needed to find a way to make their products distinct from others on the market. The consistent packaging and advertising that resulted from this challenge was the beginning of the brand movement (Blackett, 2004).

Today, many organizations, including those that provide services rather than products, try to establish a recognized brand. Allen and Simmons (2004) note, "In the 1980s, the term brand migrated from soap powders and came to mean virtually anything on the planet with an ability to sustain an attraction or influence among people" (p. 113). The Aflac duck and GEICO gecko are two examples of how organizations selling services rather than products attempt to use visual images to create an identity that sets them apart from others in the same class. Nonprofit organizations also need to pay attention to their brands. Mark and Pearson (2001) argue that nonprofits need to demonstrate to potential donors that the organization matches the donor's values better than other organizations seeking money. Branding is not just for dish soap or toothpaste—it has become critically important to nearly all organizations.

Branding is tightly linked to the canon of style. Its goal is to create a recognizable and pleasing visual and verbal identity for the organization. Schmitt and Simonson (1997) emphasize the importance of elements including color, font, sound, touch and texture, and aroma in the design and display of products, retail outlets, and Internet messages. Although designing these visual images often requires the professional work of artists and designers, an organizational rhetor must be active in the process of developing the messages that the organization wants to communicate through stylistic choices. For example, the organizational rhetor might develop a series of strategies to portray an identity that is "sophisticated," or "fun," or "dependable." The designer would then work to create aesthetic elements that help support that identity.

An organizational identity is an audience's perception of what an organization is and what it stands for. It is understood through personal experiences and media messages, both of which are heavily influenced by messages produced by the organization itself. As you think about the many organizations that you come in contact with on a daily basis, consider the role that organizational rhetoric—particularly the strategies of association, differentiation, and branding—plays in how you recognize and react to them.

❖ IDENTITY MAINTENANCE RHETORIC

Once an organization has completed the difficult task of crafting a positive and distinct identity, it must work to maintain that identity. Identity maintenance rhetoric consists of messages designed to preserve or enhance the identity of the organization in the face of anticipated or unanticipated identity-enhancing or -threatening events. Although similar to identity creation rhetoric, identity maintenance rhetoric lacks the elements of centrality and consistency over time. Identity maintenance allows an organization to capitalize on information that may not be central to its identity or may not hold true over a long period of time, but is consistent and supportive of a positive identity in the immediate situation. Identity maintenance rhetoric focuses heavily on demonstrating that the organization upholds community standards and contributes to community causes.

The Rhetorical Situation for Identity Maintenance Rhetoric

Those creating identity maintenance rhetoric must recognize exigencies that can be used to improve how audiences perceive the organization. To accomplish this goal, an organization must carefully monitor the environment in order to capitalize on identity-enhancing opportunities.

Exigence

In an identity maintenance situation, an exigence will be an event, either anticipated or unanticipated, that has the potential to improve how people think or feel about the organization. In short, the organization has good news that, if handled well, can help to reinforce or enhance its positive, distinct identity.

For example, perhaps the organization has made unexpectedly high profits, given a large contribution to charity, or received an award for an environmental innovation. Maybe the organization is hosting an event to thank the community, show customer appreciation, or recruit new stakeholders. If effectively presented, these sorts of events can reinforce or improve how people view organizations. For example, each year, several businesses in Austin, Texas, serve as sponsors of a large music festival. Their logos appear on stages, T-shirts, and posters, and their names and slogans are often announced onstage. The association of the organizations with the fun of a music festival has the potential to enhance how people perceive them. In another example, Yoplait yogurt enhances its identity as a company committed to promoting healthy living by donating money for breast cancer research based on the number of pink container tops sent in by customers.

Audiences and Constraints

The audiences and constraints for identity maintenance rhetoric are similar to those for identity creation rhetoric. All four types of audiences may be interested, and both prior organizational actions and prior organizational rhetoric may serve as negative or positive constraints. One additional constraint on identity maintenance rhetoric is the need for consistency. Because the purpose of maintenance rhetoric is to reinforce the core and enduring elements of the identity, any new rhetoric needs to be consistent with the ideas and values that have already been established. For example, a health care organization might benefit from promoting their sponsorship of a 5K run because it is consistent with the mission and identity of enhancing health. The organization would likely not get the same identity-enhancing benefit from sponsoring a pie-eating contest.

Rhetorical Strategies for Identity Maintenance

Many of the strategies used for identity creation are also key for identity maintenance. In this subsection, however, we focus most heavily on the association strategy of values advocacy because it helps explain nearly all of the examples of rhetoric that have identity maintenance as their goal.

Association

As outlined earlier in this chapter, Bostdorff and Vibbert (1994) outline four ways that rhetors present values with the goal of enhancing how audiences view an organization. They may make explicit appeals to values held by members of the audience, they may demonstrate how the products or services of the organization match societal goals, they may discuss the charitable activities of the organization, or they may praise admired individuals in order to demonstrate that the organization holds values similar to the person being saluted. Each of these strategies is well-suited to demonstrating that an organization is a contributing member of its community. By demonstrating adherence to shared values, an organization adds to the positive nature of its identity.

The concept of *company storytelling* may help clarify the ways that organizations enhance and promote their identities (Schuetz, 1990). Organizations use values to "tell a story" about who they are and what they stand for. Schuetz argues that organizations tell their stories "through value claims that make judgments about people, actions, objects and ideas. Company storytellers support value claims by descriptions (word pictures or photographs), by examples or experiences of employees, and by testimonials of customers and employees" (pp. 278–279).

A few examples illustrate the use of values advocacy and company storytelling in identity maintenance rhetoric. The first two values advocacy strategies can be illustrated by a single example. The Abundant Forests Alliance, composed of members of the wood and paper products industry, purchased an advertisement in the April 30, 2007, issue of *Time* magazine. The advertisement explicitly advocates the value of environmental protection (appealing to shared values) and promotes the fact that members plant more trees each day than are harvested. It includes a photo of what appears to be a family relaxing in a natural setting. This appeal illustrates the second strategy of values advocacy as well (matching societal goals), by linking the value with organizational practices. The copy includes the following: "The people of the wood and paper products industry have been Planting it Forward for years. We plant over 1.7 million new trees every day, more than making up for what is harvested." The rhetoric shows support for a commonly held value, and links that value with the identity of organizations producing wood and paper.

The third strategy of values advocacy—the discussion of charitable activities—is a common feature of identity maintenance rhetoric. These types of appeals often promote monetary donations made by an organization, but organizations may also focus on contributions of time and effort made by employees. For example, a Toyota advertisement in *Time*, August 25, 2003, reads, "Toyota dealers not only go out of their way for their customers; they make a difference in their communities. That's why you'll find them involved with anything from teaching job skills to helping the homeless, to organizing youth sports leagues that keep kids off the streets." The ad continues by discussing how the larger organization honors the charitable efforts of the dealers, thus linking the community service of employees with the Toyota slogan, logo, and email address included at the bottom of the page.

The fourth values advocacy strategy, expressing admiration for individuals who model key values, is illustrated in an advertisement for the Coca-Cola Company that ran in the February 3, 2006, *USA Today*. The ad ran shortly after the death of human rights activist Coretta Scott King, and praised her life and work. The ad links the identity of the organization with the work of Mrs. King by including a small logo and the sentence, "At the Coca-Cola Company, we take solace in knowing that her work, hope, passion and conviction live on."

As the above examples illustrate, the strategy of association is often delivered through paid advertisements. The strategy may also be used in annual reports, press releases, sponsorship of particular community events, or in events hosted by the organization itself. In addition, identity rhetoric is sometimes produced by trade or industry groups to enhance the identity of a large group of similar organizations. *Trade groups* are organizations that are composed of members who produce the same products and services, and therefore have similar economic, social, and regulatory concerns. Sometimes these groups produce advertisements that enhance the identity of the whole industry. The example from the Abundant Forests Alliance discussed above depicts a trade group–level effort to enhance identity. The Abundant Forests Alliance is composed of a large group of organizations that produce wood and paper products. Although the ad enhances the identity of the Abundant Forests Alliance, it also enhances the identity of all organizations in the wood and paper business, by association.

Differentiation and Branding

Differentiation and branding can also be important strategies in maintenance rhetoric. Because we discussed them in detail earlier in this chapter, we will give only brief explanations of how they can be useful in maintaining and enhancing an identity that has already been established. Using the strategy of differentiation may allow an organization to enhance its existing identity by pointing out the distinction between itself and a similar organization that has experienced some sort of scandal or controversy. For example, if one airline performed particularly poorly during a weather-related delay, the other airlines might take that opportunity to brag about their fine customer service record. Organizations want to avoid having their reputations injured simply through association with similar organizations that have made mistakes. Using elements of the organization's brand frequently and consistently in identity maintenance rhetoric is also an important way to reinforce both the overall identity and the brand itself.

❖ EVALUATING AND CRITIQUING IDENTITY CREATION AND MAINTENANCE RHETORIC

With an understanding of the rhetorical situation and rhetorical strategies at work in identity creation and maintenance, it is important to ask how rhetorical critics and creators may use this knowledge. By studying particular rhetorical situations, and particular samples of rhetoric, communication professionals could use their knowledge of identity rhetoric to determine whether the effort should have been successful, and possibly to make suggestions for how it could be improved. When conducting an evaluative reading of a sample of identity rhetoric, in addition to considering the basic ideas laid out in Chapters 2 and 3, critics may also want to ask some or all of the following questions:

- What elements of the rhetorical situation seem to most demand a certain kind of rhetorical response?
- Does the goal seem to be to build or change the organization's identity, or to maintain or defend it?
- Are there examples of association strategies in the rhetoric?
- Are there examples of differentiation strategies in the rhetoric?
- Are there examples of branding strategies in the rhetoric?
- Do the strategies do a good job of addressing the demands of the situation?

A critical reading asks how power is created and maintained in identity rhetoric. In addition to the more general critical questions introduced in Chapters 4 and 5, a critic analyzing identity rhetoric may want to consider some or all of the following questions:

- Who has the authority to determine what elements comprise the organization's identity?
- Have any elements of the organization's past practices or policies been omitted or de-emphasized in order to uphold a desired identity?
- Does the organization provide evidence for its claims about values or about charitable activities?
- How are community values identified and measured in the rhetoric? Would audiences agree with claims about the importance of particular values, and with how the organization claims it meets those values?

❖ CONCLUSION

Identity rhetoric is an important category of organizational rhetoric on its own, but in one sense, we could argue that all organizational rhetoric concerns identity. Identity rhetoric plays a central role in the other types of rhetoric we discuss in the following chapters. Cheney and Christensen (2001) write, "We observe the surprising extent to which the question of what the organization 'is' or 'stands for' or 'wants to be' cuts across and unifies many different goals and concerns" (p. 232). The identity an audience holds for an organization is the starting point from which all rhetoric addressing issues, risk, and crisis will proceed. A positive identity can simplify the task of a rhetor in one of those situations, while a negative identity will add rhetorical constraints to be overcome. We will return to questions of identity at least briefly in each of the chapters that follow. Use your understanding of identity rhetoric to analyze the situation and sample rhetoric that follow.

❖   **CASE STUDY: "WHO SAYS THE INTERNET IS ONLY**
     FOR YOUNG PEOPLE?" IDENTITY AND DISASTER RELIEF

The American Red Cross, founded in 1881, is familiar to most Americans for its work in disaster recovery; blood donation; service to military personnel and families; and education programs such as swimming lessons, first aid, and CPR. Although the American Red Cross is chartered by the U.S. Congress, "the Red Cross is not a government agency; it relies on donations of time, money, and blood to do its work" (www.redcross.org). Because it relies on volunteers and donations, and because its work often involves responding to disasters, the American Red Cross faces a number of ongoing rhetorical challenges.

Economic conditions in the United States were challenging at the time that the Web page selected for this case study was accessed (see Figure 6.2). An article by Barbara Hagenbaugh in the October 7, 2008, *USA Today* reported that "it's a challenging year for non-profits as a sluggish economy and rising prices make it more difficult for groups to raise money from cash-strapped families and businesses." As a nonprofit organization that focuses on assisting people in need, the American Red Cross must compete with many other organizations for donations and volunteers. The Salvation Army and the United Way are national-level organizations serving some of the same needs and seeking funding and time from many of the same people. In addition to national-level organizations, local charitable organizations—churches, environmental groups, arts organizations, universities, and many others—also seek volunteer time and donations from people who have limited resources. Because the Red Cross has a congressional charter and is often mentioned in association with government agencies such as FEMA (Federal Emergency Management Agency), some potential donors might mistakenly believe that the organization is also funded by the federal government.

The American Red Cross has been the source of some controversy in recent years. Along with FEMA and many other organizations, the

Red Cross was criticized for inefficiency in responding to Hurricane Katrina in 2005. The *New York Times* reported on April 12, 2006, that "the Red Cross has been under fire from regulators, politicians, volunteers and victims over its response to the hurricane, when it experienced problems that included overloaded telephone lines, lack of basic supplies and loose internal controls that have led to criminal fraud investigations in Louisiana" (Strom, 2006). Perhaps in part because disasters often evoke strong emotions and involve large amounts of money, the Red Cross often finds itself criticized (Strom, 2008). The organization also faced controversial changes in personnel. In December of 2005, in the aftermath of Hurricane Katrina, then-Executive Director Marsha J. Evans resigned (Gose, 2007). Her successor, Mark W. Everson, was fired in response to a scandal just 6 months after being hired. Diana Aviv, leader of a nonprofit trade association, told the *New York Times*, "The tragedy of this is that the American Red Cross is probably the best-known nonprofit organization in this country. . . . When the stories about it are more about governance and management and less about how it saves lives, it's sad and not just for the Red Cross" (Strom, 2007).

The Red Cross has made an effort during recent natural disasters to distribute their rhetoric through a variety of emerging sources that are probably familiar to college students. During the Midwest flooding in the summer of 2008, the organization created an "online newsroom" that "brought together information about shelter locations and feeding programs, news alerts, and press releases from Red Cross chapters in the affected states." In addition, the organization used postings on a blog called "Red Cross Chat" to communicate with audiences about the situation and the role of the Red Cross. The organization also posted photos and video to Flickr and YouTube (Wallace, 2008). In addition to these technological innovations, in 2008 the American Red Cross emblem appeared on a 3M-sponsored car in a NASCAR auto race, in an effort to increase blood donations among the 75 million fans of the sport (Olson, 2008).

When the Web page selected for this case study was accessed (see Figure 6.2), the American Red Cross was part of a major flood-fighting effort in Fargo, North Dakota, and Moorhead, Minnesota (Roepke, 2009). As you analyze this rhetorical situation and the Web page that follows, conduct the Process for Analyzing Organization Rhetoric (you may want to use the worksheets in the appendix) and answer the case study questions. You may also want to visit www.redcross.org to investigate the role of identity strategies in the rhetoric currently posted on the organization's site.

Figure 6.2   Sample Web page From American Red Cross

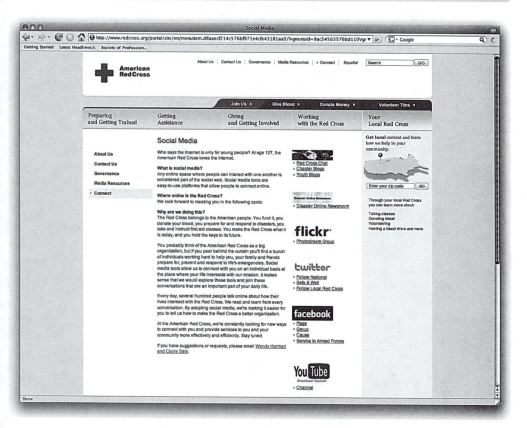

Case Study Questions

Basic Descriptive Process

1. Which of the strategies of organizational rhetoric can you identify in the sample? (You may want to refer to the Worksheet for Identifying Rhetorical Strategies in Organizational Texts in the appendix.)

   a. Does the rhetor use association strategies? If so, with what does he or she associate the organization and how?

   b. Does the rhetor use differentiation strategies? If so, from what does he or she disassociate the organization and how?

   c. Are there examples of branding strategies in the rhetoric?

   d. In what ways do these strategies help focus on what is central and enduring about the organization?

    e. How do the channels of delivery (social networking media, a race car) contribute to identity creation or maintenance?

    f. In what ways might the rhetoric use an already-existing identity to advance the goals of the organization?

2. What are the key elements of the rhetorical situation? (You may want to refer to the Worksheet for Describing Rhetorical Situations in Organizations in the appendix.)

    a. Would you say this is a situation that calls for identity-building rhetoric or identity maintenance rhetoric? Or both? Why?

    b. Which types of audiences seem to be target audiences in this situation?

    c. What constraints common to identity situations are present in this case?

Evaluative Reading

1. Compare the strategies you have identified with the elements of the rhetorical situation. Which strategies seem especially adapted to which elements of the rhetorical situation? (You may want to refer to the Worksheet for Conducting an Evaluative Reading in the appendix.)

2. Based on what you know about the rhetorical situation and what you have found out about the strategies, what did the rhetor want the reader to think, feel, or do after looking at the Web site?

3. Based on what you know about the situation and the strategies, should the rhetoric have accomplished its goal? Do you think the audiences reacted the way the rhetor intended them to? Why or why not?

Critical Reading

1. Based on what you know about the rhetorical situation and the strategies, has the organization included enough information for audience members to make an informed decision about the rhetoric? (You may want to refer to the Worksheet for Conducting a Critical Reading in the appendix.)

2. Based on what you know about the rhetorical situation and the strategies, who was and is allowed to contribute to the discussion in the rhetoric, and whose voices are not heard? Does the rhetoric indicate in any way that interested parties are invited to participate?

3. How does your evaluative reading compare with your critical reading? Are the two readings similar or different? How? What do the similarities or differences tell you?

4. Based on the three questions above, how does the rhetoric extend or limit the power of the organization in society?

Case Study References

American Red Cross. (2009a). *About us.* Retrieved March 29, 2009, from http://www.redcross.org/portal/site/en/menuitem.d8aaecf214c576bf97 1e4cfe43181aa0/?vgnextoid=477859f392ce8110VgnVCM10000030f3870aR CRD&vgnextfmt=default

American Red Cross. (2009b). *Brief history of the American Red Cross.* Accessed March 29, 2009, from http://www.redcross.org/portal/site/en/menuitem .86f46a12f382290517a8f210b80f78a0/?vgnextoid=271a2aebdaadb110VgnV CM10000089f0870aRCRD

Gose, B. (2007, July 26). Ready or not? *Chronicle of Philanthropy, 19.*

Hagenbaugh, B. (2008, October 7). Uncertainty is the enemy of philanthropy. *USA Today.*

Olson, E. (2008, June 13). National Red Cross campaign begins as a logo on a stock car. *New York Times.* Retrieved June 24, 2009, from http://www .nytimes.com/2008/06/13/business/media/13adco.html

Roepke, D. (2009, March 29). Red Cross ramping up local efforts. *INFORUM.*

Strom, S. (2006, April 12). Red Cross plans changes after hurricane problems. *New York Times.* Retrieved June 23, 2009, from http://www.nytimes.com/ 2006/04/12/us/nationalspecial/12red.html

Strom, S. (2007, November 29). Firing stirs new debate over Red Cross. *New York Times.* Retrieved June 23, 2009, from http://www.nytimes.com/2007/11/ 29/us/29cross.html

Strom, S. (2008, June 5). Red Cross in new dispute over disaster relief funds. *New York Times.* Retrieved June 24, 2009, from http://www.nytimes.com/ 2008/06/05/us/05tornado.html

Wallace, N. (2008, June 6). Red Cross experiments with disaster blogs. *Chronicle of Philanthropy, 20.*

7

Rhetoric About Issues

❖   ❖   ❖

Figure 7.1   Process for Analyzing Organizational Rhetoric (Issues Rhetoric)

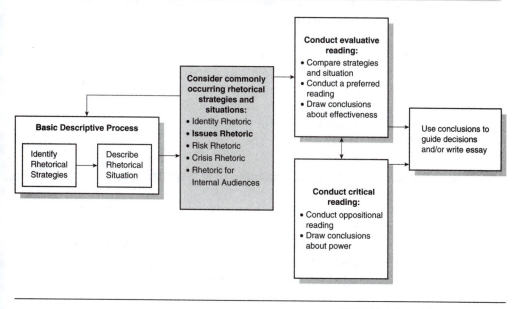

SOURCE: Adapted from Ford (1999).

In November 2000, Jim and Virginia Stowers opened the doors of the Stowers Institute, a $300-million biomedical research facility in Kansas City, Missouri. Jim Stowers is the founder of American Century Funds. He and Virginia are both cancer survivors who decided to create an endowment of over $2 billion for the institute (Neaves, 2005).

The facility houses approximately 35 independent research teams that study how genes and proteins control fundamental events in living cells. Because this research investigates specific genetic and molecular processes involved in causing disease and in repairing damage to cells, tissues, and organs, it is crucial that researchers have access to stem cell lines (Neaves, 2005).

At a time when many states were passing amendments banning stem cell research, Missouri voters had to decide whether to support a 2006 amendment to the state's constitution protecting stem cell research—including embryonic stem cell research—from government interference (Rovner, 2006). Missouri state Senator Matt Bartle (R) and groups such as Missouri Right to Life were leading the opposition to the amendment (Slevin, 2005). If the measure did not pass, stem cell research could be considered illegal in Missouri, scientists would have to leave for other states to do their work, and the Stowers Institute could be forced to close its doors or change its mission. An issue had emerged.

Organizational rhetors on both sides of the debate had the job of creating messages to influence how a wide variety of audiences understood and participated in the development and resolution of the issue. In this chapter, we discuss issues rhetoric, or messages designed to influence the development of public policy.

❖ DEFINING ISSUES AND ISSUE MANAGEMENT IN ORGANIZATIONS

Generally, an issue arises when there is a level of agreement that some problem exists, but there is not agreement on whether it is serious enough to merit action, nor on what action should be taken. Heath (1997) argues that *issues* are "contestable questions of fact, value, or policy that affect how stakeholders grant or withhold support and seek changes through public policy" (p. 44), meaning that people may disagree about what is true or false, or right or wrong on a topic, and about what, if any, action should be taken. In the chapter's opening example, there was little agreement among groups on what legislative action about stem cell research should be taken, if any.

Audiences' perceptions of these questions will then affect how they respond to organizations, and whether they seek formal action to address the topic. Parties may agree, for example, that it is a good idea to reduce the number of deaths from automobile accidents. These same parties may disagree about whether to solve the problem with a policy requiring additional safety features in autos, a policy requiring new technology on the roadway, or a policy requiring drivers to retake a road test every 5 years. Some parties may even argue that the number of deaths from traffic accidents is not high enough to merit any additional action.

Many issues or exigencies are never "'solved' in the sense of an absolute termination of discussion, but they do become 'resolved' or 'managed'" (Cheney & Vibbert, 1987, p. 175). This process of resolving or managing an issue is called *issue management* or *issue rhetoric*. The public relations campaigns designed to influence public policy decision making are called issues management campaigns. There are two primary approaches to managing issues: An organization may attempt to persuade audiences to accept its position on an issue, or it may attempt to engage interested parties in discussion in order develop a position that is acceptable to all. Because it is concerned with influence through either direct appeals or collaborative decision making, the process of issues management is inherently rhetorical (Cheney & Vibbert, 1987).

In the first approach, organizations view issue management as "an organizationally grounded struggle over dominant meanings of issues" (Kuhn, 1997, p. 193). In other words, organizations attempt to influence how various audiences perceive the information surrounding an issue in a manner that benefits the organization. Kuhn defined issue management as "public discourse in which organizations seek to define issues, as well as to influence public argumentation in a way favorable to the organization" (p. 189). This direct influence–based perspective, established in part by Heath's (1980) early rhetorical work in issue management, Cheney's (1983) dissertation focusing on U.S. Catholic bishops' attempts to influence nuclear power development, and Sethi's (1987) early study of corporate advocacy, has been supplemented in recent years by a more participative perspective on issue management.

Public relations scholars recently have argued that issue management processes should be viewed as dialogue or engagement among publics, rather than as one-way influence (Taylor, Vasquez, & Dorley, 2003). Taylor et al. explain that "engagement means that relevant stakeholders are considered, and involved, in the organization's decisions" (p. 260), consistent with key ideas in critical approaches to organizational rhetoric (see Chapter 4). They go on to say that the engagement model is grounded in two key assumptions: First, the model assumes that all organizations attempt to maximize their outcomes, and second, that publics are taking greater interest in the actions of organizations. Taylor et al. argue that organizations are most effective at maximizing their interests when they listen to their publics and anticipate and adapt to public needs. These relationships between organizations and other interested parties extend beyond any one particular issue, and need to be nurtured. The goal of engagement between organizations and publics is to generate solutions to issues that benefit all participants in the conversation.

This is an approach with limitations. For one, a collaborative approach to issue management is simply not feasible in some situations (Leichty, 1997). In addition, sometimes the goals of organizations and publics—particularly activist publics—may be truly incompatible. Leichty explains, "Intrinsically motivated activists see themselves as representing the forces of good arrayed against the evil and corrupt forces," where these activists may view collaboration as "both immoral and undesirable" (para. 19). Although this more inclusive approach opens an issue conversation to a larger number of voices, it is important to remember that organizations are still engaged in issue management in order to influence public policy *in ways that benefit the organization* (Cheney & Frenette, 1993; Heath, 1980; Kuhn, 1997).

Issues may involve a variety of players: the organization, various audiences, the government, and the media. Issues rhetoric has as its goal influencing the interpretation and resolutions of interests relevant to an organization, either through direct persuasion or through a process of negotiation with concerned parties. While early organizational rhetoric and issue management studies and recommendations focused almost exclusively on corporations (e.g., Crable & Vibbert, 1983; Sethi, 1987; Waltzer, 1988), it is now clear that many different types of organizations, including corporations, nonprofit organizations, trade associations, and activist/advocacy organizations (e.g., Greenpeace, PETA, etc.), all use rhetoric to influence the development of public policy (Botan & Taylor, 2004).

Generally, organizations that implement issue management strategies are larger ones with access to time, money, and the media (Heath,

1997). It is this access, and thus the ability to wield tremendous influence in contrast to smaller organizations and individuals, that makes it important for students of organizational rhetoric to investigate the situations that call for, and the strategies used in, these campaigns.

❖ FOUNDATION FOR UNDERSTANDING ISSUES RHETORIC: ISSUE LIFE CYCLES

Issue management is built upon two basic assumptions. The first is that most issues unfold in a fairly similar pattern (Botan & Taylor, 2004), or life cycle. It is because this cycle is predictable that issues can be managed with an end goal of influencing public policy such that it benefits the organization. Second, issue managers assume that "one issue cannot stay in the public mind forever" (Bridges, 2004, p. 63). Different issues compete for attention, and the attention span of the public and media is limited. Generally, issues arise, catch on among publics (or not), and fade away. Different rhetorical approaches are useful in each stage of the issue life cycle. Stages in a life cycle are determined in part by how many and which groups are interested in an issue (Botan & Taylor, 2004).

Building upon Jones and Chase's (1979) original issue management model, Crable and Vibbert (1985) outlined five basic levels of issue status: potential, imminent, current, critical, and dormant. Each issue status level has a slightly different focus: Some place a heavier focus on planning, while others focus more on rhetorical strategy development. Organizations must continue to conduct analysis of the issue and the rhetorical situation throughout the lifespan of the issue.

Potential Status

When an issue is in potential status, some person or group is demonstrating interest in the issue. This person or group may be a member of one or more of the organization's audiences, or it may be the organization itself. Rhetorical efforts in this stage may include monitoring the rhetorical situation, and crafting arguments to be used in this or a future stage of the model. Crable and Vibbert (1985) argue that the central questions at this level are "Should not something be done about x?" or "We think x ought to be done" (p. 6).

This first part of the potential status level is similar to Jones and Chase's (1979) issue identification step. In order to identify issues in potential status, organizations must monitor legislative, regulatory, and social aspects of the environment to discover which issues are of concern to various audiences. If an organization can address emerging problems successfully themselves, then proposed legislation or regulation may never arise. Alternatively, the organization may use what Crable and Vibbert (1985) called the "catalytic strategy," and decide to encourage legislation or regulatory action that will serve its own purposes. In essence, the organization may decide to attempt to drive forward the issue on its own terms.

The second type of organizational action that occurs in the potential issue status is issue analysis. Once an issue has been identified, the organization must carefully consider the elements in the issue. An organization should ask about the origin of the issue (if the organization did not originate the issue itself) and the organization's strengths and weaknesses in relation to the issue.

As an organization addresses issues in the potential stage, rhetors can begin to consider the types of appeals that may be useful in addressing the issue, either at the present time or as it continues to develop. Jones and Chase (1979) called this considering "issue strategy options." These issue strategies are composed of the rhetorical strategies and will be addressed shortly. The decision about which strategy to use is based on the potential success of each one in accomplishing organizational goals, as well as the costs and benefits of each option.

Imminent Status

Crable and Vibbert (1985) explain that in the imminent status level, the potential issue is beginning to be accepted by persons or groups. New audiences begin to endorse the issue. For example, in a debate about restaurant smoking bans, local public health departments may endorse the bans. Significant people see linkages between themselves and others interested in the issue; "the issue is 'coming together' or 'picking up steam'" (p. 6).

Rhetorical efforts in the imminent stage include continued monitoring of the rhetorical situation, generation of strategy options, and consideration of the costs and benefits of implementing various strategies. Building on analysis and research from previous stages, organizations begin to formalize a plan by identifying goals and objectives, and formulating strategies to achieve those goals (Jones & Chase, 1979). It is in this step and in ongoing issue stages (see below) that messages are designed and delivered to audiences.

Current Status

When an issue is in current status, it is an accepted topic of conversation. The organization and other parties interested in the issue are disseminating information on a large scale. As Crable and Vibbert (1985) describe, "Coverage of the issue has tended to dichotomize and dramatize the sides of the issue" (p. 6). Rhetorical efforts in this stage include continued monitoring of the rhetorical situation, and the development, presentation, and assessment of strategies designed to influence the issue.

Critical Status

By the time an issue reaches critical status, people have "taken sides" (Crable & Vibbert, 1985). The organization's enabling audiences are moving toward making a decision about how to vote or whether to enact a policy. The rhetorical efforts in this stage include crafting, presenting, and assessing final strategies to influence the decision. Once the policy is enacted or has failed, the organization evaluates the strategies used and the outcome in order to improve its approach in future issue debates.

Dormant Status

Once a decision about the issue has been made (i.e., the legislation passes or fails, the regulation is implemented or not, the zoning proposal is approved or not, etc.), the issue enters a dormant stage (Crable & Vibbert, 1985). However, policy issues rarely completely disappear. As Bridges (2004) notes, coalitions can reactivate the same or a similar issue, so the cycle of issue statuses is actually ongoing. If circumstances change, an issue may arise again in a new potential status. Rhetorical efforts in the dormant status focus primarily on continued monitoring of the rhetorical situation, but organizational rhetors may also anticipate arguments that they will use if the issue again becomes active.

The case of the Missouri debate over stem cell research provides an illustration of the life cycle of an issue. The amendment protecting the ability of scientists to conduct stem cell research was passed by Missourians. The issue had received growing media attention as representatives of Stowers, the Missouri business community, members of Missouri Right to Life, and other members of the public debated the issue in the legislature and in the press. After the amendment passed, the issue received less attention in the media. However, because the Stowers Institute plays a significant role in biomedical research as an economic development generator in the Kansas City and Missouri areas, related issues, such as recruitment of scientists to the Midwest, are likely to arise in the future.

❖ ISSUE MANAGEMENT: THE RHETORICAL SITUATION

The situation in which issue management discourse is created is shaped in large part by the organization's attention to the legal, political, and social environment in which it operates. Organizations must monitor their rhetorical situations and be aware of the potential threats and advantages associated with public policy (Heath, 1988). This monitoring role is often played by public relations or public affairs professionals, but the monitoring responsibility also may be diffused among employees throughout the organization. The rhetorical situations for issue management are composed of the key components of organizational rhetoric that we have discussed throughout the book: exigencies, four types of audience, and constraints and assets.

Exigencies

Very simply, the exigence (problem) for issues rhetoric is an issue. Issues, or disagreements about the best course of action, arise out of at least two broad categories of circumstances or exigencies. The first exigence occurs when, by monitoring their environment, members of organizations discover that proposed legislation or regulation could have an impact on their ability to conduct business. Such legislation or regulation is often proposed when an organization's actions do not meet societal expectations of responsible behavior (Heath, 1997; Meyers & Garrett, 1993). For example, organizations are held to standards of environmental protection, community renewal, and energy conservation, among others (Jones & Chase, 1979). Organizations are expected to treat people equally and fairly, and are expected to protect the security and safety of those with whom they interact (Heath, 1994). When organizations fail to meet any one of these standards, members of the enabling, functional, or diffused audiences may create an issue by arguing that legislation or regulation is necessary to make organizations comply.

Many people in the United States currently are debating whether all businesses should be required to provide health insurance for their employees. There is general agreement that it would be advantageous if the 40 million U.S. citizens without health insurance as of 2008 had access to insurance, but there is almost no agreement about how best to meet that goal. This expectation emerged as an issue because requiring organizations to provide health care insurance is one strategy proposed in order to achieve health coverage for all Americans. Thus, the national debate over universal health insurance is an ongoing issue for groups such as the National Federation of Independent Business, labor unions, trade associations such as the American Nurses Association, and many individual corporations and small businesses.

A second, related exigence emerges when instead of responding to an issue advanced by others, organizations propose legislation or regulation that they believe will improve their ability to conduct business. For example, organizations have proposed legislation that reduces tax burdens, changes environmental protection standards, or changes zoning or building codes.

Audiences

Although all four types of organizational audiences can be relevant in issues rhetoric, the enabling audience is usually the most important. Enabling audiences for issue management are those that can actually make the legislative or regulatory decisions at stake in the controversy. The specific audiences depend on the issue, but often include local, state, and federal governments, as well as regulatory agencies such as the Federal Communications Commission, the Federal Trade Commission, and the Internal Revenue Service. Because governmental and regulatory bodies make and enforce rules for the operation of particular industries, organizations must influence those bodies to enact legislation or regulation favorable to them, or discontinue legislation or regulation that hinders their ability to do business.

The diffused audience also plays a key role. Activist/advocacy groups are one important diffused audience. These groups often are composed of people whose societal expectations have been violated by an organization. An activist group is two or more individuals who organize in order to influence enabling or other diffused audiences through action that may include education, compromise, persuasion, pressure tactics, or force (Grunig, Grunig, & Dozier, 2002, p. 446). For example, the Physicians Committee for Responsible Medicine brought a lawsuit against the City of Phoenix accusing the city of violating the Arizona Open Meeting Act in allowing Covance Laboratories (a drug-testing organization using animals) to build a facility in the Chandler, Arizona, Airpark (Gonzales, 2008). The Physicians Committee for Responsible Medicine was a diffused audience for Covance, but became an important player when it assumed an activist role and created rhetoric.

A second important diffused audience in issue management rhetoric is the media (Leichty, 1997). Media are the primary means by which organizations can reach targeted audiences and interact with key publics (Heath, 1997). Organizational rhetors face the challenge of framing issues arguments in ways that catch and hold the attention of decision makers in media outlets. This can include editors and reporters for newspapers or magazines, television or radio, or Internet-based news organizations. Media representatives are an important diffused audience because they have the power to determine which issues come to public attention, and how those issues are framed for readers and viewers in the enabling, functional, and diffused audiences.

In issue management rhetoric, the normative audiences include those linked to the organization because they face similar problems or share values. For example, Conoco would be a normative audience to other oil companies' rhetoric about legislation concerning drilling in protected environments in Alaska. Often groups in the same industry band together to provide funding for campaigns that will attempt to influence regulation and legislation. Many industries have trade groups that include a lobbying arm (e.g., the Pharmaceutical Researchers and Manufacturers of America). In addition, a group of organizations in the same industry might agree to regulate themselves in a formal way in order to prevent regulators or legislators from imposing what might be more stringent regulations. For example, the entertainment industry created its movie rating system in part in an effort to avoid having the government create a potentially more restrictive system.

Functional audiences must not be overlooked. While the focus of issue management theory is on messages directed to audiences considered external to the organization, messages directed to external publics also have consequences for internal audiences (e.g., employees) (Cheney, Christensen, Conrad, & Lair, 2004). Consumers, employees, and members of trade organizations (e.g., teachers in the National Education Association) have the ability to put pressure on governmental and regulatory bodies. If organizations can persuade individuals that changes in regulation are beneficial in terms of cost, safety, or job creation, those individuals might testify at public hearings, protest legislation, or in other ways influence the regulatory process.

Members of functional audiences may also be members of diffused audiences for particular issues. For example, employees of a university that wants to annex land normally would be considered a functional audience for that university in the organization's issue management rhetoric about annexation. However, some of those employees may live on land that the university wants to annex, and therefore may more closely identify with the interest groups who oppose the annexation than with their employer.

Finally, messages designed for internal audiences have consequences for the organization's external publics (Cheney & Christensen, 2001; Cheney & Vibbert, 1987). This is particularly important to consider in an era of email, when the "forward" command for sending email messages outside of the organization is easily used.

Constraints and Assets

Issue management rhetoric is constrained by a number of factors and potentially supported by other factors. Organizational rhetors often face challenges of (1) being heard in an environment full of messages, (2) developing rhetoric under time limitations, (3) analyzing and presenting complex ideas, and (4) working within the context of existing organizational identity and prior organizational rhetoric.

Organizations are often constrained by a difficulty in being heard (Cheney & Christensen, 2001) for at least two reasons. First, the media is under no legal obligation to help organizations distribute their issue management messages. According to Heath (1997), Federal Communications Commission changes in regulation mean that "no program director is required by law to air any particular organization's issue advertisement" (p. 243). This means that organizations must find ways to seek media attention in order to present their side of the issue (West et al., 1996), rather than assuming that the media itself will guarantee that all sides of any particular issue will be presented. Organizations face the challenge of needing to either purchase media time or create a campaign that attracts the attention of news outlets.

The sheer number of voices in play in an issue debate also constrains organizations' ability to be heard. Issue debates rarely take place between only the organization and one opposing activist group. Often there are many players: the organization (or group of organizations) itself, opposing groups, supporting groups, governmental officials, representatives of the media, and so forth. All are creating messages that compete with each other for attention. Specific messages created by these other voices can also serve as a constraint. If a particular opposing message catches on, it must be answered (responded to) by the organization, or the original messages may be left in the minds of various audiences and become the frame through which they view the issue.

In the 1993–1994 debate over proposed health care reform, for example, President Bill Clinton's task force developed a proposal for universal health insurance (health insurance that would cover all Americans). Task force representatives sent messages about the development of the plan, as well as messages about the plan itself, to a variety of audiences. So did all of the other organizations involved in the debate. There were opposing trade association groups, such as the American Medical Association, the National Federation of Independent Business, and the Health Insurance Association of America (HIAA). There were also supporting trade association groups, such as the American Nurses Association, the AFL-CIO, and the American College of Physicians and Surgeons.

Messages from one or more of the groups served as constraints on messages of one or more of the other groups. For example, the HIAA spent over $14 million on a series of television advertisements featuring a middle-class couple named Harry and Louise. The ads tried to demonstrate the potentially negative consequences for middle-class America if the Health Security Act passed (West et al., 1996). The groups who supported the Act felt the need to respond to those messages specifically so that negative messages would not go unanswered. In other words, the HIAA messages constrained what the supporting groups could discuss, as well as what they had to spend their advertising money on, at least during the time the ads ran.

The number and nature of voices clamoring to be heard on an issue often pose a particular challenge for organizations attempting to engage all parties in the resolution of an issue. It may be extremely difficult to incorporate views of everyone in a single solution at a particular point in time. The nature of the other voices in the controversy may also serve as a constraint. For example, one of the voices in a controversy might be that of a competitor. Although the organization and the competitor may be working toward achieving a goal such as economic development in the community, the organization must be careful in deciding when to divulge proprietary information (Keyton, Ford, & Smith, 2008).

The timing of an event may also constrain rhetoric about issues. Events in an issue controversy may unfold at a fast pace, and many messages may need to be created at the same time. For example, sound bites from opposing groups may require a quick response. The need to respond quickly limits the strategies available to organizational rhetors. They may not have time, for example, to do extensive research on the arguments made in the sound bite or to find evidence to use in the response. Time is a particularly important constraint for organizations with the goal of engaging all interested parties in the resolution of an issue. Dialogue requires time, and time is not always available.

Complexity is also a potential constraint for rhetoric about issues. Issues such as health care reform (universal coverage), nuclear power, and biomedical research require debate over technical content, which is difficult for nonspecialist or generalist publics to follow, and organizational spokespersons must become interpreters and educators. In addition to the complexity of an individual issue, organizations may have to manage multiple situations simultaneously. For example, a health care facility may be in a long-term process of influencing legislation that may impact Medicare reimbursement rates. If the health care facility suddenly faces a crisis, at least two events may occur: resources (time, money, and staff) may be diverted from the reimbursement debate, at least for a time, and the agency's reactions to the crisis may have an impact on its credibility, thus influencing how audiences think about the pending reimbursement issue.

Finally, organizational identity and prior organizational rhetoric may emerge as a limitation on what can be said, or as an asset that can make generating issue messages easier. An organization that does not have a clear and positive identity may face greater challenges in persuading enabling and diffused audiences about an issue than would an organization with a positive and familiar identity. In addition, organizations must avoid creating messages that could have a negative impact on identity by making them seem focused on their own needs to the exclusion of community concerns. Kuhn (1997) argues that this "inherent tension between the interests of the stakeholders and the interests of the organization must be addressed in the discourse" (p. 196). Crable and Vibbert (1985) summarized this constraint, writing, "Issues positions must be presented as 'newsworthy,' and organizational efforts should have the charm of attractive policy potential instead of an aura of self-centeredness" (p. 13).

Prior organizational rhetoric may also constrain or expand a rhetor's options for addressing issues. Decision premises established in earlier rhetoric can affect how audiences receive new messages. In addition, past efforts to manage issues or address organizational wrongdoing will remain in the minds of audience members as they process current issue rhetoric.

In summary, organizations face highly constrained situations when managing issues. A large variety of exigencies and audiences must be accounted for in the design and implementation of issue management campaigns. A complex and constraining situation can be addressed through a variety of rhetorical strategies.

❖ STRATEGIES FOR RHETORIC ABOUT ISSUES

As the above discussion implies, it is critical that organizational rhetors addressing issues carefully monitor rhetorical situations. It is equally important, however, that they be familiar with rhetorical strategies that allow them to address those situations. Rhetorical strategies used in issues rhetoric are delivered in print, television, Web site, and radio advertising; congressional and other types of testimony; public meetings; cooperation sessions; lobbying; newsletters; press releases; public affairs programming; billboards; legislative position papers; special events; and speeches. Strategies used in issues rhetoric for congressional and other regulatory audiences often feature logical arguments and evidence. Strategies used in issues rhetoric for public audiences often feature values appeals, and appeals to credibility and identity.

Claims and Evidence in Rhetoric About Issues

Because issue management is usually linked to regulation or legislation, claims and evidence play an important role—especially in issues rhetoric directed at enabling audiences. Two specific approaches to claims and evidence are particularly useful in managing issues. We first discuss the importance of stock issues in creating and presenting arguments, and then discuss a model for presenting issue arguments (Kuhn, 1997).

The stock issues model is well known to those who study debate (Freely, 1996; Vancil, 1993). It suggests that in any issue, there are four points at which controversy can arise. First, parties can argue about whether or not a problem exists, and if so, whether the problem is significant enough to merit attention. For example, parties may agree or disagree that highway fatalities are a problem that deserves attention. Second, they can disagree about what causes the problem, or what prevents the problem from being solved. Following the example above, participants may argue about whether current laws, if more strictly enforced, might solve the problem of highway deaths.

Third, people can argue about whether or not a proposed policy can actually solve the problem. They may dispute whether improving safety features in cars can really work if people still routinely disobey speed limits. Finally, participants can debate about whether the costs (financial, social, moral) of implementing the policy outweigh the advantages. Automobile manufacturers, for example, would likely argue that changes in safety equipment would make a small difference in safety but would raise the price of cars, thus hurting consumers.

The stock issues are useful both as an analytical tool in the early stages of an issue, and as a way to invent arguments in later phases. As an analytical tool, the model helps rhetors see where points of disagreement might occur, so that they can target their arguments to the places they will be most useful. The model can also assist rhetors in crafting arguments. Depending on the analysis of the issue and the rhetorical situation, a rhetor will decide whether to argue about problem, cause, policy, or cost, or some combination of those factors.

For example, Mozisek and Hoffman (2005) found that testimony in the debate over changes to Title IX (legislation concerning equal opportunity for men and women in school-sponsored athletics) focused on several of the stock issues. Representatives of USA Wrestling and the Women's Sports Foundation presented conflicting positions on whether Title IX produced discrimination against men; whether the current policy was effective in achieving equal opportunity; whether a new policy based on "proven participation" of women in sport, rather than on the percentage of women in the student body, would reduce the disputed discrimination against men; and whether implementing the new policy would result in increased discrimination against women. Knowing the general model of the stock issues, and studying the particular issue in play, allows a rhetorical critic to discover the most relevant arguments.

Knowing which arguments to make is only part of the challenge in issue rhetoric; a rhetor also needs to know how to present them. Based upon a review of the issue management literature and his study of an issue management campaign at a large university, Kuhn (1997) describes four "layers of content" that are found in issue management discourse. His model essentially names the parts of an argument as subject, appeal, evidence, and solution. The *subject* is the issue's topic (e.g., changing the zoning regulations on Main Street), the *appeal* is a persuasive appeal to the target audience, *evidence* supports the appeal, and the *solution* is a preferred way to handle the issue (p. 197).

A pamphlet by Philip Morris USA titled "Strengthening Resolve, Building Resilience" provides an excellent example of these four types of content. It is clear from the cover of the pamphlet that the *subject* is prevention of youth smoking. The *appeal* made in the discourse is for the audience to agree that teen smoking has many causes and that Philip Morris USA is working hard to prevent many of those causes. The *evidence* for this appeal is found throughout the pamphlet in the form of examples of programs instituted by the organization to reduce teen smoking. Finally, the *solution*, though not clearly stated, seems to be for the audience to conclude that Philip Morris USA is responsibly working to decrease teen smoking, and hence further regulation and litigation are not necessary.

Evidence, particularly statistical support and testimony from opinion leaders, plays a key role in rhetoric about issues. Organizational representatives testifying on proposed legislation to Congress or other regulatory agencies (e.g., school boards, city planning commissions, etc.) rely heavily on these strategies. Statistics that illustrate the extent of damage to profits (and thus the corporate tax base) or economic growth, for example, might be incorporated into testimony against legislation to limit stem cell research.

Values Advocacy in Rhetoric About Issues

Although strategies using claims and evidence are important in issues rhetoric used in testimony delivered to Congress and other enabling audiences (e.g., school boards), these types of appeals may be much less common in issues rhetoric designed for public audiences. Issues rhetoric designed for diffused (activist/advocacy groups, the voting public) and functional audiences (employees, customers, etc.) often features values advocacy strategies. As Heath (1997) points out, the key benefit of using value appeals in issues rhetoric is to establish "common ground with key publics through the identification of mutual interests" (p. 218).

Values advocacy strategies may establish premises for use in later rhetoric. As Bostdorff and Vibbert (1994) explain, "In values advocacy, organizations do not attempt to convince their audiences that a particular value is important so much as they make implicit arguments about that value's importance relative to other values that society holds" (p. 151). In short, organizations attempt to influence how people prioritize their values, and to convince audiences that organizational values and individual values are compatible.

Although the strategies used to advance values in issue management rhetoric are similar to those in other types of organizational rhetoric (see Chapter 2), the particular values are sometimes different. Values commonly used in rhetoric about issues include profit, growth, efficiency, safety, quality, and innovation. Other examples include free enterprise, liberty, democracy, equality of opportunity, and freedom from government interference in business (Waltzer, 1988). The types of values to which rhetors appeal must be guided by their analysis of the interests and values of their audiences.

One example of values advocacy appeared in the public policy debate over pharmaceutical pricing. Merck & Co., Inc. (2008) argued that "the best way to remove inefficiencies, control costs, and improve the quality of health care is through competition and choice, the corner-stones of the free marketplace" (n.p.). The key values expressed in this statement are competition and choice in an unregulated marketplace, free of price controls set by the federal government. Many Americans share this belief in a free market, and thus may be persuaded to agree with Merck that further government regulation would exacerbate, rather than alleviate, the problem of the high cost of health care.

This process of completing an argument based on a shared premise is called *organizational enthymeme*. Although the form of the organiza-tional enthymeme is rooted in claims and evidence, its use in issue management is most often tied to values. Through ongoing values advocacy, an organization can persuade audiences to accept premises such as "What is good for the organization is good for the community," "Creating jobs is more important than preserving wildlife," "Any increased regulation means increased consumer costs," or even, "The government (or an activist group) is unfairly out to get this organiza-tion." These premises and others like them, ingrained through prior rhetoric, will help guide how audiences process new information and make decisions about whether to support or oppose organizational actions on an issue (Tompkins & Cheney, 1985).

If a resident of Round Rock, Texas, for example, has accepted the premise that "what is good for Dell is good for me," then Dell would sim-ply need to establish that a policy, such as tax relief, was good for the com-pany. What we know about enthymemes tells us that the audience will then complete the sequence and determine that, in fact, tax relief for Dell benefits the community and therefore should be enacted. A truly com-plete analysis of the issue management discourse of an organization should include a review of prior discourse of that organization that may have served to establish premises being used to manage the issue at hand.

Identification is a second emotion-based strategy used in issue rhetoric. Although the concept of identification is often associated with internal organizational rhetoric, it can also be an important positive outcome of an engagement approach to issue management (Cheney, 1983). Symbolically, by encouraging and responding to participation, an organization uses the common ground strategy of expressing con-cern for the individual. This may have two rhetorical advantages. First, individuals and groups that participate in a decision-making process will often have increased commitment to the outcome of that process (Barker, 1993). Second, simply by promoting that it encouraged participation, an organization may enhance its reputation with audiences who were not part of the process.

Credibility Strategies in Rhetoric About Issues

A number of credibility strategies may appear in organizational rhetoric about issues. Most are fairly standard and are discussed throughout this book, but the strategy of calling attention to participation is unique in issue and risk rhetoric. As we discussed earlier, an increasing number of organizations are turning to an engagement model of issue management (Kent & Taylor, 2002). Participation from multiple parties can serve both practical and rhetorical purposes. From a practical angle, multiple voices will often generate new ideas for addressing an issue, allowing for a better outcome than might have occurred with organizational ideas alone.

Participation also serves the important rhetorical function of building credibility. Organizations that can demonstrate their commitment to participation can call attention to that practice in order to enhance corporate social legitimacy and enhance identity. The community component of corporate social legitimacy requires that an organization demonstrate that it has concern for the community, and can act as a positive member of that community (Hearit, 1995). An organization that seeks, truly listens to, and incorporates community input on an issue will certainly enhance corporate social legitimacy and organizational identity.

❖ EVALUATING AND CRITIQUING RHETORIC ABOUT ISSUES

With this understanding of the goals, situations, and strategies of rhetoric about issues, it is important to think about how critics can use this information to evaluate organizational rhetoric and to determine the issues of power at work in the discourse. Critics operating from the evaluative approach would try to understand the elements of a particular issues situation, and then compare the building blocks in the rhetoric with the demands of the situation to make a judgment about potential effectiveness. From an evaluative perspective, issues management is concerned with how effectively messages serve to advance the interests of an organization.

In addition to the general questions outlined in Chapters 2 and 3, an evaluative critic studying issues rhetoric should ask some or all of the following questions:

- Are any of the constraints most common to issues rhetoric present in the rhetorical situation?
- Are there any rhetorical strategies that seem particularly well or poorly adapted to the stage of the issues life cycle?
- Which of the stock issues are mentioned in the rhetoric? How are those arguments developed or supported?
- Are there examples of values advocacy in the rhetoric?
- Are there any examples of organizational enthymeme in the rhetoric?

Because organizationally influenced public policy can have an enormous impact on the lives of individuals, and because of the inherent power imbalance between individuals and organizations, it is very important to consider issue management rhetoric through a critical lens (Cheney & Dionisopoulos, 1989, p. 149; see also Deetz, 1992). In addition to the general questions about choice and voice outlined in Chapters 4 and 5, someone conducting a critical reading of issue management rhetoric should consider some or all of the following questions:

- How does the organization portray itself as qualified or authorized to speak about a particular issue?
- Is there evidence in the rhetoric that interested audiences have been consulted and have had a reasonable opportunity to influence the process?
- "What is said about an issue and what is not said" (Cheney & Dionisopoulos, 1989)?
- Based on your knowledge of the rhetorical situation and the rhetoric, does the organization appear to conceal or de-emphasize information that might influence the issue?

❖ CONCLUSION

Organizations spend a great deal of time and money attempting to influence public policy and perceptions of public policy. The complex rhetorical situation, the changing nature of issues throughout their life cycle, and the range of available strategies make issues rhetoric an important and interesting element of what organizations do to influence the thoughts, feelings, and behaviors of audiences. Use your understanding of issues rhetoric to analyze the case study and rhetoric that follow.

❖ CASE STUDY: MENU LABELING—HEALTHY IDEA OR BIG BROTHER?

A food fight of sorts broke out among restaurant owners, health advocates, and the City of New York in late 2007 and early 2008. In a climate of increasing concern for food-related health issues, city officials proposed a policy requiring any restaurant with more than 15 locations to post calorie information in a prominent spot near the menu board. The issue quickly gained the attention of a variety of parties. The city based its rationale for the policy on concerns about increasing obesity and lack of access to nutritional information. According to the *New York Times* (Rivera, 2007b), Dr. Thomas R. Frieden, city health commissioner, stated, "The big picture is that New Yorkers don't have access to calorie information," and "Not everyone will use it, but many people will, and when they use it, it changes what they order, and that should reduce obesity and, with it, diabetes."

The initial New York City food fight emerged in the midst of debates about menu labeling across the country. On September 18, 2007, the *Christian Science Monitor* reported that as California debated such a bill, similar measures were either in place or being considered in counties in the states of Washington, Maryland, and Connecticut, the city of Philadelphia, and at least 12 other municipalities (Wood & Tully, 2007). New York City Mayor Michael Bloomberg had also attained a reputation, and the nickname of "Nanny Mayor," for supporting health reforms such as smoking bans and limitations on the use of trans fats (Rivera, 2007b). *Business Week* claimed, "Many health experts have shifted their emphasis from tobacco to diet as Public Enemy No. 1" (Orey, 2008, p. 36).

In September of 2007, Federal District Court Judge Richard J. Howell struck down an initial New York City policy on menu labeling but, in doing so, suggested ways in which a reformulated policy would meet legal requirements (Rivera, 2007a). The policy came under review because of a lawsuit filed by the National Restaurant Association claiming that it was unconstitutional. *Business Week* reported that the association was represented by a law firm that had extensive experience as counsel to Philip Morris (Orey, 2008).

In October of that same year, the city introduced a revised policy scheduled to take effect on March 31, 2008. The *New York Times* estimated that it would affect about 10% of the approximately 23,000 restaurants located in the city. Two hurdles then stood in the path of enacting the new policy: a public hearing that was scheduled for November 27, 2007, and the approval of the city's board of health (Rivera, 2007a). The policy was subsequently passed by the city on January 22, 2008 (Orey, 2008). With the introduction and approval of the new policy, the controversy moved back into public attention and generated a variety of responses from interested parties.

Several organizations associated with health care or the restaurant business quickly responded with either enthusiasm or concern to the city's proposal. The National Restaurant Association again expressed its concern, including the argument that the policy would place a financial burden on individual franchise owners, that it was an infringement on business, and that it would fail to effectively address the health problems it sought to solve (Orey, 2008).

The New York State Restaurant Association filed suit to overturn the policy, and the national association paid David B. Allison, a nutrition professor at the University of Alabama, to write a brief arguing that there was no scientific evidence to support the idea that posting calorie content of foods would have a positive impact on health. Allison's actions attracted negative attention from members of the Obesity Society (a research group focusing on issues of weight), of which he was a member, who suggested that Allison "had crossed the line into paid advocacy" (Stark, 2008). Other experts also filed briefs in support of the policy. Organizations such as the Center for Science and the Public Interest (pro-labeling) and the Center for Consumer Freedom (anti-labeling), described as a "not-for-profit initially funded by Philip Morris, and now backed largely by food and restaurant companies," weighed in on the issue of menu labeling (Orey, 2008, p. 36).

On February 17, 2009, the 2nd U.S. Circuit Court of Appeals rejected the New York State Restaurant Association's challenge of the policy (Chan, 2009). The National Restaurant Association (2009) responded to the court's decision with a press release arguing that a state-by-state approach was not the most effective way to solve obesity problems in the United States. Many states around the country continue to consider similar menu-labeling policies. The press release that follows was distributed by the National Restaurant Association and archived on its Web site at www.restaurant.org. As you analyze this rhetorical situation and the press release (Figure 7.2, p. 160) that follows, conduct the *process for analyzing organizational rhetoric* (you may want to use the worksheets in the appendix), and answer the case study questions.

Figure 7.2   News Release From the National Restaurant Association,
                 January 31, 2008

NATIONAL RESTAURANT ASSOCIATION ®
The Cornerstone of the Economy, Career Opportunities and Community Involvement
1200 SEVENTEENTH STREET NW, WASHINGTON DC, 20036 | WWW.RESTAURANT.ORG

FOR IMMEDIATE RELEASE
Thursday, January 31, 2008

CONTACT: Sue Hensley
202-331-5964

Mike Donohue
(202) 331-5902

media@dineout.org

National Restaurant Association Reacts to NYC Court Filing to Stop Onerous Government Regulation on Menu Labeling

(Washington, DC) – The National Restaurant Association issued the following statement in response to today's filing by the New York State Restaurant Association in federal district court to strike down a New York City Board of Health regulation which dictates how nutrition information should be provided in some of the city's restaurants.

The regulation, passed January 22nd, is punitive against multi-unit restaurants operating in New York City that have 15 or more outlets nationwide. Many of these restaurants provide nutrition information to consumers in a variety of ways through point-of-sale materials, posters, tray liners, kiosks and Web sites. A similar version of the same regulation was stuck down by the court in New York last September. The new regulation would take effect March 31st.

"The New York City Board of Health has once again pushed forward a misguided regulation that would punish the city's restaurants, many of whom are already providing comprehensive and accurate nutrition information to customers in convenient ways, both in the restaurant and on the Web," said John Gay, senior vice president for government affairs and public policy at the National Restaurant Association.

"Last September, we were encouraged by the court's decision to strike down the Board of Health's flawed regulation. We hoped that the court's action would send a message to the city's regulators that there must be more thought given to pursuing this complex issue.

"We believe this newly-concocted regulation, very similar to the last one, is confusing to consumers, onerous for restaurants, and will not achieve its intended purpose. We strongly affirm our support for the legal action taken today by the New York State Restaurant Association."

###

The National Restaurant Association, founded in 1919, is the leading business association for the restaurant industry, which is comprised of 945,000 restaurant and foodservice outlets and a work force of 13.1 million employees - making it the cornerstone of the economy, career opportunities and community involvement. Along with the National Restaurant Association Educational Foundation, the Association works to represent, educate and promote the rapidly growing industry. For more information, visit our Web site at www.restaurant.org.

Case Study Questions

Basic Descriptive Process

1. Which of the strategies of organizational rhetoric can you identify in the press release? (You may want to refer to the Worksheet for Identifying Rhetorical Strategies in Organizational Texts in the appendix.)

   a. Which of the stock issues are mentioned in the rhetoric (problem, current system, solutions, advantages and disadvantages)? How does the rhetor discuss each one?
   b. What kinds of claims and evidence are found in the rhetoric?
   c. Does the rhetor use values advocacy? If so, what values does he or she appeal to and how? Can you identify any possible examples of organizational enthymeme?
   d. In what order are the arguments presented? Does this sample follow Kuhn's (1997) model?

2. What are the key elements of the rhetorical situation? (You may want to refer to the Worksheet for Describing Rhetorical Situations in Organizations in the appendix.)

   a. Is there an issue in the rhetorical situation? How do you know that?
   b. In what stage of the life cycle does the issue seem to be?

Evaluative Reading

1. Compare the strategies you have identified with the elements of the rhetorical situation. Which strategies seem especially adapted to which elements of the rhetorical situation? How are strategies adapted to audiences and the stage in the life cycle?

2. Based on what you know about the rhetorical situation, and what you have found out about the strategies, what did the rhetor want the reader to think, feel, or do after looking at the press release? (You may want to refer to the Worksheet for Conducting an Evaluative Reading in the appendix.)

3. Based on what you know about the situation and the strategies, should the rhetoric have accomplished its goal? Do you think the audiences reacted the way the rhetor intended them to? Why or why not?

Critical Reading

1. Based on what you know about the rhetorical situation and the strategies, what level of choice is given to the audience of this rhetoric? What information about the issue is shared, and what is not shared? (You may want to refer to the Worksheet for Conducting a Critical Reading in the appendix.)

2. Based on what you know about the rhetorical situation and the strategies, who is allowed to contribute to the discussion in the rhetoric, and whose voices are not heard? Does the rhetoric indicate in any way that interested parties are invited to participate?

3. How does your evaluative reading compare with your critical reading? Are the two readings similar or different? How? What do the similarities or differences tell you?

4. Based on the three questions above, how does the rhetoric exercise or challenge the power of the organization in society?

Case Study References

Chan, S. (2009, February 18). Court upholds the city's rule requiring some restaurants to post calorie counts. *New York Times.* Retrieved July 1, 2009, from http://www.nytimes.com/2009/02/18/nyregion/18calorie.html

National Restaurant Association. (2009, February 17). *News release: National Restaurant Association statement regarding federal court ruling on menu labeling in New York City.* Retrieved July 1, 2009, from http://www.restaurant.org/pressroom/pressrelease.cfm?ID=1739

Orey, M. (2008, February 11). A food fight over calorie counts. *Business Week,* p. 36.

Rivera, R. (2007a, September 13). Fight to put calories on menus may widen. *New York Times.* Retrieved June 25, 2009, from http://www.nytimes.com/2007/09/13/nyregion/13calories.html?_r=1&fta=y

Rivera, R. (2007b, October 25). New York City reintroduces calorie rule. *New York Times.* Retrieved June 25, 2009, from http://www.nytimes.com/2007/10/25/nyregion/25calories.html

Stark, K. (2008, February 16). Weighty issue: Money and science. *Philadelphia Inquirer.*

Wood, D. B., & Tully, A. (2007, September 18). Must menus in California count calories, carbs, fats? *Christian Science Monitor.* Retrieved June 25, 2009, from http://www.csmonitor.com/2007/0918/p02s01-ussc.html

8

Rhetoric About Organizational Risk

❖   ❖   ❖

Figure 8.1 Process for Analyzing Organizational Rhetoric (Risk Rhetoric)

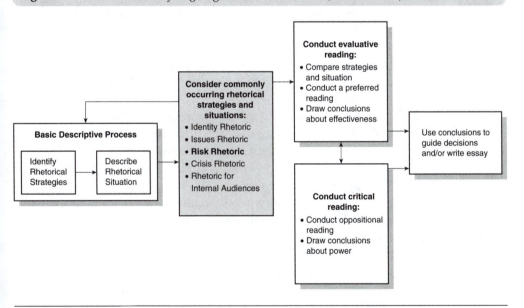

Figure 8.1 Process for Analyzing Organizational Rhetoric (Risk Rhetoric)

SOURCE: Adapted from Ford (1999).

After decades in which no new nuclear power plants were built in the United States, the Nuclear Regulatory Commission began accepting applications for new plants in 2007 (Mufson, 2007).

For energy companies wanting to build new plants, the greatest challenge may be persuading communities that doing so will not endanger the health and safety of residents. With public memory of incidents such as a leak at the Three Mile Island facility in 1979 or the catastrophic incident at Chernobyl in 1986, many people are at best uninformed and at worst terrified of nuclear energy. Organizational rhetoric has an important role to play in how these organizations and communities negotiate the risks of building new nuclear facilities in the United States.

On a smaller level, you make decisions about risk every day. You consider if you want to risk going to the movies the night before your midterm exam, or to risk driving faster than the posted speed limit. These examples suggest a decision about something that has potentially negative consequences—a lower grade, a speeding ticket, or perhaps even an accident. In making your decision, you must weigh the possible benefits of the pleasure of a movie or the convenience of spending less time in the car against the potential costs of poor grades or a speeding citation. Organizations must make similar sorts of judgments about risk and must explain and justify their choices to audiences.

As we have discussed throughout this text, in order for organizations to operate in their communities they must create a perception of corporate social legitimacy among their audiences (Hearit, 1995). Sometimes organizations, either by their nature or because of a particular action they plan to take, pose potential risks to their communities. An energy company may want to construct a nuclear reactor, a retailer may want to open a store in an environmentally sensitive area, or a city might want to build a landfill near a residential neighborhood. Any of these scenarios could cause anxiety among local audiences about health, safety, quality of life, or property values.

Situations like these can threaten an audience's perception of both an organization's competence and its concern for the community, and threaten the organization's positive identity. These challenges require a special type of rhetoric. In this chapter, we define organizational risk rhetoric, discuss the rhetorical situation surrounding it, and explore the rhetorical strategies organizations most commonly use to address risk.

❖ DEFINING RISK IN ORGANIZATIONS

In order to understand what risk rhetoric is, it is first necessary to understand the idea of risk by itself. Elliot (2003) explains that even though we often think about a "risk" as a thing, it is "not a physical entity subject to direct sensory perception... it is a judgment" (p. 215). *Risk* is a judgment made by individuals. Heath (1997) defined risk as "a dialectic of benefit and harm" (p. 325). People make their judgment of risk based on how likely it is that an event will occur, and how severe the negative impact of the event might be, if it does occur (Elliot, 2003). On a personal level, you make a risk decision every time you cross a street. You usually determine that although the result of being hit by a car would be highly negative, the likelihood that you will be hit is quite low. In the same way, you may decide that although it is very likely that you will get knocked down playing recreational basketball, the chance of any resulting injury being serious is small. Since risk is a perception, rather than an objective fact, rhetoric can serve to influence how people form and modify their ideas about risk.

Although she specified risks linked to technology, Mirel's (1994) definition helps explain the general idea of *risk rhetoric:* "Risk communications [rhetoric] provide evidence and assessments of potentially hazardous technologies in order to persuade audiences to discuss, decide, and act on issues in particular ways" (p. 41). Risk rhetoric, then, has the task of influencing how a variety of audiences understand and respond to hazards potentially posed by organizational actions. Organizational decisions about risk sometimes result in new public policy, so in many cases, risk rhetoric is a subset of issues rhetoric (see Chapter 7). Although many of the ideas discussed in the chapter about issues will apply, risk rhetoric is unique in significant ways.

Messages about risk generally emerge for one of two purposes. Some messages seek to encourage people to avoid a risk. As a college student, you have probably seen lots of posters encouraging people to avoid risks. Students are advised to call an escort rather than walking alone on campus after dark, to wash their hands often during flu season, and to avoid unhealthy drinking or unsafe sexual practices. These types of messages are often the focus of health campaigns and have been frequent subjects of scholarship in health communication (e.g., Murray-Johnson & Witte, 2003). The second type of risk rhetoric—and the focus of this chapter—is designed to persuade audiences to take a risk by convincing them that the chances of the event happening are low, that the negative effects would be minor if the event did happen, or that the benefits of the action outweigh the potential costs. In order to accomplish this, audience members must be persuaded to focus on a risk; ask questions about the risk; and decide "whether the risk can be trustworthily managed, and whether the risk is acceptable" (Elliot, 2003, p. 215).

In the above example about crossing the street, you make a decision about whether or not to take a risk based on your own assessment of the situation. When organizations make a decision about risks, they are often deciding whether hundreds or even millions of people should be exposed to a risk. The use of a new food production or protection technique, or the construction of a new production facility, will create some chance of a negative event occurring, and some chance that the results of that event will have significant negative consequences. Since organizations often take the decision about whether or not a risk is acceptable out of the hands of individuals, they must craft rhetoric to explain the risks to audiences and convince them of the acceptability of the risk.

❖ FOUNDATIONS FOR UNDERSTANDING RISK RHETORIC

In order to understand the strategies and situations associated with risk rhetoric, it is important to discuss two foundational concepts: risk frames, and the *elaboration likelihood model* of persuasion.

Risk Perception Frames

"Frames" serve as filters that shape how we perceive the world and events in it. Different frames will lead to different interpretations. *Risk perception frames* filter how interested parties process information about risks (Elliot, 2003). Elliot argues that experts (often those who work for organizations or regulatory agencies) and lay publics (often members of the enabling, functional, and diffused audiences) measure and process, or frame, elements of risk differently. These differences may make it difficult for experts to create rhetoric for lay publics, and for lay publics to make arguments to influence organizational action on risk.

It is important to understand how expert and public frames differ. Table 8.1 lays out the four basic areas of difference as identified and described by Elliot (2003).

The table demonstrates why differing perceptions of the idea of risk can create daunting challenges for people creating risk rhetoric. First, if public audiences place value on the experiences of others in the community, and on the perhaps sensational stories they have heard on the news, they will not likely be receptive to statistics

Table 8.1   Expert and Nonexpert Risk Frames

	Experts	Nonexperts
What does "risk" mean?	Level of risk is framed by a "big picture" approach based on scientific models that address likelihood of occurrence and seriousness of consequences.	Level of risk is often framed by possibility of extreme outcomes rather than models that address likelihood and severity.
How is evidence about risk gathered?	Questions and evidence use the scientific method. Data about risks across a population are trusted.	Questions and evidence are often experiential and anecdotal. Individual experiences and observable examples are trusted.
What is important in how risks are managed?	Physical and technical systems are responsible for controlling risk. Past performance of such systems is used as evidence.	Social systems and individual actors are responsible for controlling risk. Past performance of people and social systems may be used as evidence.
What level of risk is acceptable?	The potential costs of a risk are weighed in order to make a mathematical judgment.	The preference is often for a zero-level chance of risk.

SOURCE: Adapted from Elliot (2003).

presented by expert rhetors. For example, individuals hesitated to accept a risk if it was "potentially catastrophic (a nuclear power accident)" (Elliot, 2003, p. 215). In addition, lay audiences may believe that no matter how effective a physical system is at limiting the possibility of an accident, corrupt or inept people or organizations can cause that physical system to fail, thus leading to negative consequences in the community. As Mirel (1994) summarized from Douglass and Wildavksy (1982), public audiences "do not selectively choose to attend to some risks while ignoring others because scientific evidence or specialized knowledge proves actual dangers to health and safety. Rather, people select risks because of a constellation of other factors" (p. 44).

Conversely, if lay publics who try to influence risk topics use only anecdotal evidence and argue only for zero-risk levels, they will not likely be effective in persuading experts to modify risk practices or policies. If either party in a risk dialogue fails to recognize the challenge presented by diverse risk perception frames, they are unlikely to be successful in modifying the exigence.

The Elaboration Likelihood Model of Persuasion

A second concept useful in understanding rhetoric about risk is the *elaboration likelihood model* (ELM) of persuasion developed by Petty and Cacioppo (1986). Although this theory applies to all persuasive messages, it is especially helpful in understanding rhetoric about organizational risk. These scholars argue that people are persuaded not only by messages designed to be persuasive, but also by other cues. Audience members may *elaborate,* or think, to differing degrees in processing messages about attitude change.

In order to understand ELM, you need to understand the continuum of ways that people might arrive at attitude change. On one end of the continuum is the *central route.* People use a central route to persuasion when they seek information, and carefully measure claims and evidence. On the other end is the *peripheral route.* People take the peripheral route when they attend to other sorts of cues, including credibility, liking, and the views of other people (O'Keefe, 2002). In organizational rhetoric about risk, peripheral cues may include appeals to emotion, organizational identity, and organizational identification messages either from the organization itself or from other interested parties.

Whether an individual uses the central or peripheral route is influenced by two factors: motivation and ability. People who have an interest in the topic (i.e., are motivated)—for example, those who live across the street from the proposed landfill, or whose children attend the school that may contain asbestos—will be more likely to use the central processing route. People with less interest or motivation will be more likely to use the peripheral route. The second factor is ability, or the degree to which audience members can understand and attend to the arguments. People with higher levels of ability are likely to take the central route. The variables of motivation and ability have important implications for creators and critics of risk rhetoric. As suggested by our discussion of risk frames, risk situations often involve highly complex technical information and strong emotions. Thus, the choice of strategies for addressing risk can have an impact on which route an audience member takes.

Both the central and peripheral routes may lead to persuasion, so both can be effective. It is important, however, for a rhetorical critic to consider the ethics of an organization encouraging audience members to take the peripheral route. Though emotion and credibility can be acceptable criteria to consider in making decisions, rhetors may limit audience choice by failing to present information in ways that enhance audience motivation and ability to use the central route.

With an initial understanding of risk frames and the elaboration likelihood model, we can see how these two concepts may influence the rhetorical situation facing organizations addressing risk.

❖ THE RHETORICAL SITUATION FOR RISK RHETORIC

The rhetorical situation for risk is most commonly characterized as anticipated and potentially threatening. Organizations are generally able to anticipate when proposed actions may cause audiences to perceive a risk. Because risk is concerned with potentially negative outcomes, concerns about proposed actions may threaten positive impressions of the organization. A discussion of the exigencies, audiences, and constraints related to rhetoric about risk will present a more complete picture of the rhetorical situation.

Exigencies

Organizations often encounter risk-related exigencies. At the most basic level, the problem in these rhetorical situations is that the organization wants to take some action that one or more audiences may perceive as a risk. The ideal outcome would be that the organization can involve interested audiences in a dialogue that ultimately leads to a decision about risk that is acceptable to both the organization and other interested parties.

Interested parties may resist risk for a number of reasons. Heath (1997) argues that "safety, fairness, equality, and environmental quality are motivators people use when deciding whether a problem exists that affects them and deserves their attention" (p. 324). Organizational actions can pose risks in a number of possible areas that may attract the attention of audiences. Actions can pose perceived threats to the environment, to human health and safety, or to the economics or social identity of a community. Whether an organization anticipates a negative reaction to a potential risk or already faces opposition from interested parties, its challenge is to convince audiences that either the risk does not exist or the risk is not as significant as it is being perceived or presented.

Audiences

The exigence of persuading audiences to accept a risk is more easily understood when we add a consideration of the audiences and constraints that contribute to the rhetorical situation. In risk rhetoric, audiences play a key role in defining the exigence. Members of enabling, functional, and diffused audiences in particular may be active in the rhetorical situation in several ways. They may call attention to the risk situation, challenge organizational accounts of the risk, demand legal or political action, or participate in finding an acceptable compromise about the risk.

All four types of audience have an interest in rhetoric about risk and can be important audiences. *Enabling audiences* are particularly important if the topic of the risk becomes a public policy issue. As discussed in the previous chapter, legislators and members of regulatory bodies have the ultimate ability to pass or defeat policy changes. Risk issues are tied to public policy because legislation and regulation are often used to control or limit risky actions by organizations.

For example, the Environmental Protection Agency (EPA) dictates how many parts per million of chemical compounds can be released into the air in order to control health risks in the United States; the Federal Aviation Administration (FAA) and Transportation Security Administration (TSA) determine what safety practices must be in place on jets and in airports in order to reduce risks associated with air travel; and the U.S. Department of Agriculture (USDA) sets conditions on how animals are raised and slaughtered in order to reduce risks of food-borne illness. These agencies; dozens of others on the local, state, and federal levels; as well as legislative bodies on those same levels may be influenced by rhetoric about risk. They are audiences of both the organization's messages seeking to mitigate the perception of risk, and the messages created by individuals and organizations seeking to defeat the implementation of whatever is believed to cause the risk.

Functional audiences are also important in risk rhetoric. Given the human sense of self-preservation, employees generally prefer to work in environments that don't endanger their own health and safety or that of others. Customers and suppliers also prefer to affiliate with safe and fair organizations rather than with organizations perceived to operate in ways that put people or the environment at risk.

Normative audiences are important in risk rhetoric for many of the same reasons that they are important in issues rhetoric. Organizations that share similar interests may join together to produce rhetoric that attempts to influence thoughts and feelings about risk.

Diffused audiences are very important to organizations using rhetoric to influence perceptions of risk. Diffused audiences may include physical neighbors of the organization's facilities, local and national activist groups with an interest in the topic, and representatives of the news media. For example, in the TXU power example used earlier in this book, the large number of groups that assembled both in favor and against building additional coal-fired power plants was key in influencing how people thought about the risk elements of the situation. Groups in favor of the plants pointed to risks of blackouts and power shortages if the plants weren't built, and groups opposed emphasized potential for decreased air quality if they were built. The media coverage of the debate also kept these potential risks high in the minds of enabling and functional audiences.

Constraints and Assets

The constraints facing people crafting risk rhetoric may be a bigger challenge than in almost any of the other types of rhetoric discussed in this book. The common constraints facing risk rhetoric include diverse risk frames, the complexity of risk topics, the emotionally laden nature of risk topics, and the status difference between organizations and audiences. Elements that may be either limitations or assets include existing organizational identity, prior organizational rhetoric, current thinking about related topics, and the current regulatory or legislative climate.

First, as the above discussion indicated, experts and laypeople often perceive and respond to information about risk differently. This conflict between risk perception frames presents a possible constraint. Experts must attempt to take the perspective of lay audience members and craft messages compatible with that perception frame. At the same time, lay audiences wishing to influence risk decisions may need to learn to take the perspective and speak the language of the experts.

The elaboration likelihood model helps explain a second possible constraint, complexity and uncertainty. Because debates about risk often involve scientific and technical topics, they can quickly become quite complex, and complexity can limit an audience's ability to elaborate on an issue. Rowland (2008) asserts that arguments based on claims and evidence may be particularly difficult for audiences to understand when they address highly complicated topics. When rhetors and audiences must address risk topics such as whether a particular technical system can adequately reduce the risk posed by a technology, or when they must discuss complicated statistics related to likelihood of accidents occurring, complexity becomes a significant constraint.

Linked to the constraint of complexity is the high level of uncertainty often associated with risk-related topics (Mirel, 1994). The possible long-term effects of many potential risks, especially those linked to emerging technology, are often unknown. Elliot (2003) argues that "people tend to judge risks more harshly when they appear to be . . . not well understood" (p. 215). He gives the example of genetically modified food products. Most average people do not understand the processes behind modification of plants and animals for food production. In addition, the long-term results of people consuming this type of food are unknown.

A third constraint evident in this type of rhetorical situation is that dialogues about risk can often involve a very high level of emotional involvement. High emotional involvement can often be incompatible with topics that rely heavily on logical and technical arguments (Rowland, 2008). One way that the emotional nature of risk topics is manifested is through *outrage*, which Mirel (1994) describes as "intense public concern, distrust, fear, intolerance, or resistance" (p. 44). It makes sense that topics concerned with health and safety would generate high levels of emotion. In addition, concerns about risk are often tied to basic values such as self-determination or family.

As individuals become involved in controversies concerning risk, their personal identities also may become tightly tied to their perception of the risk. Elliot (2003) found that "as the conflicts intensified, so did the activists' sense of identity, shifting from interest-based concerns with safety to rights-based concerns with safety to rights-based concerns with freedom from assault" (p. 219). He also found that as controversy intensified, experts became more tightly linked to their identities as rational scientists. When the outcome of the risk situation becomes so closely tied to people's perceptions of their identities, emotion may widen the gap between risk perception frames. When individuals begin to see their role in fighting a risk as a key part of their identity, they may hold even more tightly to elements of their risk perception frames, such as zero tolerance for risk. Likewise, as experts become more invested in their role as scientific professionals, they may hold more strongly to elements of the expert frame, thus making it even more difficult for the two groups to communicate effectively with one another.

A fourth possible constraint is the power imbalance between organizations proposing a risk and individuals and community groups opposing that risk. Mirel (1994) argues, "Regardless of statistically probable risks to health, life, or the environment, citizens may become outraged at a technology and concomitantly perceive it to be unacceptable if, for example, they believe they have no control over where it is situated" (p. 44). Audiences also view risks more skeptically if they "appear to be involuntary (living adjacent to a pesticide manufacturer)" or "inequitable (a cluster of toxic landfills in a neighborhood)" (Elliot, 2003, p. 215). These responses are linked to the difference in power between individuals and organizations. In addition, public audiences may perceive that organizations have access to financial and political resources not available to individuals or community groups, and that organizations will take advantage of those resources to impose risks on the less-empowered groups.

Although many organizations act ethically in assessing and implementing risky actions, it is the perception of power imbalance that produces a challenge for organizational rhetors. For example, in 2008 the village of Webberville, Texas, was concerned with the risk posed by a proposal from the much more powerful city of Austin to build a landfill just outside of the Webberville village limits. Much of the discourse surrounding the topic featured concerns about how a small municipality could have any success in fighting a city with the resources of Austin (Toohey, 2008).

Outrage may be further emphasized if issues of race/ethnicity and economic status are also involved. Heath (1997) identified an "emerging concern that the placement of manufacturing companies, waste disposal facilities, and hazardous occupations do not equitably expose rich persons to risks as often or as severely as poor persons and those of color" (p. 326). If risks appear to be unfairly distributed in a society, outrage and the accompanying emotions of fear and distrust may be increased.

In contrast to the very imposing constraints of perception frames, complexity, emotion, and status differences, three factors may emerge that can ease or intensify a rhetor's task of influencing audiences to tolerate a risk. First, as has been true in several other types of rhetoric we have discussed, organizational identity and earlier rhetoric produced by the organization can serve as either limitations or assets in risk rhetoric. If an organization has a strong, positive identity that includes a reputation for competence and concern for community, audiences may be more willing to trust organizational messages and accept arguments about risk. On the other side, a rhetor who has a negative organizational identity will have a much more difficult task. For example, imagine being asked to write risk rhetoric for Exxon following the *Valdez* oil spill, or for Union Carbide following an accidental leak that killed 2,000 people in Bhopal, India (Ice, 1991). If audiences already have negative associations with an organization, the challenge of addressing risk is that much greater. If information is complex, and an audience member moves to the peripheral processing route, organizational identity may become a key peripheral cue.

Second, as is true in issue management, the general legislative and regulatory climate can also serve as either a limitation or an asset. In a climate of decreasing regulation, regulatory and legislative bodies may be more receptive to arguments made by business and industry. This can serve as an asset for an organizational rhetor, as it may lower the level of scrutiny and the burden of proof that organizations have taken all available steps to mitigate risks. In a climate of increasing regulation and legislative oversight, however, legislators and regulators may be more receptive to the arguments of individuals and groups expressing concern with organizations' risk proposals. This can pose an additional constraint for risk rhetors, who may then need to refute additional arguments and meet a higher standard of proof.

❖ STRATEGIES FOR RHETORIC ABOUT RISK

There are several rhetorical strategies important in helping rhetors manage risk-related situations. Each of them is based on one or more of the rhetorical strategies discussed in Chapter 2. By now, you are familiar with many of the strategies outlined below, though a few are uniquely suited for negotiating risk issues with audiences. Because the rhetorical situation in risk rhetoric is so complex, organizations will use credibility and identity-based appeals, values appeals, and logical arguments and evidence. In addition, they will craft their language carefully to present their arguments in the most effective way.

Rhetorical strategies addressing risks are delivered in a wide range of forms, including Web sites, newsletters, and television and radio ads. Unlike some other forms of organizational rhetoric, though, rhetoric about risk often occurs in the context of public meetings. These public meetings allow organizations to present their case for a risk-related action to public audiences, and to receive feedback.

Organizational Credibility

Because audience reactions to questions about risk are closely linked to an organization's reputation, strategies to promote corporate social legitimacy and to maintain and enhance identity will be common in risk rhetoric (Hearit, 1995). Although appeals to the community element of corporate social legitimacy are still important, competence is more likely to be a key strategy in rhetoric about risk. Recall that in order to be perceived as competent, "a corporation must meet socially constructed standards of quality and desirability as well as perform in accordance with accepted standards of professionalism" (p. 2). It will be easier for a company that is perceived to uphold standards of quality to reassure audiences that it will be able to successfully mitigate risk than it would be for an organization that is not perceived as competent.

Competence may be created in rhetoric by explaining policies that have been enacted to minimize the threat that a risk-related event will occur or that it will have significant negative effects. In a September 24, 2007, news release reassuring audiences about the safety of one of its nuclear power facilities, NRG Energy wrote, "Nuclear power plants are among the most secure industrial systems in the United States. In addition to their extraordinary structural strength and multiple safety systems, they are protected by numerous barrier and intrusion detection/prevention systems." This reassurance of competence fits with the expert frame idea that reliable physical systems are keys to reducing risk.

The organization supplemented this technical claim with information that may better establish competence in the eyes of nonexpert audiences by emphasizing control of human elements (Elliot, 2003). The rhetoric of NRG continued, "The plants are also constantly patrolled by highly trained, heavily armed officers with SWAT-level skills and capabilities," and "All STP [Nuclear Operating Company] employees must pass extensive background checks that include criminal, personal, psychological and drug screening. In addition, employee behavior is monitored through continuous observation and random drug testing programs of everyone with access to the plant."

Issues of identity are also important in risk rhetoric. Organizations pursuing actions that may be perceived as posing risks to the community may use association and differentiation to connect themselves with positive values (as will be discussed shortly), or to separate themselves from other organizations that may have misjudged the potential risk and caused harm to their communities. For example, if one pharmaceutical company produced a product later found to cause dangerous side effects, other drug manufacturers would want to distance themselves from those negative perceptions by creating rhetoric that emphasizes differences in testing philosophy or procedure.

Values Advocacy

If, as Bostdorff and Vibbert (1994) argue, shared values serve to create premises for decisions made by individuals about organizations, the strategy of values advocacy will be common in rhetoric about risk. Organizations may create agreement with audience members that a variety of commonly held values are important, and then offer risk-related ways in which to uphold those values. Values advocacy may also be useful in risk because of its ability to defuse criticism and enhance organizational image. The same approaches for building common values outlined in earlier chapters apply in risk.

For example, an organization may make explicit appeals to values, talk about its products or practices in a way that reinforces common values, praise individuals who uphold the values, or present its charitable activities as evidence of common values. Wal-Mart's most recent campaign, featuring the slogan "save money, live better," appeals to the common values of economy and quality of life, and creates a premise that says that economic value *leads* to quality of life (Wal-Mart Stores, Inc., 2008b). Once the organization has encouraged audiences to accept the premise that economic value leads to quality of life, it has established the grounds on which to build later arguments about risk. For example, if the company wants to build a new store in an environmentally fragile area, it may be able to persuade the audience that potential risk of environmental damage is outweighed by the advantage of the increased economic value, and therefore quality of life, promised by a new Wal-Mart store.

Claims and Evidence

Although claims and evidence play some role in almost all organizational rhetoric, they are generally more developed in rhetoric about issues and risk. Because these two types of rhetorical situations are so complex, the need to present claims and provide evidence is particularly important. Organizations may present claims and evidence about the likelihood that a particular risk-related event could occur, or about how serious or harmless consequences of that event might be. In addition, arguments generated through use of the stock issue of cost (see Chapter 7) may encourage rhetors to frame arguments in terms of a balance of the risks inherent in a project against the potential benefits of the project. According to Elliot (2003), this type of argument is generally more acceptable to those using an expert frame rather than a nonexpert frame to interpret risk.

It is also important to consider the types of evidence that may be offered to support claims about organizational risk. Recall that experts tend to rely on statistics to address risk questions, while nonexperts tend to use experiential or anecdotal evidence. The ability to draw from both types of evidence may help reduce the constraint produced by diverse risk perception frames (Elliot, 2003). In considering the role of evidence in risk rhetoric, Mirel (1994) suggests that rhetors explain and qualify methods for gathering statistics and "personalize risk-related numbers and statistics through examples, anecdotes, and concrete images" (p. 49).

An additional argumentation strategy common in risk rhetoric is the process of anticipating and refuting arguments that may be made by those who oppose the organization's action. By carefully monitoring the environment and listening to audiences, organizational rhetors can predict the sorts of arguments that may be made. They can then respond to them proactively rather than reactively. For example, the NRG Energy rhetoric quoted above spends a great deal of space offering reassurances about the safety of its facility. Because of past events and public attitudes toward nuclear power, communication professionals anticipated the need to carefully address the risk of safety failures.

Community Participation

As is true in rhetoric about issues (see Chapter 7), community participation in controversies over risk can serve both practical and rhetorical functions. Practically, seeking input from all interested parties can help ensure that the best possible decisions are made. Rhetorically, participation establishes a sense of concern for the community, and may help reduce somewhat the constraint that results from the perceived power imbalances between parties in a risk situation. The use and promotion of participation may also help alleviate the sense of outrage that may emerge if an audience feels they have no control over how a risk decision is made (Mirel, 1994).

A portion of risk-related participation usually happens at public meetings. Elliot (2003) argues that it is important for organizational representatives to listen actively at these meetings because the information can increase understanding of local issues and audience values, and because it may encourage parties in opposition to also listen more openly to the messages of the organization. One example of community participation in a risk decision occurred following the events outlined in the case study about TXU in Chapter 3. As part of the deal that authorized the buyout, environmental groups and the proposed buyers met and agreed on a plan to minimize environmental risk caused by the operations of the newly formed organization (Koenig, 2007).

Stylistic Strategies

What is said in risk rhetoric is important, but *how* it is said is equally important. Language and other stylistic choices are important in a situation where complexity, high emotions, and power imbalances present significant constraints. Organizational rhetors may be tempted to use technical language to intimidate the audience into accepting a risk. This approach, however, may widen the gap between expert and nonexpert perceptions of risk and thus increase emotions of distrust and outrage. Many scholars who write about risk discuss the importance of using language choices that make information more, rather than less, accessible to nonexpert audiences.

❖ EVALUATING AND CRITIQUING RHETORIC ABOUT RISK

With an understanding of the rhetorical situation and rhetorical strategies associated with risk, it is important to consider how rhetorical creators and critics may use this knowledge. An evaluative critic will identify the constraints present in a particular risk situation and then study the rhetorical strategies in order to evaluate whether the messages were likely to have been successful. On the flip side of evaluation, creators of rhetoric may learn from the efforts of others how to best address the many constraints associated with persuading audiences to trust organizations to effectively manage risk. In addition to the general questions suggested in Chapters 2 and 3, a critic conducting an evaluative reading of risk rhetoric should consider some or all of the following questions:

- Are any of the constraints most common to risk rhetoric present in the situation?
- What risk perception frames do people in the audiences appear to have?
- Are there strategies in the rhetoric that seem to account for those frames?
- Are there strategies in the rhetoric that seem designed to enhance the organization's credibility?
- Are there strategies in the rhetoric that appeal to emotion?
- Are there strategies in the rhetoric that appeal to values?
- Are there strategies that use claims and evidence?

With their interest in how power is constructed and maintained through organizational rhetoric, critics doing a critical reading will be interested in analyzing rhetoric about risk. As is evident in the constraint of power imbalance between individuals and organizations, questions of power are abundant as we consider rhetoric about risk. In addition to the general questions laid out in Chapters 4 and 5, a critic conducting a critical reading should consider some or all of the following questions:

- How does the organization portray itself as qualified or authorized to speak about a particular risk topic?
- Does the rhetoric appear to try to shrink or expand the power distance between the organization and other interested parties? If so, what rhetorical strategies does it use?
- Does the rhetoric invite or limit participation in the risk assessment process? If so, which rhetorical strategies accomplish the invitation or limitation?
- Does the organization present information in ways that allow audiences to make fully informed choices about whether a risk situation is likely to occur and what the consequences of that occurrence might be?
- Does the organization present information in ways that encourage participants to use peripheral instead of central processing?

❖ CONCLUSION

Contemporary organizations often have to propose actions that audiences perceive to involve threats to health, safety, or the environment. The purpose of rhetoric about risk is to involve audiences in a dialogue that can ultimately lead to decisions about risk that are acceptable to the organization and to other interested parties. The rhetorical situation is characterized by an extremely large number of constraints, including complexity, emotion, and diverse perceptions of risk. The discourse surrounding risk often contains rhetorical strategies of credibility, appeals to values, claims and evidence, language, and participation that offer the potential for rhetors to create messages capable of resolving the controversy. Use your understanding of risk rhetoric to analyze the description of the rhetorical situation and the sample rhetoric that follow.

❖ CASE STUDY: NO BODIES IN MY BACKYARD

Although forensic crime dramas like *CSI: Crime Scene Investigation* are very popular, it seems that many people don't want to get too close to the action. A proposal by Texas State University-San Marcos to build a forensic research facility generated concern among many residents of the surrounding city of San Marcos. The proposal was discussed in a public meeting and attracted media coverage, both in local papers and in papers from Bismarck, North Dakota, to Boston.

The purpose of a forensic research facility like the one proposed by the university is to study how human bodies decompose in various circumstances in order to improve law enforcement officials' ability to study crime scenes. Dr. Jerry Melbye, the director of the proposed facility, told the *San Antonio Express News*, "There is an enormous amount of research to be done," and "We are going to make Texas a pretty hard place to commit homicide" (Croteau, 2006). Melbye described the proposed facility as "a 6-acre tract, surrounded by prison-style 12-foot chain-link fencing topped with razor wire and monitored by video surveillance in an isolated location" (Croteau, 2006). He also specified that at most, the facility would do research on no more than 10 bodies at any given time (Bloom & Osborne, 2007).

Over the course of the controversy, the university proposed building the facility on mostly rural, university-owned land about 2 miles from an outlet mall, on university-owned land near the city airport, or on a parcel of land on the university's ranch. Discussion of the project began in 2006 and finally concluded in February 2008, when the university announced that it would build the facility at the ranch location.

Media coverage of the proposal created some very different ideas about the forensic research facility. Howard Witt (2007) of the *Chicago Tribune* wrote, "But some folks in the small central Texas city of San Marcos recently dodged the ultimate NIMBY nightmare: a forensic research facility comprised of dozens of dead human bodies left out in the open to rot." This same article described concerns with the site initially proposed by the university: "City officials were concerned that visiting bargain hunters might discover a little more than they bargained for. Nearby residents worried about bugs being attracted to the body farm and coyotes gnawing on body parts and dropping them in their back yards" (Witt, 2007). Much of the media coverage used the phrase "body farm" to describe the facility. The term was coined by crime fiction author Patricia Cornwell, and is not the label preferred by those doing forensic research. Melbye was quoted as saying, "Body farm is an emotional term. . . . It was good for her book because it conjures up a lot of emotion" (Croteau, 2006).

The *San Antonio Express-News* reported that shortly after the initial announcement, fliers opposing the facility were passed out in one neighborhood in San Marcos. The fliers warned residents that "the facility would reek of death, that coyotes and vultures could carry off body parts and leave them in people's yards, and the flies could pick up germs from the bodies and spread diseases" (Croteau, 2006).

Although the university did not need zoning permission from residents or the city to build the research site, officials did hold a public meeting in April of 2007 to share information and hear the concerns of local residents (Mendez, 2007). The residents had plenty of concerns to share. People who lived near the proposed sites were worried about the possibility that the bodies would attract coyotes that might then prey on local livestock; that rain water runoff from the facility would pollute nearby bodies of water; that diseases could be spread; that the odor of decaying bodies would be carried on the wind; and that, as a result, property values would decrease (Bloom, 2008; Witt, 2007; Zarazua, 2007).

The *San Antonio Express-News* quoted one participant as saying, "You can have this thing somewhere other than a community that has homes" (Zarazua, 2007). According to the *Austin American-Statesman*, another landowner said he feared the facility would add to an existing problem with coyotes that had killed farm animals. The man said, "'Leaving a dead body out in the open is not a good idea" (Bloom & Osborne, 2007).

An additional concern was that vultures, attracted to the bodies at the facility, would create a hazard for aircraft taking off and landing at the nearby San Marcos Airport. One pilot wrote in an email to the *Houston Chronicle,* "If I hit a vulture, I am assured of either a quick death or a nasty crash landing" (Mangan, 2007). Airport Manager Kenny Johns also expressed concern that pilots flying over the facility would be able to see the bodies (Witt, 2007).

Ultimately, the university decided not to build on the airport site, but instead to locate the facility on a portion of the Freeman Ranch—a university-owned property used for research on agriculture. The press release that follows was put out by officials at Texas State to announce the final decision and was archived on the university's Web site. As you consider the rhetorical situation and the press release (Figure 8.2), conduct the *process for analyzing organizational rhetoric* (you may want to use the worksheets in the appendix), and answer the case study questions.

Figure 8.2   News Release From University News Service, February 12, 2008

Texas State Forensic Research Facility to locate at Freeman Ranch

Posted by Jayme Blaschke
University News Service
February 12, 2008

Texas State University-San Marcos will locate its planned Forensic Research Facility on the 3,000-acre Freeman Ranch, a move announced by Provost Perry Moore today.

The Forensic Research Facility will be an open-air lab of approximately five acres surrounded by high security fencing. Within this lab, human bodies that have been donated to the facility will be allowed to decompose in a natural environment under the study of forensic anthropologists. The facility will be located in an area of Texas State's Freeman Ranch that is away from all properties bordering the ranch. The closest bordering properties are approximately one mile away. It will be operational by late spring, Moore said.

The facility, which will be an integral part of a graduate program in forensic anthropology at Texas State, will train scientists and assist law enforcement officials in establishing the time of death and the nature of death when bodies are found. It will also provide training in the identification of skeletal and dental remains. Workshops for law enforcement at the facility will include crime scene training, human identification, cadaver dog training and numerous other workshops.

"There is a real need for a laboratory such as this in our region," said Moore. "What we learn at the facility will be of extraordinary value to the law enforcement community."

Support for the facility has come from many law enforcement agencies in Texas and nationally.

During the first several years of operation, there will be no more than five or six bodies at the facility at any one time. The total decaying matter at the facility will be no greater than several dead deer or one large cow, therefore, the facility will not significantly increase the total decaying material on the Freeman Ranch or in the area of the ranch.

All bodies in the facility will be treated with respect and according to regular protocol for the study of human remains. A Hazard Analysis Critical Control System will be utilized to protect workers at the facility as well as individuals outside the facility. Netting and fencing will be used to keep intruders out of the facility, including scavengers and predators such as vultures and coyotes.

"Given that only five acres will be fenced out of more than 3,000 on the Freeman Ranch, coupled with the extensive measures planned to assure the security of the facility, the Forensic Research Facility will have minimal impact on the general operation of the ranch and will in no way undermine the use of the ranch for agriculture, ranching and range management education," said Moore.

University News Service, 860 J.C.Kellam
Phone: 512.245.2180. Fax: 512.245.8153

Case Study Questions

Basic Descriptive Process

1. Which of the strategies of organizational rhetoric can you iden-tify in the sample? (You may want to refer to the Worksheet for Identifying Rhetorical Strategies in Organizational Texts in the appendix.)

   a. Does the rhetor use credibility strategies?

   b. Does the rhetor use values advocacy strategies? If so, to what values does he or she appeal and how?

   c. Does the rhetor use claims and evidence?

   d. Do any of the strategies in the rhetoric seem to address people using a layperson's risk frame? An expert risk frame?

   e. Do any of the strategies in the rhetoric seem to encourage readers to take the central processing route? The peripheral route?

2. What are the key elements of the rhetorical situation? (You may want to refer to the Worksheet for Describing Rhetorical Situations in Organizations in the appendix.)

   a. How would people using a layperson's risk frame perceive this rhetorical situation? How about people using an expert risk frame?

   b. Which types of audience seem to be target audiences in this situation?

   c. What constraints common to risk situations are present in this case?

Evaluative Reading

1. Compare the strategies you have identified with the elements of the rhetorical situation. Which strategies seem especially adapted to which elements of the rhetorical situation? (You may want to refer to the Worksheet for Conducting an Evaluative Reading in the appendix.)

2. Based on what you know about the rhetorical situation and what you have found out about the strategies, what did the rhetor want the reader to think, feel, or do after looking at the press release (Figure 8.2)?

3. Based on what you know about the situation and the strategies, should the rhetoric have accomplished its goal? Do you think the audiences reacted the way the rhetor intended them to? Why or why not?

Critical Reading

1. Based on what you know about the rhetorical situation and the strategies, has the organization included enough information for audience members to make an informed decision about the rhetoric? (You may want to refer to the Worksheet for Conducting a Critical Reading in the appendix.)

2. Based on what you know about the rhetorical situation and the strategies, who was and is allowed to contribute to the discussion in the rhetoric, and whose voices are not heard? Does the rhetoric indicate in any way that interested parties are invited to participate?

3. How does your evaluative reading compare with your critical reading? Are the two readings similar or different? How? What do the similarities or differences tell you?

4. Based on the three questions above, how does the rhetoric extend or limit the power of the organization in society?

Case Study References

Bloom, M. (2008, February 13). "Body farm" finally has a place to rest. *Austin American-Statesman.*

Bloom, M., & Osborne, C. (2007, April 14). "Body farm" unwelcome as neighbor. *Austin American-Statesman.*

Croteau, R. (2006, December 7). Texas State University lab would allow study of decomposing human remains. *San Antonio Express-News.*

Mangan, K. S. (2007, May 18). Stiff opposition. *Chronicle of Philanthropy.*

Mendez, A. (2007, April 10). Forensics facility will set Texas State U.-San Marcos apart in field. *University Wire.*

Witt, H. (2007, June 15). Texas finds trouble securing location for "body farm." *Chicago Tribune.* Retrieved June 26, 2009, from http://www.jameslogancourier .org/index.php?itemid=2226

Zarazua, J. (2007, April 12). Despite "ewww" factor, body farm "done deal." *San Antonio Express-News.*

9

Crisis Rhetoric

❖ ❖ ❖

Figure 9.1 Process for Analyzing Organizational Rhetoric (Crisis Rhetoric)

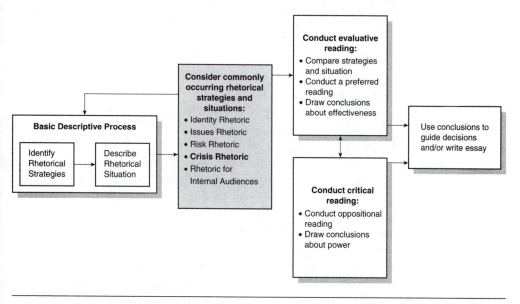

SOURCE: Adapted from Ford (1999).

On March 24, 1989, an oil tanker named the *Exxon Valdez* ran aground on Bligh Reef in Alaska, spilling 270,000 barrels of oil into Prince William Sound, and creating the largest tanker spill in U.S. history (Shabecoff, 1989). While no humans lost lives or were injured,

185

thousands of birds and animals were killed and gas prices climbed in the United States (Associated Press [AP], 1989; Shabecoff, 1989). The ship's commander, Captain Joseph J. Hazelwood, was charged with operating a vessel while intoxicated (AP, 1989). Exxon immediately began cleanup processes, but the progress was slow. Thus, Exxon faced two major threats to its identity: the problem of the oil spill itself, and negative reports about the cleanup efforts (Benoit, 1995a). The response of Exxon is now considered a classic case of what *not* to do in a crisis (Hearit, 2006).

Anyone who reads online news or newspapers, or surfs through various news channels on television or radio, knows that organizations face challenges to their reputations every day. These challenges often are both potentially threatening and unanticipated. Some challenges are more threatening than others because they happen unexpectedly and endanger the faith and trust audiences have placed in those organizations. Accidents happen that endanger, or even end, the lives of customers or neighbors; calculated risks may result in economic disaster; or a natural event, such as Hurricane Katrina in 2005, may send an organization into chaos. These types of situations result in rhetoric about what is called an *organizational crisis.*

Classic examples of organizational crisis situations include the 1982 poisoning of several packages of Johnson & Johnson's Tylenol capsules and the 1984 deadly leak of gas from a Union Carbide facility in Bhopal, India. Other examples of organizational crisis include the situation faced by companies who had offices in the World Trade Center on September 11, 2001; Ford Explorer rollovers partially caused by underinflated Firestone tires; NASA's 1986 Space Shuttle Challenger and 2003 Space Shuttle Columbia explosions; and the situations faced by organizations such as AIG that needed to explain how lending practices led to financial problems.

Situations like these are managed in part through actions by the organization (paying restitution, cleaning up spills, correcting procedures, making changes in policy), and in part by how the organization uses rhetoric during and following the crisis event. No crisis facing an organization can be effectively managed without the strategic use of messages (Hearit, 2006). In this chapter, we explore the rhetorical situation created by crisis events, and highlight the role of rhetorical strategies in planning for and responding to crises in organizations.

❖ DEFINING RHETORIC ABOUT CRISIS

Key to distinguishing rhetoric about crisis is a definition of crisis itself. The term *crisis* is used very casually in our everyday conversation. For example, a student might say, "I'm in crisis mode because my term project is due Friday." However, a definition of a crisis in organizations takes a very specific form. According to Ulmer, Sellnow, and Seeger (2007), an organizational crisis is "a specific, *unexpected,* and *nonroutine* event or series of events that create high levels of *uncertainty* and *threaten* or are perceived to threaten an organization's high priority goals" (p. 7, emphasis in original). Coombs (1999) notes, "A crisis has the potential to disrupt or affect the entire organization" (p. 3). How these definitions translate into constraints for organizational rhetors will be discussed later.

Ulmer et al. (2007) also argue that two key elements comprise an organization's response to a crisis: (1) the practical, physical actions it takes in addressing the situation (conducting environmental cleanup, caring for victims, changing policy to prevent future problems, etc.) and (2) how it uses discourse to present its role in the crisis and the aftermath to audiences. Both elements are key. If organizations act, but no one knows about the action, their reputations will continue to suffer. At the same time, organizations can create massive amounts of rhetoric, but if they do not follow through with promised actions, their reputations will likely be harmed even further.

Rhetorical strategies for managing threats to organizational reputation are grounded in the strategies discussed in Chapter 2. In addition, scholars in rhetoric, public relations, and organizational communication have used their knowledge of the strategies to identify some approaches especially adapted for response to crisis. For example, in this chapter we study two of these specialized strategies: corporate or organizational apologia (e.g., Hearit, 1995, 2006; Rowland & Jerome, 2004) and image repair theory (e.g., Benoit, 1995a).

Coombs (2004, 2006) has proposed the *situational crisis communication theory* (SCCT) to frame the rhetorical choices organizations have to make to manage crises. SCCT fundamentally assumes that the "content of the crisis response must match the crisis situation" (Coombs, 2006, p. 175; see also Heath & Millar, 2004; Ulmer et al., 2007). With these assumptions in mind, the discussion of crisis rhetoric must begin with consideration of the crisis life cycle.

❖ FOUNDATION FOR UNDERSTANDING CRISIS RHETORIC: LIFE CYCLE OF A CRISIS

Ideally, crisis management should be an ongoing function in organizations (Coombs, 1999). Lessons learned from the resolution of their own and others' crises should help guide future organizational decisions (e.g., Venette, 2008), and organizational members at all levels (but especially public relations professionals and other members of the management team) should be scanning all environments in order to plan effectively. For our purposes of learning to evaluate crisis rhetoric, we foreground the life cycle of a crisis from these ongoing organizational processes.

Scholars of organizational crisis have developed at least two models to describe the way in which crisis situations unfold. Heath and Millar's (2004) framework features stages of response. Ulmer et al.'s (2007) framework addresses communication demands at each stage of a crisis. We discuss Ulmer et al.'s (2007) suggestions in the context of Heath and Millar's (2004) stages: pre-crisis strategies, crisis response strategies, and post-crisis response strategies.

Pre-Crisis Stage

As is true in issues and risk rhetoric, planning is an important step in successfully addressing crisis in organizations. Argenti (1998), Heath and Millar (2004), Coombs (2006), and Ulmer et al. (2007) all argue that organizations need to assess the risks facing their organizations. Communication professionals, including public relations professionals, must be closely involved in the planning process as part of the management team because they will be expected to execute the plan and speak for the organization (Heath, 1997; Ulmer et al., 2007). Rhetorical efforts in this stage fall into three main areas: anticipating crisis, avoiding crisis, and managing relationships with potential crisis audiences.

An organization must constantly monitor its organizational environment in order to determine what types of crises are most likely to occur. The determination of potential crises will be based in part on the nature of the organization. Some industries are inherently more dangerous for employees and neighbors (e.g., industrial and power plants); some organizations manufacture products that are vulnerable to sabotage or quality problems (e.g., pharmaceutical companies). The physical location of some companies makes them prone to natural disasters (e.g., oil rigs during hurricane season in the Gulf of Mexico).

Finally, negative public attitudes about an industry or a particular organization may also increase the chance that a group will draw negative attention from organizational audiences. For example, the activist organization PETA (People for the Ethical Treatment of Animals) sometimes faces negative public attitudes despite its goal to prevent cruelty to animals because of the extreme strategies it has used to draw attention to its cause. Regardless of what risks a particular organization faces, organizational leaders must attempt to anticipate what might go wrong in order to be as prepared as possible should that incident actually occur.

As they anticipate possible situations, rhetors may also attempt to anticipate the types of arguments that could be made should the crisis occur. Rhetoric, in the form of policy statements and training materials, may also help to avoid crisis by effectively persuading employees to follow established safety and security practices. The specific strategies most successful for crisis rhetoric are discussed later in this chapter.

Finally, in the pre-crisis stage, rhetoric may be used to build relationships with audiences. One emerging model of crisis management argues that organizations must begin building and maintaining relationships with key publics prior to any crisis situation (Hearit, 2006; Heath, 1997; Heath & Millar, 2004; Ulmer et al., 2007). Ideally, a positive prior relationship will make audiences more receptive to organizational rhetoric during a crisis. In addition, relationships with various stakeholder groups prior to a crisis may help the organization consider ideas for preventing a crisis from occurring in the first place. Broadening the number of perspectives considered in planning for a crisis may help an organization develop more effective preventive strategies than it could on its own (Waymer & Heath, 2007).

Crisis Response Stage

Both physical and rhetorical actions play important roles in this stage of the crisis. During this stage, public relations professionals (or other employees responsible for creation of messages) and other organizational leaders become the key actors in crafting and presenting organizational messages. In this stage, organizations must coordinate activities, disseminate information, and reduce uncertainty (Ulmer et al., 2007). There are a number of activities that organizations may need to coordinate. For example, the physical rescue and care of any victims must always happen first in a crisis situation. Rhetorical efforts may include explaining the rescue or recovery efforts and influencing how various audiences assign meaning to, and responsibility for, the events of the crisis. Organizations may need to simultaneously conduct rescue operations and construct messages reducing uncertainty and justifying their efforts (Ulmer et al., 2007).

Although we will discuss specific strategies later in this chapter, it is also important to think about how rhetoric is delivered during the crisis response stage. A centralized message and source of communication can increase consistency and decrease uncertainty during a crisis. Massey (2001) found that organizations that produce consistent messages across stakeholders will enhance their legitimacy, while organizations that produce inconsistent crisis responses (conflicting messages to different audiences) will reduce their legitimacy.

Communicating clearly with those audiences affected by the crisis is one of the actions recommended by Argenti (1998) in managing crisis. He also recommends that organizations (1) gather as much information as possible on an ongoing basis, (2) set up a centralized communication center, and (3) communicate with the media early and update them frequently. The first and third actions seem to contradict each other, and to some degree they do. Although it is important to be sure that all information released is accurate, it is also important that the media hear from an organizational spokesperson early. Sometimes early messages must simply communicate a lack of information, a concern for the victims, and the intention to get and share information as quickly as possible (Ulmer et al., 2007), but those early, relatively simple messages are extremely important in the organization's goal to recover its corporate social legitimacy.

Post-Crisis Stage

Rhetoric takes center stage in the post-crisis stage of the rhetorical situation. In this phase, organizations take the practical actions of learning the cause of the crisis, implementing changes to prevent the same problem in the future, and compensating victims. Rhetorically, organizations must regain trust from their enabling, functional, normative, and diffused audiences, in order to reestablish corporate social legitimacy. In addition, organizations in the post-crisis stage should also assess their crisis response in order to improve future efforts.

❖ CRISIS MANAGEMENT: THE RHETORICAL SITUATION

As stated above, a crisis is defined as "a specific, *unexpected,* and *non-routine* event or series of events that create high levels of *uncertainty* and *threaten* or are perceived to threaten an organization's high priority goals" (Ulmer et al., 2007, p. 7, emphasis in original). First, the event is unexpected and nonroutine. Even if the organization has considered what to do in the event something does not go as planned, the specifics of what actually goes wrong, the exact group of people who suffer the consequences, the exact cause of the event, and the exact timing of the event cannot be predicted (Gilpin & Murphy, 2006). Thus, every situation faced by organizational representatives must be approached as a new event. Second, the event is nonroutine, so it cannot be managed by routine organizational procedures (Ulmer et al., 2007). Crises often require measures tailored specifically to the situation the organization faces. A discussion of the exigencies, audiences, and constraints emerging in a crisis will paint a more complete picture of the rhetorical situation.

Exigencies

As you might expect, the exigence in crisis management rhetoric is a crisis. These exigencies are often quite controversial because they may involve danger to human life, and they may determine whether an organization will continue to do business. In this subsection, we will describe more specifically the exigence for crisis based upon the types of crises that organizations face, and the timing of them (Coombs, 2004, 2006; Ulmer et al., 2007).

The exigence in any crisis situation is influenced by the nature and seriousness of what has occurred and by how audiences perceive organizational responsibility for it (Benoit, 1995a; Rowland & Jerome, 2004). For example, one category of crisis occurs when "stakeholders hold strong attributions of organizational crisis responsibility" (Coombs, 2006, p. 183) and includes intentional management misconduct (e.g., the Enron crisis). The other categories include those in which "stakeholders hold moderate attributions" and "stakeholders hold weak attributions" of organizational crisis responsibility (p. 183).

Ulmer et al. (2007) categorize the types of common crises faced by organizations into two groups according to the cause of the crisis in relation to the type of harm experienced by the organization. Intentional crises are those created by acts deliberately designed to harm the organization. Intentional crises include terrorism, sabotage, workplace violence, poor employee relationships, poor risk management, hostile takeovers, and unethical leadership. In contrast, unintentional crises are basically unforeseeable or unavoidable, such as natural disasters, disease outbreaks, unforeseeable technical interactions, product failure, or downturns in the economy.

Rather than discussing exigencies in terms of intention, Hearit (2006) focuses on responsibility. He writes, "Contrary to popular belief, most crises are not the result of an external [or even internal] psychopath but instead are self-generated, the result of internal screw-ups on the part of companies . . . organizations are more often than not the victims of their own misdeeds" (p. 2). Crises in this category would feature human error, such as errors that cause product defects, violations of law, or errors in judgment such as pilot error. Rowland and Jerome (2004) also address the issue of responsibility when they discuss whether some responsibility for the crisis could be shared by another organization or individual.

Audiences

All four types of audience may be important in crisis rhetoric. Enabling audiences such as regulators need to be persuaded that the organization meets industry requirements. Functional audiences, including stockholders and employees, will need to be reassured of the financial viability of the organization. Customers and employees will need to be reassured of their health and safety. Other organizations (normative audiences) will be interested in how the affected organizations respond so that they might emulate their successes and avoid their failures (J. McMillan, personal communication, September 2008). The media as diffused audiences are key to getting the word out to various publics during and after the crisis.

As is the case in so many types of organizational rhetoric, the fact that multiple audiences exist serves as a constraint on the available means of persuasion. Addressing the concerns of one audience may have the effect of causing concern for or alienating another audience

(Leichty, 1997). Organizations facing a crisis must figure out how to address the often-conflicting goals of the various audiences involved.

Some audiences will be more directly affected by crisis situations than others. An organization can protect its reputation by communicating as directly and personally as possible with those persons. For example, when several miners in Pennsylvania were trapped underground during the summer of 2002, spokespersons for the rescue agencies made progress reports to the families prior to releasing information to the media, thus demonstrating their commitment to the individuals involved and managing the demands of multiple audiences.

Constraints

Much like with issue and risk rhetoric, those creating crisis rhetoric face a large number of constraints. In this subsection, we address five of the most obvious constraints: the timing of crisis, the uncertain nature of crisis situations, prior organizational actions and rhetoric, legal and social expectations, and the emotional nature of many crisis situations.

First, crises are, by definition, unexpected. The immediate events in a crisis also unfold at a very fast pace. Although the long-term effects can take years to be resolved, timing is a significant constraint on the creation of rhetoric (Argenti, 1998; Marcus & Goodman, 1991). Many organizational crises, particularly those events that can cause physical harm (e.g., workplace violence or natural disasters), emerge very quickly. For example, the 2007 shooting of customers and employees at the Von Maur store in Omaha, Nebraska, unfolded in less than 20 minutes. In essence, the main part of the event had ended before any response could begin. Even events that have been developing over time (e.g., financial mismanagement) can reach the crisis stage and attract media attention quite suddenly.

The Timing of Crisis Situations

Not only does a crisis response have to be formulated quickly, it also needs to emerge in an appropriate order. For example, Coombs (2006) argues, "The primary concern during a crisis is human lives and safety—people come first. After a crisis hits, stakeholders must learn how the crisis might/will affect them and what, if any actions they must take to defend themselves" (p. 184). Addressing the safety of those injured in the crisis (physically and/or financially, depending on the type of event) must come before an organization's defense of its actions, in order to avoid the perception (or reality) that the organization is unconcerned with the human impact of the crisis. Although crisis situations usually demand an immediate response, the organization must continue to monitor the crisis long after the immediate impact has passed. It may take many years for a full understanding of a crisis event to emerge (Marcus & Goodman, 1991).

For example, in 2007, the Interstate 35 bridge over the Mississippi River in Minneapolis, Minnesota, collapsed. Several people were killed, many others were injured, and the collapse created a traffic problem that lasted over a year during the bridge's repair. At the time that the collapse occurred, it was clearly a crisis for the construction companies involved and for state and local governments, all of which created rhetoric to respond. The story of the cause of the collapse, however, will be incomplete for several years. As a result, each time information about the investigation is released, organizations will need to create rhetoric to help audiences make sense of the findings in ways that either defend or enhance organizational identity.

Uncertainty in Crisis Situations

The second constraint, uncertainty, is related to the constraint of time. Because events unfold so quickly, there is often a high level of uncertainty associated with most crisis situations. Crisis events produce uncertainty for an organization and for members of nearly all of the organization's audiences. There may be uncertainty about what happened or what is going on as the crisis emerges (Sellnow, Seeger, & Ulmer, 2002), what is being done to rectify the situation, who bears primary responsibility, and how the organization can withstand the impact of the crisis. To make the situation even more challenging, organizations, even though they may know more than the public, often don't know *much* more, and thus, may not be able to release information or explain the situation at the pace audiences would like.

Prior Organizational Rhetoric and Actions

As is true in all types of rhetoric, past organizational actions and messages can serve as a constraint on an organization's ability to create rhetoric in a crisis situation. This may be especially true if it is not the organization's first crisis. Coombs (2004) found that an organization's history of crises "intensified the attributions of crisis responsibility [in the new crisis] and lowered perceptions of organizational reputation" (p. 282). For example, FEMA's (the Federal Emergency Management Agency's) reputation was severely damaged following its slow response in helping victims of Hurricane Katrina. This well-publicized failure to respond appropriately influences how people receive new information about the organization. For instance, news items reported that FEMA trailers distributed to Katrina victims had to be recalled due to concentrations of formaldehyde that were reportedly causing illness. Because people already had questions about FEMA's actions, they were unlikely to give the organization the benefit of the doubt when passing judgment on the developing situation.

Legal, Financial, and Societal Limitations

The rhetorical response of organizations to crisis is constrained by legal and financial limitations, and by the expectations society holds for particular types of organizations. Coombs (2006) argues that legal and financial ramifications are entangled because "the legal ramifications will come with a price tag" (p. 185). For example, although some audiences may want to hear an apology when an organization is perceived as causing harm, that same apology can be perceived by another audience as an invitation to bring suit against the organization (Tyler, 1997). Coombs (2006) also notes that sometimes organizations will accept punishments rather than arguing for their innocence, simply in order to avoid the cost of defending themselves.

Sometimes the social expectations of the type of industry or service in which the organization is engaged constrains the type of responses from which it can choose in crisis situations. Organizations such as schools, religious institutions, and social service agencies may be constrained by heightened societal expectations. People expect religious organizations to behave in keeping with moral precepts, and they expect government agencies to obey the law. When they fail to do so, they not only face the immediate crisis (an injured child or a financial scandal, for example), but also face the crisis created by their failure to operate in keeping with societal standards for industries of their type. For instance, Tracy (2007) argues that one school board's perceived dual role as an elected body and a corporate entity complicated its ability to respond to crisis when a deficit of millions of dollars was reported.

The Emotional Nature of Crisis Situations

Finally, the heightened emotional climate surrounding many crisis situations serves as a constraint on how an organization may respond. In discussing emotional appeals, Aristotle argued that people make decisions very differently depending on their emotional states. Audiences of crisis rhetoric are often under the sway of powerful emotions, including fear, anger, anxiety, and sadness. These emotions can present a challenge to rhetoric (Rowland, 2008). Ulmer et al. (2007) argues, "Crises are often so disturbing that they change the way we think about the world" (p. 29). Think about how you felt in the wake of a major event such as the terrorist attacks of September 11, 2001, or the 2007 shootings at Virginia Tech. Even though you may not have been affected directly, the nature of the events, the loss of human life, and the uncertainty surrounding the events likely created some anxiety and difficult emotions.

In sum, the timing of crisis situations; uncertainty during crisis situations; legal, financial, and societal limitations; and the emotional nature of crisis situations present a complex set of constraints for organizational rhetoric in times of crisis. It is a challenge for those crafting messages (public relations professionals and others) to respond in unanticipated, potentially threatening situations.

❖ STRATEGIES IN CRISIS RHETORIC

Rhetoric plays an important role in all three stages of the crisis life cycle. Since crisis situations are very complex, responses may include the basic strategies outlined in Chapter 2 and some strategies designed especially for crisis situations. Recall that the goals of crisis rhetoric are to restore audiences' trust in an organization following a crisis event. In this section, we discuss three primary strategies—instructional strategies, apologia strategies, and differentiation strategies—as well as use of the strategies in combination.

Instructional Strategies

Instructional strategies initially may seem to be more informative than persuasive. However, these approaches can accomplish both goals. As Coombs (2006) points out, the "primary concern during a crisis is human lives and safety—people come first" (p. 184). Building upon Sturges's (1994) and Bergman's (1994) work in his *situational crisis communication theory*, Coombs (2006) argues that the first messages an organization should craft are instructing information. Stakeholders need to know what to do to care for or protect themselves from further danger. Instructing responses should include a detailed example of what happened, as well as recommendations for what audience members should do to protect themselves from the effects of the crisis. These responses address stakeholders' basic safety and security needs to get through the crisis. Care of the victims, while clearly ethically mandatory, also helps reestablish at very basic levels corporate social legitimacy by demonstrating that the organization is still in control of itself and cares for those harmed. For example, the organization should advise audiences whether neighbors near a chemical spill or a fire should evacuate. Coombs and Holladay (2002) go so far as to advocate that no other crisis response strategies should be implemented until the instructing information is given. Rhetorically, instructional messages may draw from the strategies of appeals to needs and values, and the use of claims and evidence.

Apologia Strategies

A second set of strategies for crafting crisis rhetoric is described by the term *organizational apologia* (Hearit, 2006; Rowland & Jerome, 2004). This approach can be particularly useful in the response and post-crisis stages if the organization must bear some responsibility for the crisis. Although the term apologia suggests an apology in the traditional sense of saying, "I am sorry," Hearit (2006) distinguishes between the two. He states, "Apologia refers to the act of giving defense, whereas apology typically means the offering of a mea culpa [admission of fault]" (p. vii). Apologia is the act of defending oneself, and that defense strategy may or may not include admitting responsibility for a negative event. In some cases, an organization may choose to apologize for the crisis in our everyday sense of apology, but that is only one of the strategies described in apologia.

Long before the concept of corporate apologia was developed, Ware and Linkugel (1973) argued that individuals speaking in defense of themselves used one or more of four basic strategies: denial, bolstering, transcendence, and differentiation. We briefly define these four basic strategies and discuss how they have been adapted for understanding organizations speaking in defense of themselves.

The strategy of *denial* is fairly self-evident: The speaker simply denies any association with, or positive feeling about, whatever is viewed negatively by the audience. Depending on the facts of the case, an organization may deny that the event happened, that they were involved in any way, or that they intended to cause any harm. Benoit and

Lindsey (1987) argued that Tylenol succeeded in defending themselves when sabotaged capsules caused cyanide poisoning in seven people, in part by being able to deny that the poisoning was their responsibility. They were able to blame it on an unknown individual not associated with the organization by characterizing it as the action of a madman who had tampered with the product after it had left the factory.

Bolstering creates an association between the rhetor—in our case, the organization—and something viewed positively by the audience. Bolstering may involve the use of the basic rhetorical strategy of values advocacy. For example, in defending itself against charges of pollution, an organization may call attention to the contributions it has made to society in other ways. Bolstering will often be accompanied by denial, thereby allowing the organization to deny involvement with the negative element while also reinforcing the positive associations. However, if the accusation is very serious, and the organization cannot deny responsibility, it seems logical that bolstering will have limited effectiveness.

The strategy of *transcendence* tries to attach a new, more favorable meaning to an event or charge by attempting to move deliberations from the specific action to a more general principle. For example, an organization may admit to being part of a negatively viewed event, but then attempt to show how in reality, its participation served to advance some higher cause. Animal rights groups might admit to violating laws such as breaking and entering to release animals, but will justify or defend their actions by pointing to the higher good of saving the animals' lives.

The strategy of *differentiation* attempts to take the action in question out of its immediate context and place it in a larger context that is viewed more favorably by the audience. Ice (1991) has argued that Union Carbide attempted to differentiate between the disaster in India and its usual operating record. In other words, rhetors for the organization tried to take the disaster out of the immediate context in which it was the dominating event, and place it in the larger context of the overall safety record of the organization.

In developing the idea of organizational apologia, Benoit (1995b) catalogues a group of strategies that he refers to as *organizational image restoration strategies* (in later work [1997, 2000], he called these *image repair strategies*). His broad categories of denial, evading responsibility, reducing the offensiveness of the act, corrective action, and mortification built upon Ware and Linkugel's (1973) original strategies and provided more specificity. For example, "reducing the offensiveness of the act" includes an organization's offer of compensation to the victim of a crisis.

Hearit (2006) identifies five prototypical stances that organizations implement to defend their actions. This model includes or implies many of the ideas developed by Benoit (see above) and Coombs (2004). However, Hearit contributes another apologia strategy that he labels as *counterattack*. In a counterattack, an organization combines denial of guilt with pointing the finger at its accuser. Media organizations often are the target of counterattack strategies. For example, a reporter or producer may be counter-accused of unfairly editing the story about a crisis or using the story to increase ratings rather than explain what happened (Hearit, 1996; 2006). Organizational apologia strategies may incorporate the rhetorical strategies of appeals to values (bolstering, transcendence) and the use of claims and evidence to support any of the four types of arguments.

Dissociation Strategies

A third large category of rhetorical strategies is composed of dissociation strategies. Hearit's (2006) concept of organizational apologia is grounded in the results of several studies that focus on how dissociation strategies function rhetorically for organizations facing crises. He found that in answering accusations, organizational rhetors draw distinctions between (1) the opinions of the public or media and the "true" knowledge possessed by the organization, (2) the action of an erring individual in the organization and the organization as a whole, and (3) a single act and the larger essence of the organization.

Opinion/Knowledge Distinction

The first strategy—drawing a distinction between opinion and knowledge—consists of organizational rhetors making the argument that the public possesses only partial or inaccurate information about the event, while the organization has the complete and correct version of the facts. Hearit (1995) illustrated this strategy with the discourse of Domino's Pizza when it was accused of endangering drivers and the public with its 30-minute delivery promise. The company's spokesperson frequently claimed that the delivery promise was not a result of quick drive times between store and customer, but was instead a result of highly efficient work before the pizzas ever left the store. This strategy allowed the organization to discredit some outside information and reframe other information in ways less damaging to its image.

Individual/Group Distinction

The second strategy identified by Hearit (1995) is drawing a distinction between the actions of an individual in the organization and the organization as a whole. When using this strategy, organizational rhetors attempt to show that the unfavorable events are the responsibility of one "renegade" individual in the organization, and do not represent the nature of the organization—a form of scapegoating (Benoit, 1995a). Hearit also identified this strategy as part of Domino's response. The company acknowledged that an individual driver might speed or drive recklessly, but emphasized that the company in no way encouraged those behaviors, and in fact, asked the public to report any dangerous drivers.

Exxon also used this strategy (in combination with others) when it suggested that the captain of the *Valdez* was intoxicated at the time the ship ran aground and spilled over 100,000 barrels of oil. This strategy was an attempt by the organization to demonstrate that it should not be blamed, and that instead the individual was at fault. This strategy might logically be accompanied by corrective action, such as removing, punishing, or educating the erring individual in order to assure audiences that a similar event will not happen again.

Act/Essence Distinction

The final strategy in this group is drawing a distinction between the particular act or event in question, and the larger nature or essence of the organization. In this strategy, the rhetor argues that although this event has happened, it is not typical of the record of the organization. Hearit (1995) found that Exxon used this strategy by arguing that it had the technology ready to combat this "disastrous event" (not in their control), thus suggesting that the organization's true nature was to use technology to improve the environment. An organization may argue that this is a single, isolated event in a long and proud tradition of safety, service, and so forth. It attempts to minimize the impact of the crisis event by asking the audience to judge the organization on its total record rather than on this single, negative event.

Crisis Strategies in Combination

The strategies advanced by Ware and Linkugel (1973), Benoit (1995a, 1995b), Coombs (2004, 2006), and Hearit (2006) may be used singly or in combination to address challenges to corporate social legitimacy. Clearly, not all strategies work smoothly together. For example, a company that denies any responsibility, but then also distinguishes between individual and group actions, may be perceived as contradictory. Similarly, the strategy of bolstering is not likely to work if the organization already has admitted to doing something that is a serious negative violation of expectations. For example, if an organization has negligently caused someone's death, it will not likely be able to regain trust simply by promoting its donations to charity (Rowland & Jerome, 2004).

On the other hand, some combinations work more naturally together. For example, a rhetor can deny any intent to do harm and combine it with corrective action to ensure the event will not recur. Because repairing a reputation and rebuilding social legitimacy is a long-term process, successful organizations will employ different strategies across the life cycle of the crisis, all adapted to events and audiences.

❖ EVALUATING AND CRITIQUING ORGANIZATIONAL RHETORIC ABOUT CRISIS

With an understanding of the rhetorical situation and most common strategies of crisis rhetoric, it is important to ask how this information can be used by those who study organizational rhetoric. Critics using either the evaluative or critical approaches can pose interesting and important questions about crisis rhetoric. Evaluative critics are concerned with how well the strategies in the rhetoric were constructed to meet the demands of the rhetorical situation. In addition to the general questions introduced in Chapters 2 and 3, a critic doing an evaluative reading of crisis rhetoric should consider some or all of the following questions:

- Which of the constraints most common to crisis rhetoric are present in the rhetorical situation?
- Are there examples of instructional strategies in the rhetoric?
- Are there examples of apologia strategies in the rhetoric?
- Are there examples of disassociation strategies in the rhetoric?
- Are there any rhetorical strategies that seem particularly well or poorly adapted to the stage of the crisis life cycle?
- In the words of Heath and Millar (2004), does the rhetoric "demonstrate concern, empathy, and compassion; orient the audience to solutions; demonstrate that the organization is responsible and responsive; and reveal open-mindedness and receptivity to comments and criticism"? (p. 13)

Because organizational crisis sometimes results in severe negative consequences such as injury and loss of life, it is important that critics examine crisis rhetoric with a focus on the construction and maintenance of organizational power. In addition to the general questions introduced in Chapters 4 and 5, someone conducting a critical reading of crisis rhetoric should consider some or all of the following questions:

- How does the organization portray itself as qualified or authorized to speak about the crisis situation? Are other interested voices included in the rhetoric?

- How does the organization accept or assign responsibility for the crisis? Would other interested parties dispute or concur with that assessment?

- Based on your knowledge of the rhetorical situation and the rhetoric, does the organization appear to conceal or de-emphasize information that might influence interpretation of the crisis situation?

❖ CONCLUSION

Contemporary organizations exist in an atmosphere primed for crisis. Media scrutiny and public demands for accountability present constant challenges to corporate (organizational) social legitimacy. Monitoring an organization's multiple environments, identifying potential crisis areas, planning to respond, and employing appropriate rhetorical strategies are all key elements in how well an organization will be able to respond when negative events occur. Use your understanding of crisis rhetoric to analyze the description of the rhetorical situation and the sample rhetoric that follow.

❖ CASE STUDY: THE PERFECT STORM

In early February 2007, JetBlue Airways celebrated the seventh anniversary of its inaugural flight—marking 7 years of what it called a "customer-centered" approach to air travel. In those 7 years, JetBlue had expanded service to markets across the United States, received awards for outstanding customer service from a wide variety of organizations, and seen its stock prices increase 20% during 2006. The airline was finding success in an industry that had been plagued by bankruptcies among major carriers such as Northwest Airlines and United Airlines. The February 20, 2007, *Los Angeles Times* reported that JetBlue was "ranked above most of its peers in the federal government's most recent survey of industry performance in such areas as baggage handling, flight cancellations and 'bumped' travelers" ("Airline failed its passengers," 2007). In short, in February of 2007, JetBlue was flying high as a successful, well-respected airline.

Then, over Valentine's Day weekend, the company recognized as the "Best Airline for Customer Satisfaction" by Market Metrix in 2007, and "Best Domestic Airline" by *Conde Nast Traveler's* Readers' Choice Awards in 2006, ran into weather that it couldn't fly through, both literally and metaphorically. A major ice storm along the East Coast caused a 6-day crisis that led to the cancellation of one-third of all JetBlue flights, including nearly 1,000 at JFK airport in New York. The delays had an impact on more than 130,000 passengers (Zimmerman, 2007). Some of these passengers were stranded in JetBlue planes on runways for up to eight hours. A *New York Times* ("Trapped on an airplane," 2007) editorial vividly described the situation at JFK: "At the storm's worst, JetBlue had nine planes sitting on the tarmac at Kennedy Airport for six to ten hours while passengers were trapped in sweltering cabins with only snacks for food and stinking toilets."

A February 19 article in the *New York Daily News* related the stories of several passengers, including one who spent $1,700 on extra hotel rooms while stranded for several days, and another (scheduled to depart the previous Wednesday) who said, "Now they told us we'll be going out Tuesday, but I don't have any faith in that" (Fowle & Egbert, 2007). A *New York Times* article (Bailey, 2007b) included a comment from one passenger, Irving Fain, who said, "It was really a disaster. Passengers screaming, 'we pay your salary.' The security guy screaming back. Fifteen minutes into this ruckus, they finally cancelled the flight." This passenger (Fain) said he would not book another flight on JetBlue. In a February 22 letter to the editor in the *Los Angeles Times,* a passenger stated,

> We don't hold JetBlue responsible for the weather, but as JetBlue attempts to spin the meltdown as purely an operational failure, we and every other passenger in New York that day know that the reason we won't be flying JetBlue again was its failure in customer relations and communications. (Bloomberg News, 2007b)

A *New York Times* ("Trapped on an airplane," 2007) editorial called the airline's performance "horrendous" and attributed its failure to a variety of causes including a poor estimate of the strength of the storm, failed management of flights allowed to take off and land, poor crew management, and poor communication. A February 19 *New York Times* article reported, "Most airlines responded by canceling more flights earlier, sending passengers home and resuming their schedules within a day or two. JetBlue thought the weather would break and it would be able to fly, keeping its revenue flowing and its customers happy" (Bailey, 2007c). Several articles mention that the "lean" and "efficient" system that allowed JetBlue to charge lower fares and make good profits was unable to handle the demands of a crisis such as this storm.

Over the past few years, incidents in which weather or other delays have left passengers stranded on jets in very uncomfortable conditions have become fairly common. The *New York Times* (Bailey, 2007c) reported that an American Airlines plane sat for 8 hours in December 2006 in Austin, Texas, and passengers on a 1999 Northwest Airlines flight that had already been delayed 22 hours were kept on the tarmac in Detroit, Michigan, for 7 hours. Some airlines have been making policy changes to attempt to prevent or rectify these sorts of situations, but according to the *New York Times* (Bloomberg News, 2007a), the JetBlue incident has increased calls for legislation to prevent future problems.

CNNMoney.com (Wong, 2007) reported that the crisis cost the airline about $30 million including ticket refunds, providing vouchers to stranded passengers, and expenses such as overtime. According to the *Los Angeles Times* ("Airline failed its passengers" 2007), the airline warned that the cancellations might lead to a loss in first-quarter profits and reduced profit for the year. A February 17, 2007, *New York Times* (Bailey, 2007a) article may have asked the most pertinent question: "Can one very bad week for JetBlue Airways wipe out years of industry-leading customer satisfaction ratings?"

The advertisement that follows ran in the *Austin American-Statesman* shortly after the crisis unfolded (Figure 9.2). As you consider the rhetorical situation and the advertisement, conduct the *process for analyzing organizational rhetoric* (you may want to use the worksheets in the appendix), and answer the case study questions.

Case Study Questions

Basic Descriptive Process

1. Which of the strategies of organizational rhetoric can you identify in the newspaper advertisement? (You may want to refer to the Worksheet for Identifying Rhetorical Strategies in Organizational Text in the appendix.)

    a. Does the rhetor use instructional strategies?

    b. Does the rhetor use apologia strategies?

Figure 9.2   Newspaper Advertisement, JetBlue

Dear Austin,

We are sorry and embarrassed. But most of all, we are deeply sorry.

Last week was the worst operational week in JetBlue's seven-year history. Many of you were either stranded, delayed or had flights cancelled following the severe winter ice storm in the Northeast. The storm disrupted the movement of aircraft, and, more importantly, disrupted the movement of JetBlue's pilot and inflight crewmembers who were depending on those planes to get them to the airports where they were scheduled to serve you. With the busy Presidents' Day weekend upon us, rebooking opportunities were scarce, and hold times at 1-800-JETBLUE were unusually long or not even available, further hindering our recovery efforts.

Words cannot express how truly sorry we are for the anxiety, frustration and inconvenience that you, your family, friends and colleagues experienced. This is especially saddening because JetBlue was founded on the promise of bringing humanity back to air travel, and making the experience of flying happier and easier for everyone who chooses to fly with us. We know we failed to deliver on this promise last week.

We are committed to you, our valued customers, and are taking immediate corrective steps to regain your confidence in us. We have begun putting a comprehensive plan in place to provide better and more timely information to you, more tools and resources for our crewmembers and improved procedures for handling operational difficulties. Most importantly, we have published the JetBlue Airways Customer Bill of Rights — our official commitment to you of how we will handle operational interruptions going forward — including details of compensation. Our CEO, David Neeleman, has a personal message to you about this that you can find at jetblue.com/promise.

You deserved better — a lot better — from us last week, and we let you down. Nothing is more important than regaining your trust, and all of us here hope you will give us the opportunity to once again welcome you onboard and provide you with the positive JetBlue Experience you have come to expect from us.

Sincerely,

jetBlue
AIRWAYS*

jetblue.com/promise

   c. Does the rhetor use dissociation strategies?

   d. Can you identify any combinations of strategies used by the rhetor?

2. What are the key elements of the rhetorical situation? (You may want to refer to the Worksheet for Describing Rhetorical Situations in Organizations in the appendix.)

   a. In what stage of the life cycle does the crisis seem to be?

   b. Which types of audience seem to be target audiences in this situation?

   c. What constraints common to crisis situations are present in this case?

Evaluative Reading

1. Compare the strategies you have identified with the elements of the rhetorical situation. Which strategies seem especially adapted to which elements of the rhetorical situation? (You may want to refer to the Worksheet for Conducting an Evaluative Reading in the appendix.)

2. Based on what you know about the rhetorical situation and what you have found out about the strategies, what did the rhetor want the reader to think, feel, or do after looking at the statement?

3. Based on what you know about the situation and the strategies, should the rhetoric have accomplished its goal? Do you think the audiences reacted the way the rhetor intended them to? Why or why not?

Critical Reading

1. Based on what you know about the rhetorical situation and the strategies, has the organization included enough information for audience members to make an informed decision about the rhetoric? (You may want to refer to the Worksheet for Conducting a Critical Reading in the appendix.)

2. Based on what you know about the rhetorical situation and the strategies, who was and is allowed to contribute to the discussion in the rhetoric, and whose voices are not heard? Does the rhetoric indicate in any way that interested parties are invited to participate?

3. Based on your knowledge of the rhetorical situation and the rhetoric, does the organization appear to conceal or de-emphasize information that might influence possible interpretations of the crisis?

4. How does your evaluative reading compare with your critical reading? Are the two readings similar or different? How? What do the similarities or differences tell you?

5. Based on the four questions above, how does the rhetoric extend or limit the power of the organization in society?

Case Study References

Airline failed its passengers. (2007, February 22). *Los Angeles Times.*

Bailey, J. (2007a, February 17). Long delays hurt image of JetBlue. *New York Times.* Retrieved June 28, 2009, from http://www.nytimes.com/2007/02/17/business/17air.html

Bailey, J. (2007b, February 18). JetBlue cancels more flights, leading to passenger discord. *New York Times.* Retrieved June 28, 2009, from http://query.nytimes.com/gst/fullpage.html?res=9F06E1DE153EF93BA25751C0A961 9C8B63

Bailey, J. (2007c, February 19). Chief "mortified" by JetBlue crisis. *New York Times.* Retrieved June 28, 2009, from http://query.nytimes.com/gst/fullpage.html?res=9B0DE4D7153EF93AA25751C0A9619C8B63&sec=&spon=&pagewanted=all

Bloomberg News. (2007a, February 23). Airlines' proposals on long runway delays. *New York Times.*

Bloomberg News. (2007b, February 22). JetBlue expects wider losses. *Los Angeles Times.*

Fowle, N., & Egbert, B. (2007, February 19). JetBlue hopes to fly high by Wed. *Daily News* (New York).

Trapped on an airplane. (2007, February 23). [Editorial]. *New York Times.*

Wong, G. (2007, February 20). JetBlue fiasco: $30M price tag. *CNNMoney.*

Zimmerman, M. (2007, February 21). A contrite JetBlue offers a plan. *Los Angeles Times.* Retrieved June 28, 2009, from http://articles.latimes.com/2007/feb/21/business/fi-jetblue21

10

Organizational Rhetoric for Internal Audiences

❖ ❖ ❖

Figure 10.1   Process for Analyzing Organizational Rhetoric (Internal Rhetoric)

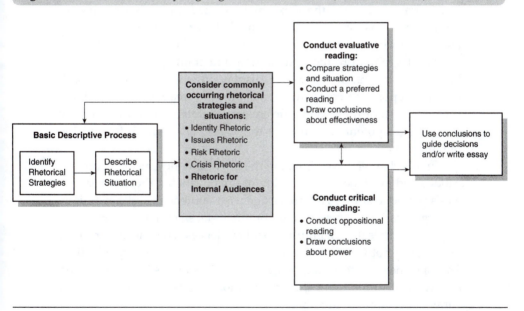

Figure 10.1   Process for Analyzing Organizational Rhetoric (Internal Rhetoric)

SOURCE: Adapted from Ford (1999).

In the movie *Cast Away* (Zemeckis & Broyles, 2000), Tom Hanks plays FedEx executive Chuck Noland who embodies the principles of timeliness and customer service held sacred by his organization. After

Chuck is stranded on a deserted island as the result of a plane crash, he carefully collects and sorts the FedEx packages that have washed up on shore with him. He then waits several days, until his survival finally demands it, to open the packages. At the end of the film, we see Chuck deliver one package that he has refused to open and has protected for 4 years.

What makes an employee so willing to uphold the values of an organization, even when his supervisors are thousands of miles away and presume that he is dead? Although the movie is a work of fiction, Chuck's experiences lead us to ask questions about the role of rhetoric in influencing the thoughts, feelings, and behaviors of employees, volunteers, and others we might think of as being "inside" the organization.

Up to this point, we have focused primarily on organizational rhetoric designed for audiences external to the organization. Although for-profit and not-for-profit groups spend a large amount of time and money creating messages to build identity, and to address issues, risk, and crisis, these external messages are only a portion of the complete picture of organizational rhetoric. Organizations also create rhetoric aimed at functional audiences. When businesses and nonprofit groups produce orientation and training materials or in-house newsletters, or when they display an employee-of-the-month plaque or sponsor a company picnic, they are creating organizational rhetoric. Each of these symbolic creations attempts to influence how members (or potential members) think, feel, and behave toward the organization.

In this chapter, we explore the rhetorical situation inside of organizations and examine how a variety of organizational rhetorical strategies are used to address internal exigencies, audiences, and constraints. All organizations, whether large or small, face similar challenges, or exigencies, in dealing with functional audiences. They need to recruit, retain, and motivate individuals to do the work of the organization. They also need to encourage organizational members to change when needed, and to represent the organization to external audiences in a variety of rhetorical situations.

From a theoretical perspective, it is nearly impossible to designate an "inside" and an "outside" of an organization. As we discussed in presenting the idea of rhetorical situations, no single situation can be described as purely internal or purely external because the interests of various kinds of audiences are intertwined. From a practical perspective, there are some kinds of messages that, while available to a variety of audiences, are directed primarily at internal audiences. In this chapter, we review the theoretical foundations, situations, and strategies most relevant to internal organizational rhetoric.

❖ THE RHETORICAL SITUATION IN INTERNAL ORGANIZATIONAL RHETORIC

We present a variety of rhetorical situations that internal rhetors may face by discussing organizational socialization, retention, and organizational change, and by reviewing how the primarily external exigencies surrounding issues, risk, and crisis rhetoric present unique challenges to rhetors addressing internal audiences.

Exigencies, Audiences, and Constraints for Organizational Socialization

The concept of organizational socialization provides a helpful framework for understanding the role of rhetoric in meeting the goals outlined above. *Organizational socialization* is the process an individual experiences in becoming part of an organization (Bullis, 1993; Jablin & Krone, 1987). The process is generally described as taking place in three stages. Although the stages are labeled in a variety of ways, we will refer to them as *anticipatory socialization, organizational entry,* and *metamorphosis* (Jablin, 2001; Jablin & Krone, 1987; Miller, 2006). Organizational communication scholars have been particularly interested in the communication processes that happen as new members gather information, accept and test new roles, and learn the culture of organizations. Although socialization is an individual and largely interpersonal experience, rhetoric created by organizations also plays a key role in influencing members' thoughts, feelings, and behaviors at each step in the process. We discuss the rhetorical situation presented to rhetors in each of the three stages of socialization.

Anticipatory Socialization to the Organization

Scholars recognize that the process of thinking about our working lives begins very early (Jablin, 2001). Recall the time you may have spent during childhood thinking about whether you were going to be a firefighter, a teacher, a doctor, a lawyer, a professional athlete, or a rock star. Although rhetoric, mostly in the form of mass media, does influence our early thinking about what it means to work, this initial phase is not directly addressed by most organizational rhetoric. Organizations do, however, spend considerable effort attempting to influence the second process of anticipatory socialization. This process also happens in the context of a particular organization. As you complete your college degree, you are probably thinking about where you want to work; perhaps you have even begun doing research to find out about particular organizations. If so, you are engaged in the initial stages of organizational anticipatory socialization.

Organizations must compete for people like you, so they need to create messages that will recruit new members—this is the exigence for rhetoric in the anticipatory stage. Organizations need to establish themselves as attractive and rewarding places to work (or volunteer), and must demonstrate that the benefits to a new member will outweigh any costs.

The audience for this type of rhetoric is composed of individuals who are able to meet the needs of the organization. Organizations face a number of constraints when recruiting new employees. Competing messages from other organizations, a questionable organizational identity, or an uninviting geographical location are just a few of the possible challenges facing rhetors trying to persuade potential newcomers. The strategies and forms of rhetoric used to addresses the challenges of anticipatory socialization are discussed later in the chapter.

Organizational Entry

Once a rhetor has persuaded individuals to associate with the organization, the next step is to introduce newcomers to the organization and to persuade them to begin making decisions with the interests of the group in mind. Almost any new job begins with at least a few hours, and even up to a week, of orientation. Employee orientation serves both a task function and a rhetorical function. The task function simply means that newcomers need to learn how to do the job, whether that involves learning to operate new equipment or becoming acquainted with procedures. The rhetorical function is a bit more challenging. The rhetorical function in the entry phase is to persuade newcomers to behave like other members of the organization. As discussed in Chapter 3, newcomers need to adopt the "decision premises" of the organization and begin thinking, feeling, and behaving in ways that uphold the organization's best interests (Tompkins & Cheney, 1985). After studying the orientation program at a company producing medical equipment, Pribble (1990) argued, "During socialization, differences between personal values and ethics of newcomers and those of an organization are most salient, as would be rhetorical efforts to convince newcomers to embrace the organization's ethical stance" (p. 255). Because new employees are seeing the organization's values for the first time, and comparing them with their own values, it is important that orientation programs take advantage of this opportunity to establish premises (Bostdorff & Vibbert, 1994; Tompkins & Cheney 1985).

The audience for this type of rhetoric is new employees (or volunteers), and the constraints may include attitudes, beliefs, or values that conflict with those of the organization, as well as any preconceived notions a new employee might bring to the situation. The strategies and forms used to address this rhetorical situation are discussed later in the chapter.

Metamorphosis

The final stage in the socialization process is often referred to as *metamorphosis* and is accomplished when the newcomer is accepted as, and feels like, an insider. At this point, it may seem that all of the organizational rhetoric in the anticipatory and entry phases has done its job, and the employee or volunteer is "finished." In reality, though, rhetoric remains of central importance long after a newcomer has been socialized into the organization and identifies with it.

There are a number of possible exigencies for rhetoric following the metamorphosis phase. First, organizational rhetoric must help retain employees and reinforce their loyalty to organizational values and practices. Second, organizational rhetoric may need to address the challenge of promoting change in an organization. Third, organizational rhetoric should help prepare members to serve as informal representatives of the organization's interests to external audiences in a variety of rhetorical situations. These three exigencies are discussed in the following sections.

Exigencies, Audiences, and Constraints for Reinforcement and Retention

Organizations cannot simply create identification and assume their rhetorical work is finished. Identification is an ongoing process. The level of connection an individual may feel with an organization can increase and decrease over time. Competing demands for identification, a change in values of the individual, or a change in the perceived values of the organization can all strain organizational identification (Hoffman & Medlock-Klyukovski, 2004; Russo, 1998; C. R. Scott, 1997). These sorts of changes require organizations to demonstrate that they are worthy of employee loyalty. The audience for this type of rhetoric is current organizational members, and the constraints may include cynicism; changes in beliefs, attitudes, or values; and threats to organizational reputation. The strategies used to address this rhetorical situation are discussed later in the chapter.

Exigencies, Audiences, and Constraints for Organizational Change

After building and reinforcing organizational decision premises through identification, organizational leaders often find themselves in the challenging position of asking employees to participate in a change that may alter or threaten some points of identification. Organizational change is a complex process, and communication about change relies on both face-to-face and rhetorical channels. Change is a continuous process in any organization. It may be incremental or dramatic, and although it may be planned or unplanned, we focus on the role of rhetoric in planned change.

Kuhn and Corman (2003) define change as "planned interventions . . . to modify elements such as formal structures, labor processes, or record systems" (p. 198). This type of change requires employees to "buy into" decisions often made at higher levels of the organization, and to make changes to long-established ways of operating. For example, many hospitals are in the process of converting from paper record keeping to electronic charting and data storage. This involves major changes in daily procedures and may require employees to learn many new skills. Other types of change may alter reporting lines in an organization or change the way work is performed. For example, several manufacturing organizations in the United States have restructured their companies into "self-managing teams" in which work groups make and enforce their own policies, and schedule and design their own work procedures (Barker, 1993). Convincing employees to learn to work in an environment so dramatically different from the traditional assembly line provides a challenge for those creating organizational rhetoric about change. Some changes are even more threatening to individuals. Mergers, for example, often involve lost jobs or mandatory relocation.

Organizational rhetoric plays an important role in how change—the need for the change, the components of the change, and the expected results of the change—is understood and accepted (or rejected) by organizational members. The exigence facing rhetoricians addressing change is essentially the need to encourage insiders to think, feel, and behave positively toward a proposed change. The constraints may include a lack of trust in the organization, anxiety related to uncertainty, fatigue and skepticism due to a perception of never-ending change, or a perception of increased workload or decreased benefits. Larger changes such as mergers or plant closings will include the added constraint of heightened emotional involvement.

External Challenges, Internal Exigencies: Situations Requiring Member Advocacy

The final set of rhetorical situations facing those who create internal rhetoric mirrors the exigencies discussed in previous chapters. Concerns with organizational identity, issue and risk management, and crisis require rhetoric for both external and internal audiences. Sometimes insiders are the primary audience for this type of rhetoric. In other cases, they are included as an audience so that they can serve as advocates for the organization with external audiences. Cheney and Christensen (2001a) argue that "Many organizations have begun to realize the difficulties of convincing an external audience about their deeds (e.g., their protection of the environment or defense of human rights) if the internal audience does not accept the message—and vice versa" (p. 232). Because there is so much overlap between internal and external audiences, rhetors must be certain to create consistent messages that are persuasive to both groups.

A few examples may help clarify this idea. Threats to organizational identity may have a negative impact on the morale and commitment level of employees. When this sort of situation occurs, the organization would benefit from crafting identity messages for both internal and external audiences (Dutton & Dukerich, 1991). Once the employees have been reassured about the reputation of the organization, they can then become advocates of that message to external audiences.

Internal audiences may play a similar role in issue management discourse. Internal rhetoric must convince members that it is to their advantage that an issue be decided in a particular way. They must also be encouraged to take some action such as attending a public meeting or contacting an official to support or oppose the policy. Employees of companies that manufacture automobiles, for example, may be persuaded that some policy such as increased fuel efficiency standards does not benefit the organization, or will not create the promised environmental benefit. Those employees may then contact their government representatives to encourage them to oppose the policy.

Risk rhetoric may also be directed internally. Although we have studied the ways that organizations manage risks that they pose in their communities, there is a great deal of risk that may be internal to organizations. Risk rhetoric aimed at internal audiences may attempt to persuade them to accept or avoid risks within the workplace. For example, organizational newsletters may include messages about the number of accident-free days at a job site in an effort to encourage people to avoid unnecessary risks. On the other hand, some organizational rhetoric may reassure employees that a level of potential risk such as when working near toxic materials, is low, and thus persuade employees to continue working as usual.

Finally, organizations may face both internal and external crises that require rhetorical responses. As with identity rhetoric, the internal audience may be a target audience if the crisis happens primarily within the organization. If an accident occurs that does not affect outsiders, and does not become public information, then the organization must reassure a primarily internal audience that either company policies were not to blame, or that corrective action has been taken. If the crisis is primarily external, then messages directed at members may encourage them to help with recovery efforts or defend the reputation of the organization in the face of the crisis. When accusations were made against Major League Baseball about widespread drug use, for example, many owners, managers, and players spoke out in defense of the sport and argued that the few who used drugs were exceptions to the rule. Although many of the identity, issue, risk, and crisis strategies identified in early chapters will apply to internal audiences as well, specific strategies for internal rhetoric are addressed later in the chapter.

❖ RHETORICAL STRATEGIES FOR INTERNAL MESSAGES

Organizational rhetoric designed for internal audiences is built from the same strategies as rhetoric designed for external audiences. Particular elements will be more important, however, depending on the situation. In this section, we review the strategies most commonly found in internal organizational rhetoric.

Rhetorical Strategies for Socialization Messages

Anticipatory Strategies

The anticipatory stage of organizational socialization relies heavily on the strategies associated with identity creation and organizational identification. Association (particularly values advocacy), differentiation, branding, and identification strategies are especially common in recruitment rhetoric. Potential members will identify with, and then join, organizations with distinct and positive identities, and organizations whose goals and values seem to match their own. In order to do so, they need to be persuaded that the organization is a positive place, and that their values are compatible.

The Web site of discount retailer Wal-Mart (www.walmart.com) provides a clear example of these strategies in recruitment rhetoric. In a video clip, likely designed to be shown at employment fairs, Wal-Mart promotes itself to potential management executives who would work at the organization's headquarters. The video segment includes values advocacy designed to address specific concerns with the organization's identity and the constraint that the headquarters is located in a small southern city. Values of innovation, ethnic diversity, and environmental responsibility are addressed through direct statements and visual images during the video.

Many organizational Web sites include sections for potential employees that utilize several of the common-ground identification strategies identified by Cheney (1983) and discussed in Chapter 2. In its section on jobs in the United States, IBM's Web site (www.ibm.com) includes six main pages of information. One page, and its links, is dedicated to benefits available to employees; it reads in part, "When it comes to having competitive compensation and benefits—tangible and intangible—IBM has long been a leader, and remains so today." This single sentence is an example of both advocacy of benefits and differentiation from other employers. The Target Web site (www.target.com) uses testimony from current employees to encourage future workers to apply to the organization. The "Meet Our Team" page includes video testimony from employees of both sexes and various ethnicities. The page reads in part,

> At every level of the company—from our stores to Distribution Centers to corporate locations—Target team members share a common goal: to provide our guests with the best shopping experience possible. Here are just a few of the people who bring a Fast, Fun and Friendly energy to work every day. (n.p.)

The importance of branding and visual style is evident in many samples of recruiting rhetoric. Web sites and other publications always include organizational logos and slogans, and many recruiters also distribute pens, notepads, and other items imprinted with the organization's brand. These products keep the identity of the organization in the minds of potential members. These strategies, as well as many of the other basic strategies related to identification, values advocacy, and identity, are important in rhetoric addressing the anticipatory phase of organizational socialization.

Entry Phase Strategies

Identification, values advocacy, and identity strategies are important in rhetoric for the entry phase because the goal is to persuade new members to accept and enact the decision premises of the organization. Pribble (1990) studied the orientation program of a company that designed and manufactured heart pacemakers. She discovered that the slide and audio presentation and speech by the founder created identification by introducing employees to the key values of the organization. She wrote, "It [the ethical stand endorsed in the program] also provides guiding values, rules, and assumptions for decision-making, problem-solving, conflict resolution and leadership" (p. 266). Orientation programs often provide premises against which employees can weigh decisions they make while they are members of the organization.

Pribble's (1990) research provided examples of how orientation programs incorporate testimony from both employees and outsiders in order to build identification. Other identification strategies noted by Cheney (1983) are also prevalent in rhetoric used in the entry phrase. The common-ground techniques of expressing concern for individuals in the organization, recognizing the work of specific individuals, advocating shared values, promoting benefits and activities provided by the organization, quoting outsiders who have praised the organization, and providing testimonials by employees speaking positively about the organization may all build identification during the entry phase. The strategy of the assumed "we" is common in many orientation documents, and most materials include slogans and logos for the organization. Dell Corporation tells visitors to its employment Web site (www.dell.com), "We take pride in our diverse workforce and the richness of culture and perspective it lends to our global work environment." Finally, organizations may build identification with new employees by distinguishing themselves from the competition or creating a common enemy. One employee testimonial quoted on Apple's Web site (www.apple.com) reads,

> I have friends who recently started their careers at [other large companies], where the teams are much bigger. They tell me they feel lost in the crowd and are frustrated because they are doing work that isn't so important. At Apple, things are different. The teams are small and everyone has a huge role.

Values advocacy strategies are also important during organizational entry. By identifying shared values, an organization can begin establishing decision premises for use in later rhetoric. For example, on the employment page of its Web site, Sheraton tells prospective employees, "You can feel the comfort as soon as you step through the front doors of the Sheraton—a warm and inviting atmosphere that puts you instantly at ease. The Sheraton experience is shaped around the understanding that we all share a natural, human need to belong." From the beginning of an employee's experience, "comfort" is a key value. The ideas of comfort and welcome are key decision premises for employees of this hotel corporation because they help guarantee customer satisfaction.

Finally, the identity strategies of association, differentiation, and branding may also be important during the entry phase. New students at Texas State University are all given free tee-shirts decorated with the school's logo and colors during orientation. Students thus enact their membership in the organization by wearing the university's brand. While not all organizations will distribute shirts to newcomers, most do emphasize the brand in one way or another during orientation.

Strategies Following Metamorphosis

As outlined above, rhetoric following metamorphosis may seek to accomplish several things. It may attempt to reinforce identification; to promote change; or to address identity, issues, risk, or crisis situations.

Rhetorical Strategies for Reinforcement and Retention

Rhetoric directed at organizational members who have passed the metamorphosis phase must reinforce identification with the organization, and thus, reinforce decision premises. As Cheney (1983) discovered, items in organizational newsletters often attempt to build and reinforce identification among current employees. The strategies of appeals to common ground, identification by antithesis, the use of transcendent language, and the use of common organizational symbols all help to connect the interests of members with the interests of the organization.

One specific identification strategy—expression of concern for the individual—is sometimes evident in workplace participation programs. These programs take a variety of forms including organizational democracy (in which employees influence a range of organizational decisions), focus groups to improve quality or conditions, or even suggestion boxes. Both the promotion of these initiatives and the promotion of the results serve a practical function of enhancing organizational practices, and a rhetorical function of demonstrating concern and appreciation for the contributions of individual organizational members. The rhetorical function can backfire, however, if employees feel they have made an effort to contribute, only to have their ideas ignored or dismissed (Cheney, 1995).

Newsletters, ongoing training, posters, and companywide announcements may all be used to deliver strategies intended to reinforce employee connections with the organization. Just as orientation programs serve both a task and rhetorical function, continuing training may focus on what members need to know to do their jobs, and on how they think, feel, and behave toward the organization. Even events such as picnics, award dinners, and employee appreciation weeks, may reinforce identification by demonstrating organizational concern for the needs of the individual.

Rhetorical Strategies for Organizational Change

The second goal of rhetoric following metamorphosis is to address organizational change. Change is a common element of life in many contemporary organizations, and both popular press and academic literature are full of information about how change can be managed (Zorn, Page, & Cheney, 2000). Rhetoric is a key element in managing any change, because employees and others need to be persuaded that the work required to enact a change will pay off for both the organization and the individuals. The strategies of values advocacy, identification, and identity are all prevalent in rhetoric addressing change.

Since values are such an important part of securing individuals' connections to an organization, any alteration (actual or perceived) in organizational values will require careful attention to rhetoric. In setting up their study of change in a local government, Zorn et al. (2000) highlighted the importance of advocating organizational values. They argued that the values of service, quality, and excellence are pervasive in contemporary organizational rhetoric on change. The frequency of these particular values illustrates how value premises and organizational enthymemes can influence later decisions. If employees embrace organizational values of service, quality, and excellence as important, the theory suggests that they will be more receptive to later change arguments that promise to enhance those values. Zorn et al. quote an observation from Moreland and Clark (1998) concerning the engrained value of quality: "If one opposes the changes, then one opposes 'quality'" (p. 317).

Identification strategies are important as well. As change occurs in organizations, individuals' connections with the organization will be challenged. Organizations pursuing change initiatives can use identification strategies to emphasize the core elements of the organization that will not be altered. In addition, organizational newsletters can be used to share the rationale for change, as well as the process of change, with members, thus demonstrating concern for individuals. As mentioned above, employee participation in change can serve both a practical function of improving the process and a rhetorical function of increasing employee acceptance by expressing concern for their input.

Finally, identity strategies can help promote change and encourage positive thoughts, feelings, and behaviors toward change. Sometimes it is the identity of the organization that is changing in some way. Organizations merge (Sprint and Nextel, Cingular and AT&T), or change their names (Philip Morris to Altria, Anderson Consulting to Accenture). When the identity itself is the change, internal audiences need to be persuaded that the things with which they most strongly connect will not change. Strategies such as values advocacy and identification can help provide this reassurance and maintain employee loyalty. Sometimes the outward markers of identity remain the same, while other elements change. In this situation, strategies using the brand can help to reassure insiders of a level of consistency.

Rhetorical Strategies for Identity, Issue, Risk, and Crisis Situations

Employees may also be persuaded to act as advocates for the organization in situations involving identity threats, and issue, risk, and crisis management. Rhetoric may informally prepare employees and then persuade them to take the organization's messages to key outside audiences. A document produced by Texas State University-San Marcos is an example of rhetoric asking insiders to serve as advocates for organizational identity. University faculty received a small folder decorated with the school colors, a new logo, and the new slogan, "The Rising Star of Texas." The folder contained a decal of the university's new symbol and recently changed name. The inside of the folder included a note from the university president that read as follows:

> Dear Colleagues,
>   As part of our strategic plan, we are implementing a comprehensive marketing effort. New signage, publications, banners and advertisements are just a few examples of the good work that is occurring. To aid in this effort, we have enclosed a decal for your car so that whenever you travel, Texas State will be there with you. I hope you will use this decal to help strengthen our brand and show your ongoing pride in this great institution.

This piece of organizational rhetoric asks insiders both to embrace the new brand of the university themselves and to help advocate the brand to external audiences by applying a sticker to their cars. This example illustrates the importance of branding and identification strategies in persuading insiders to become advocates for the identity of the organization. The brand is both in the rhetoric and the focus of the rhetoric. The artifact also illustrates the identification strategies of concern for the individual (giving faculty and staff a free sticker, asking for their help) and advocacy of shared values (pride in this great institution). This also illustrates the importance of addressing internal audiences on issues of organizational change.

Internal messages may also encourage organizational members to support a particular stance on an issue, or defend the organization's role in a risk or crisis situation. Convincing members to advocate for the organization's interests rests heavily on the major premise that what is good for the organization is good for the individual member (Scott & Hart, 1979). If employees accept this idea, then they are more likely to advocate for policies that benefit the organization, and to defend organizational actions.

The strategies of claims and evidence, enthymeme, and the use of the stock issues, all important in crafting external issues messages, are important in internal issue and risk messages as well. By demonstrating costs and benefits to the employees, organizational rhetors can influence their understanding of the effects of a proposed policy or risk and encourage them to take action to support the organization's interests.

Clearly, organizations face a wide array of challenges in addressing functional audiences. They must recruit and retain members, and persuade those members to accept and enact the decision premises of the organization. They must also use rhetoric to persuade employees to embrace change in the organization, and to serve as advocates of organizational interests to external audiences. As students of organizational rhetoric, we need to ask both about the practical challenge of meetings these needs, and about the ways in which internal organizational rhetoric provides space for domination as well as resistance.

❖ EVALUATING AND CRITIQUING INTERNAL ORGANIZATIONAL RHETORIC

Just as we have taken both an evaluative and a critical perspective on external forms of organizational rhetoric, it is important to examine both potential effectiveness and potential questions of power in internal rhetoric. As we have discussed in Chapter 5, a critic doing an evaluative reading would compare the specific internal rhetorical situations with the strategies present in the rhetoric. The critic could then judge whether or not the rhetoric was well suited to situational demands, and perhaps make suggestions for how more successful messages could be crafted in the future.

In evaluating the change rhetoric of a public sector organization, Zorn et al. (2000) articulated an important assumption of what we call the evaluative approach to internal organizational rhetoric. They wrote, "Getting workers to put in extra hours and performance beyond the call of duty is justified because workers are paid a reasonable wage in exchange for their efforts, and their work is underwritten by citizens who are demanding more for their money" (p. 535). The idea of a fair exchange of personal efforts for reward from the organization is inherent in the idea of organization as defined early in this text. These authors also posed some valuable questions for those studying the effectiveness of internal rhetoric: "Does such communication motivate workers to embrace and implement the changes? Does it inspire them to work to full capacity? Does it enjoin them to provide outstanding customer service?" (p. 535). These questions, and variations on them, can be useful in evaluating a wide range of internal organizational rhetoric.

In addition to the general questions introduced in Chapters 2, 3, and 5, a critic doing an evaluative reading of internal organizational rhetoric should consider some or all of the following questions:

- What sorts of exigencies does this internal rhetoric seem to address? Does the rhetoric promote socialization, change, or advocacy for the organization?
- What sorts of identification strategies are used in the artifact?
- What sorts of value strategies are used in the artifact?
- Are identity strategies (association, differentiation, branding) used in the rhetoric? If so, how?

Studying internal rhetoric from a critical perspective is important because of the often widely accepted link between employee interests and organizational interests. As Zorn et al. (2000) summarized from their analysis of the literature, internal value messages can be viewed as "empowering and exciting" or as "leading them [employees] to toil longer and harder for reduced rewards and increased insecurity" (p. 523). Critical analysis of internal messages can serve to challenge the assumption that what is good for the organization is good for the individual (Scott & Hart, 1979). In addition to considering the general questions presented in Chapters 4 and 5, a critic conducting a critical reading of internal organizational rhetoric should consider some or all of the following questions:

- How does the organization construct its right to address the topic in question?
- Are there taken-for-granted assumptions in the rhetoric about the appropriate power relationship between the organization and its members?
- Does the rhetoric seem to expand or limit member choices?
- To what degree does the organization seek participation from interested parties in making the decisions it discusses in internal rhetoric?

❖ CONCLUSION

If we want to understand how organizations operate effectively, as well as how they exercise influence in individual lives, it is important to study rhetoric crafted for both external and internal audiences. Internal organizational rhetoric serves to socialize new members to the practices and values of the organization, to reinforce feelings of belonging among existing members, to promote change in the organization, and to encourage insiders to accept and advocate organizational positions on a variety of topics. The strategies of identification, values advocacy, differentiation, and branding are all important in addressing internal organizational audiences. Use your understanding of internal organizational rhetoric to analyze the rhetorical situation and organizational newsletter that follow.

❖ CASE STUDY: A NEW RECORD—TRANSITIONING TO ELECTRONIC MEDICAL RECORDS

Thomas Goetz (2007) commented in the *New York Times*,

> Go into almost any medical office, hospital or clinic in the United States and your records will still be handled the old-fashioned way—on paper. You can use a computer to pay your taxes, to program your TiVo or to read a message from your great-aunt, but your doctor has to practically level a forest just to examine your medical files.

This observation about the status of electronic medical records (EMRs) in the United States sheds some light on the challenge faced by the University of Kansas Hospital and other health care facilities as they transition from paper-dependent to paperless processes. According to *Modern Healthcare* (DoBias, 2006), just 24.9% of physicians report using some sort of EMR, and just 10% of hospitals use EMRs to their fullest potential in moving patient information electronically between departments.

Despite this fairly slow rate of adoption, many sources argue that using EMR can create significant advantages in improving patient care ("Market Analysis," 2007; Scott, Rundall, Vogt, & Hsu, 2005). Gregory Lopes (2007) reports that "fewer medical errors, early diagnoses and improving patient care are a few of the promises of health-information technology." Because of the potential benefits of EMR, the George W. Bush administration announced and supported a goal to make electronic medical records available to every American by 2014 (DoBias, 2006). In order to achieve this goal, the federal government proposed giving financial incentives to some physicians, and eased some laws governing whether or not physicians can accept hardware and software from private companies.

There are a number of reasons why medical facilities and personnel have been reluctant to adopt EMR technology. Concerns about security and financial costs are often cited as reasons to continue to use traditional systems. More interesting factors, however, include the finding that care-provider productivity can drop as much as 25% in the first 6 months as personnel adjust to the new system (Mostovy-Eisenberg, 2006). For health care facilities, lower productivity means treating fewer patients, and in this era of economically competitive health care, fewer patients means less income. Scott et al. (2005) suggest that people may also resist implementation because EMR "may challenge beliefs about how health care should be organized; using physicians to enter data may be inefficient and perceived as demeaning, and clinicians and managers may need to learn how to use specific software, causing frustration" (p. 331).

At the University of Kansas Hospital, transitioning to EMR meant that, according to one organizational newsletter, "some 4,200 hospital staff, physicians, residents and medical students" would begin using a new system on a phased-in schedule beginning on November 12, 2007. The new system would be used to transmit physician care orders to other medical staff, to document clinical observations, to prescribe medication, to do emergency department triage and patient tracking, to make electronic copies of documents, and to manage records at three clinics in addition to the hospital. For staff members, the change might mean learning new hardware and software; readjusting division of labor among staff members (for example, early on, implementation clerks were scheduled to assist physicians with some data entry), and explaining the changes to concerned or curious patients.

The process of implementing EMR began over 2 years before the "go live" date and involved selecting a software vendor, selecting and receiving new hardware, and training employees. All through the process, individuals across the organization received information and the organizational perspective on the change via newsletters titled *For the Record*. The newsletter that follows was distributed throughout the hospital and affiliated medical school just prior to the launch date for the EMR system. As you consider the rhetorical situation and examine the newsletter (Figures 10.2 and 10.3, pp. 227–230), conduct the *process for analyzing organizational rhetoric* (you may want to use the worksheets in the appendix), and answer the case study questions.

Figure 10.2   *For the Record,* November 2007 Newsletter, University of Kansas Hospital (pp. 1–2)

November 2007

For the Record

One patient. One record. One goal. Safe, high quality care.

O₂ Goes Live

At 1 p.m. Monday, Nov. 12, The University of Kansas Hospital reaches the O₂ journey milestone that will put our new electronic health record system to the test. This is when the first phase of O₂ "goes live."

About 4,200 hospital staff, physicians, residents and medical students will use O₂ to help deliver an even higher level of safe, high quality care to our patients. Although the switch to O₂ will bring changes to the way we work, it also will bring us closer to our goal of providing the very best care possible.

In the months leading up to go-live, the O₂ Team and many other staff have been working behind the scenes to prepare the system for use. Information for current inpatients is being preloaded into O₂ with the help of staff from Nursing and Pharmacy.

Staff has entered additional data into O₂, including lab, radiology and pulmonary results, and transcribed reports for patients who have been in our hospital in the past two years. Allergy and infection information for those who have been here in the past year also is documented.

On the first day of go-live, staff will begin using O₂ at 1 p.m. and, in most

continued page 2 ...

On Oct. 15, we welcomed O₂ hardware to the hospital with a "calf drive." From left are Brad House, Jim Williams and Pat Bates, clinical analysts, O₂ Team; Mike Hastings, quality outcomes coordinator, Organizational Improvement; Christine Kober, application analyst, O₂ Team; Doug Erich, director, O₂ Team; and Shirley Weber, director, Clinical Labs.

Give It Time ...

Ask any veteran of a large system implementation, and you'll hear about the "big dip."

"During the first few days of go-live, all the positive feelings you have about the system are going to run smack-dab into your struggle to remember what you learned in training," said Vance Brison, new training manager for the O₂ Team. "The end result can be frustrating, and you may find yourself longing for the good old days."

Brison, who has witnessed a dozen go-lives at other hospitals, says this situation is always temporary.

"After a few days, a light suddenly goes on and things start clicking. Give it time," he advises.

There's always help available. If you have questions or need assistance, call on your nearby Go-Tos or contact the ITS Service Desk, 8-4894.

(Continued)

Figure 10.2 (*Continued*)

O₂ Goes Live *continued…*

cases, will no longer document on paper. The most current patient profile for each inpatient will be in the system, minimizing nurses' workload of entering new information. Nurses can then update patient assessments in O_2.

Nurses will see a significant change in the way they document the administration of medications. Once O_2 is live, clinicians will document directly on a computer on wheels (smaller than our current "COWs," so clinicians have taken to calling them "calves") at the bedside. This process will make the documentation of medication administration more accurate.

All clinical staff will benefit from having a single record across the enterprise, with the ability to view results and vital patient information from any location.

Practice, Practice, Practice

Practice makes perfect. End-users are encouraged to practice with O_2 before go-live on Nov. 12. To devote a little time to practice, click the O_2 icon on your desktop, log in and enter the "play" environment. You also can practice with one of the tablets or "calves" in your department.

Give Your Feedback

O_2 was designed understanding that the system always can be improved – and using the system will reveal opportunities to make changes. As you begin using O_2 during and after go-live, you may think of ways the system could work better. Your input can help make significant, lasting improvements.

Hospital staff will have solid support through this important part of the O_2 journey. During go-live, "O_2 Go-Tos" will be in units and departments to assist end-users with questions or problems. Staff also are urged to call the ITS Service Desk, 8-4894, when they need assistance.

An O_2 Command Center will function 24 hours a day, seven days a week for the first four weeks of go-live. Members of the O_2 Team, along with representatives from Epic Systems and ChartMaxx (document imaging vendor), will staff the center and visit units to ensure a smooth switchover.

It's critical that staff provide feedback on O_2. The system, which was designed with the help of hundreds of hospital clinicians, will

During the first weeks of go-live, our change approach will be cautious. Making a change in one place can affect system performance elsewhere. So, at first, the focus will be on any changes most urgently needed. Your input is crucial for future enhancements, and your requests will be recorded and prioritized.

continue to be improved as we move forward. Clinical leadership will help the O_2 Team prioritize staff feedback, focusing on the most significant issues first.

"For the first month or so, we encourage everyone to report any serious problem they might find," said **Doug Erich**, O_2 Team director. "After that, they should tell us about other improvements they have in mind for the system."

Know Your Log-In Information

To log into O_2, you must know your user ID and Novell password. If you don't know your ID and password, see your manager for assistance.

Continue Using PSN during Go-Live

As we go live, patient safety will be monitored constantly so any system issues affecting safety can be addressed immediately.

Staff can help in this effort by continuing to use the University

HealthSystem Consortium's Patient Safety Net (PSN). This technology will help us monitor safety during and after go-live. PSN, which the hospital has used for some time, is a confidential tool for reporting any event where harm or near-harm occurred.

During go-live, PSN reports will be consistently monitored.

Any hospital employee can use PSN. It's located on the Hospital Links page under "UHC-PSN." All reports are confidential.

Figure 10.3   *For the Record,* November 2007 Newsletter, University of Kansas Hospital (pp. 3–4)

Rely on Your O₂ Support System

Most hospital employees already know the Information Technology Services (ITS) Service Desk number. If you're an O₂ end-user, this means you already know how to get help for any questions you have when O₂ goes live Monday, Nov. 12.

And there's more good news. Throughout go-live, floor support will come in the form of "O₂ Go-Tos," O₂ Team members, and Epic and ChartMaxx representatives who will be on hand to assist you around the clock in patient care areas. You can identify these people by the blue "O₂ Go-To" shirts they'll be wearing.

Physicians also will get assistance from O₂ Go-Tos who have knowledge specific to physician tasks. You can spot these specialized Go-Tos by their burgundy O₂ shirts.

If you don't see a Go-To nearby, don't worry. You can call the ITS Service Desk for any O₂ question, at any time. The Service Desk staff will put you in touch with people who can answer your question, whether it's about logging into the system, placing orders, administering medications, running reports or any other topic.

KUPI Support

Hospital staff are not the only people who will use O₂. KUPI staff will access O₂ to review patient information. KUPI staff can call the ITS Service Desk, 8-4894, or the KUMC IT Help Desk, 8-7995.

If You Need Help
- Talk to a Go-To, who will help you immediately or take the issue to the ITS Service Desk for a solution.
- Call the ITS Service Desk, 8-4894.

Functions of the ITS Service Desk
- Triage and handle basic issues.
- Refer more complicated issues to the O₂ Command Center, where O₂ Team members will work with you to find a solution.

The O₂ Team will send daily, or more frequent, communication to all staff. They will notify you about frequently asked questions, any changes to O₂ and tips for using the system.

Beat the Stress of Go-Live

Let's face it. Health care can be stressful work. We also know it's the most rewarding profession possible because of the difference we make in the lives of our patients and their families. Go-live will add to the stress most of us feel. It also will be rewarding because O₂ will improve patient safety and the quality of care we provide.

To make the go-live experience a happier one, here's a list of stress busters. Try them out and share them with co-workers.

O₂ Stress Busters
- **Give yourself permission to ask for help.** No one is perfect, and we all learn at our own pace. Your

Go-Tos, along with the ITS Service Desk staff, are ready to help. It's okay to ask for help every time you need it. Our go-live goal is for everyone to succeed using O₂, so speak up!
- **Don't look too far ahead.** Focus on your task at hand, not on everything you need to do in one day.
- **Look for the upside.** It's easy to be positive about O₂ if you keep the goal in mind: safe, high quality patient care.
- **Take a breather.** Take time to relax and refresh. Don't forget to breathe!
- **Communicate.** Talk to your co-workers about how they are using O₂ – it's probably the most

powerful way to learn. Share your tips, shortcuts and "ah-ha!" moments with each other.
- **Exercise.** Whether you walk the dog or hit the gym, you'll feel better when you get your blood pumping.
- **Eat right.** Start with a healthy breakfast, and eat nutritious meals and snacks throughout the day. Your body will thank you for it.
- **Get enough sleep.** Sleep fuels your mind and body. Feeling tired will only add to your stress.
- **Laugh.** Laughing physically helps your body fight stress. Don't forget to smile. You'll survive go-live!

3

(Continued)

Figure 10.3 *(Continued)*

Tell Your Patients about O₂'s Benefits

Our patients may notice the increased activity in patient care areas during go-live, so take this opportunity to briefly explain how this new system will benefit them. Here are just a few of the many patient benefits.

- O₂ is the hospital's new electronic health record. It's designed to increase patient safety, as well as the quality of care we provide.
- O₂ is a shared record, which means all staff will have real-time access to important information, such as allergies, test results or clinician notes. This makes care safer, especially when patients move from one unit to another unit or service.
- The system has "decision support" features that alert caregivers to potential medication interactions, dosage issues and other key information.
- Staff no longer must decipher individuals' handwriting, reducing the chance of medication errors.

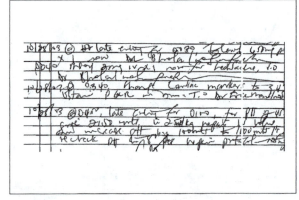

"Handwriting analysis" will be a thing of the past with O₂.

- Patient information is securely stored in O₂, and it's there whenever patients come to the hospital or visit one of our physicians. Patients no longer must answer the same questions over and over again.
- Staff members spend less time on paperwork or searching for a chart, so they can spend more time with patients.

The O₂ Journey Continues

At The University of Kansas Hospital, we're committed to improving the quality and safety of the patient care we provide. O₂ will help us continue improving patient care.

The O₂ Journey...
- Summer 2005 – We searched for a system vendor that would best match our goals for high quality patient care. Hundreds of hospital and medical center staff judged the products of three vendor finalists. Epic Systems Corporation emerged as the preferred vendor.

- October 2006 to April 2007 – The O₂ Team and advisors from around the hospital met for Design-Build-Validate (DBV) sessions. Our O₂ Team built decisions about how specific tasks should function into the system. Then advisory groups and other clinicians validated whether the designed system met expectations.
- May to July 2007 – The O₂ Team tested how O₂ integrated with other hospital systems, such as Lab, PACS, billing, etc. Each problem was addressed and fixed.

- September and October 2007 – Almost 50 in-house trainers taught nearly 5,000 end-users to use the system in real-life situations.
- Today – We're poised for staff to begin using the system in patient care units. Staff feedback will help us update the system.
- Future – With O₂ and a staff committed to improving patient safety and quality of care, our journey will continue to lead us to become the nation's best hospital.

Case Study Questions

Basic Descriptive Process

1. Which of the strategies of organizational rhetoric can you iden-tify in the newsletter? (You may want to refer to the Worksheet for Identifying Rhetorical Strategies in Organizational Texts in the appendix.)

   a. Does the rhetor use values advocacy strategies? If so, to what values does he or she appeal and how?

   b. Does the rhetor use identification strategies? If so, which ones?

   c. Can you identify any appeals to decision premises?

   d. Does the rhetor use strategies related to organizational iden-tity? If so, what kind?

2. What are the key elements of the rhetorical situation? (You may want to refer to the Worksheet for Describing Rhetorical Situations in Organizations in the appendix.)

   a. Which type or types of internal organizational exigencies are present in the situation—socialization, change, or the need for member advocacy?

   b. Which types of audience appear to be target audiences in this situation?

   c. What constraints common to internal situations are present in this case?

Evaluative Reading

1. Compare the strategies you have identified with the elements of the rhetorical situation. Which strategies seem especially adapted to which elements of the rhetorical situation? (You may want to refer to the Worksheet for Conducting an Evaluative Reading in the appendix.)

2. Based on what you know about the rhetorical situation and what you have found out about the strategies, what did the rhetor want the reader to think, feel, or do after looking at the newsletter?

3. Based on what you know about the situation and the strategies, should the rhetoric have accomplished its goal? Do you think the audiences reacted the way the rhetor intended them to? Why or why not?

Critical Reading

1. Based on what you know about the rhetorical situation and the strategies, what level of choice is given to the audience of this rhetoric? What information about the issue is shared, and what is not shared? (You may want to refer to the Worksheet for Conducting a Critical Reading in the appendix.)

2. Based on what you know about the rhetorical situation and the strategies, who was and is allowed to contribute to the discussion in the rhetoric, and whose voices are not heard? Does the rhetoric indicate in any way that interested parties are invited to participate?

3. How does your evaluative reading compare with your critical reading? Are the two readings similar or different? How? What do the similarities or differences tell you?

4. Based on the three questions above, what does your analysis reveal about the relationship between management and membership at the medical center?

Case Study References

DoBias, M. (2006, October 16). EHR adoption "pitifully behind"; Study: Only 10% of physicians use IT to its fullest. *Modern Healthcare, 36*(41), 8–9.

Goetz, T. (2007, May 30). Physician, upgrade thyself [Op-ed]. *New York Times.* Retrieved June 28, 2009, from http://www.nytimes.com/2007/05/30/opinion/30goetz.html

Lopes, G. (2007, March 5). Paper still rules patient records; Health-information technology is seen as useful but costly. *Washington Times.* Retrieved June 28, 2009, from http://mhcc.maryland.gov/electronichealth/presentations/paperpatrec.pdf

Market analysis; U.S. electronic medical records market primed to jump by 400, Kalorama report says. (2007, February 19). *Biotech Business Week.*

Mostovy-Eisenberg, M. (2006, October). Eye on EMRs: Implementation obstacles. *Review of Ophthalmology,* 73–80.

Scott, J. T., Rundall, G. T., Vogt, T. M., & Hsu, J. (2005, November 3). Kaiser Permanente's experience of implementing an electronic medical record: A qualitative study. *British Medical Journal.* Retrieved February 23, 2008, from http://bmj.com

Epilogue

The Ancient Art of Rhetoric in a Complex Organizational World

I n an early chapter of this book, we said that in some ways, to study organizational rhetoric was to study both the oldest and one of the newest areas of communication. Although nearly 2,500 years have passed, and the world has changed drastically since Greek scholars recorded the first debates over the art of rhetoric, rhetorical inquiry remains a powerful way of understanding the world.

As much as the world has changed since the days of Aristotle, it will continue to change even more quickly in the coming years. Many of the changes in contemporary society involve organizations, and how individuals and organizations interact. In this short epilogue, we outline several of these changes and discuss how and why they merit attention from scholars of organizational rhetoric. In particular, we discuss the rhetorical implications of three main changes: the increasingly global nature of organizations, the trend of nonprofit organizations to use corporate rhetorical strategies, and the proliferation of types of channels through which organizational rhetoric can be transmitted. We also discuss one subject that appears with greater and greater frequency in the rhetoric of contemporary organizations—environmental responsibility.

❖ RHETORIC IN A GLOBALIZED ORGANIZATIONAL WORLD

In the past few decades, many organizations in the United States and other industrialized nations have become multinational or have begun to do at least some of their business outside of their home nations. Stohl (2001) writes, "Indeed, it is now virtually impossible to conceive of a completely domestic, unicultural organization or organizational communication practices that do not have intercultural dimensions" (p. 324). As organizations move manufacturing facilities, service centers, and other corporate processes to countries and cultures other than their own, the task of influencing the thoughts, feelings, and behaviors of audiences important to the organization becomes more complicated. If, as we have discussed, the idea of audience is more complex in organizational rhetoric than it is in traditional rhetoric, then the audience of *global* organizational rhetoric is even more complicated. Not only is the average rhetor now designing messages for two or more sets of enabling, functional, normative, and diffused audiences, the experiences and cultures of those audiences also may be quite different from those of the rhetor.

The study of organizational rhetoric can play a key role in constructing, evaluating, and critiquing the process and effects of globalization. Organizations operating in the global economy need communication professionals who are able to analyze a variety of domestic and global rhetorical situations and craft messages to meet those needs. Because organizations are such powerful forces in any culture or nation, critics must also pay attention to how power is constructed. This is especially true when organizations move operations to communities where the economic power of the organization vastly outweighs the economic power of even the wealthiest members of the community. Most organizations with global operations have developed codes of conduct both to govern their practices and to make the argument that they are operating responsibly. A critical reading of this sort of rhetoric could help shed light on how organizations view and exercise power in global situations.

❖ CORPORATE RHETORIC IN NONPROFIT ORGANIZATIONS

A second trend that should be of interest to those who study organizational rhetoric is the increasing use of corporate rhetorical strategies in nonprofit organizations. Churches are just one example of how principles generally developed and used by communication professionals in for-profit organizations have moved to nonprofit organizations. For example, the *Washington Post* (Crabtree, 2007) reported on an advertising campaign by the United Universalist Association (UUA) that hoped to "amplify the church's voice on national issues, increase name recognition and inspire pride in the UUA identity." The article notes that in recent years, other mainline churches, including the United Church of Christ and the United Methodist Church, have run similar campaigns. Speaking on national issues, increasing name recognition, and creating organizational pride are all rhetorical functions that are frequently found in corporate organizational rhetoric.

Many colleges, universities, philanthropic organizations, activist groups, and NGOs (international non-governmental organizations) have also adopted many of the strategies used by organizational rhetors in for-profit organizations. The rhetoric created by these nonprofit organizations offers scholars an even larger pool of organizational messages to analyze, and provides an opportunity both to enhance message effectiveness, and to ask important questions about how these organizations construct and maintain power through rhetoric. It also encourages scholars to further explore how the rhetoric produced by one or more organizations can have an impact on rhetorical situations faced by other organizations, and potentially other nations.

❖ TRADITIONAL RHETORICAL STRATEGIES IN CONTEMPORARY FORMS

A third emerging topic of interest is the rapidly growing variety of channels available to organizations for the delivery of rhetoric. In addition to the traditional forms and outlets, today organizations choose from such diverse channels as text messages, blog or Twitter posts from CEOs or others, podcasts, and a presence on social networking sites or in virtual worlds. Some organizations may even try to figure out how to make their messages persuasive while they fly by in fast-forward during a show being replayed on a digital video recorder (DVR).

The virtual world or 3-D digital environment called *Second Life* offers an interesting example of an emerging channel for organizational rhetoric. Various organizations have a presence on the site and have used it to recruit and screen job candidates, to seek audience input about organizational products and services, and even to host virtual events for the *avatars* (screen identities) of up to 1,000 participants (Maddox, 2007). In September 2007, a group of Italian employees of IBM used *Second Life* to challenge the power of their organization by conducting a virtual strike. Reporter Wency Leung (2007) wrote that "during the 12-hour online strike, avatars of all appearances turned up . . . where they raised placards and shouted demands through bullhorns."

While most of the traditional building blocks still apply in these new channels, the channels themselves produce interesting new constraints for those who design rhetoric. For example, how long is too long for a text message, or a podcast? How can an organization make sure that audience members even get to a Web site where they can find these messages? In addition, new channels lead to interesting questions about how rhetoric constructs and maintains power in organizations, and how new forms of rhetoric may allow other groups and organizations to challenge power.

❖ THE ENVIRONMENT AS SITUATION AND STRATEGY

Finally, the rapidly emerging issue of the environment opens important new areas of study in organizational rhetoric. Although individuals and small groups have long expressed concern about the potential destruction of the physical environment, the topic has gained enormous levels of attention in the past decade, and organizational rhetors have taken notice. Many organizations include on their Web sites a link to several pages explaining either how they try to prevent environmental damage or how they promote environmental growth. In addition, organizations that produce or sell oil, automobiles, paper, plastic, and a variety of consumer goods have undertaken advertising campaigns to promote themselves as friends of the environment.

Questions of environmental responsibility are particularly interesting because they can be elements of the rhetorical situation and may be used as rhetorical strategies. On one hand, an organization proposing an issue or addressing a risk or crisis must consider the environmental concerns of audiences. On the other hand, an organization trying to enhance its identity, or deal with an issue, risk, or crisis might use appeals to the value of the environment to do so.

The use of appeals to environmental awareness raises important questions about how organizations construct the meaning of "environmentally friendly," and how that meaning may be accepted or contested by organizational audiences. Some scholars have labeled the danger of empty environmental promises as "greenwashing" (Ihlen, 2006). This and other environmental questions merit the attention of those who study organizational rhetoric.

With your knowledge of organizational rhetoric situations and strategies, and your understanding of the importance of using both an evaluative and critical lens to view organizational rhetoric, you are prepared to ask and answer important questions about messages on these and other topics. As the world continues to shrink, and channels for organizational rhetoric continue to expand, you will have the advantage of understanding the role of organizational rhetoric in society.

Appendix

Worksheets for Analyzing Organizational Rhetoric

This section contains the following four worksheets that critics may use as a guideline for conducting analysis of any sample of organizational rhetoric:

- Worksheet for Identifying Rhetorical Strategies in Organizational Texts
- Worksheet for Describing Rhetorical Situations in Organizations
- Worksheet for Conducting an Evaluative Reading
- Worksheet for Conducting a Critical Reading

WORKSHEET FOR IDENTIFYING RHETORICAL STRATEGIES IN ORGANIZATIONAL TEXTS

In order to describe the rhetorical strategies in the artifact that you have selected, please identify and give examples of statements in the rhetoric that fall into the following areas.

Ethos: Appeals to Organizational Credibility

Competence

Community

Pathos: Appeals to Emotions

Needs: Identify the need being created or appealed to

Values: Identify the value being appealed to

Values advocacy

Explicit appeals to values

Demonstration of how products or services uphold values

Discussion of philanthropic activities consistent with values

Praise of individuals who embody values

Identification

Common ground

Assumed "we"

By antithesis

Unifying symbols

Logos: Use of Claims and Evidence

Claims

Evidence

Statistics

Testimony

Examples

Reasoning

Inductive reasoning

By example

By analogy

Causal reasoning

Deductive reasoning

Strategies for Organizing Appeals

Introduction

Main body

Conclusion

Navigation (Web-based materials)

Stylistic Strategies

Language choices

Visual choices

Branding

Strategies for Delivering Appeals

What form is the rhetoric presented in (press release, newsletter, Web site, blog, event, etc.)?

Remember to consider whether the sample of rhetoric is similar to any of the types of rhetoric that occur with regularity in organizations (identity, issue, risk, crisis, or internal). If so, also consider the specific strategy questions posed at the end of the relevant chapters.

WORKSHEET FOR DESCRIBING RHETORICAL SITUATIONS IN ORGANIZATIONS

In order to systematically describe the rhetorical situation, please answer the following questions based on information that has been provided in a case or that you have gathered through research.

Exigencies: What elements in the situation appear to be challenges or opportunities for the organization? Is there an imperfection or opportunity? Was it anticipated or unanticipated? Is it marked by urgency? What are some options for how organizational rhetors might frame the elements?

Audiences: What types of audiences seem to be the most appropriate target in the situation—enabling, functional, normative, or diffused? What are the characteristics or interests of members of these audiences?

Constraints and Assets: What things might make it more difficult or easier for the organization to answer the exigencies? Are there preexisting beliefs, attitudes or values, or past rhetoric or experiences that will affect how the message is interpreted by audiences?

Recurring Situations: Is the rhetorical situation similar to any of the types of situations that occur with regularity in organizations (identity, issue, risk, crisis, or internal)? If so, also consider the specific elements of situations discussed in the relevant chapters.

WORKSHEET FOR CONDUCTING AN EVALUATIVE READING

Remember that before moving to this step, you should complete the basic descriptive process by identifying rhetorical strategies and describing the rhetorical situation.

Step I. Compare Rhetorical Strategies
With Demands of the Rhetorical Situation

Situational Elements: From Worksheet for Analyzing Rhetorical Situation	*Rhetorical Strategies:* From Worksheet for Identifying Rhetorical Strategies
Exigencies:	Identify strategies that seem to address the exigence.
Audiences:	Identify strategies that seem specifically tailored for a particular audience or audiences.
Constraints:	Identify strategies that seem specifically designed to address particular constraints.
	Identify strategies that appear in the rhetoric but don't seem to match specific elements of the situation.

Step II. Conduct a Preferred Reading

Answer the following question: Given what you know about the rhetorical strategies and rhetorical situations, what did the rhetor want the audience to think, feel, or believe after viewing or hearing the rhetoric?

Step III. Draw a Conclusion About Effectiveness

Your preferred reading allowed you to make an argument about what the rhetor likely wanted to accomplish. Now, use the comparison you made in Step I to make an argument about how well the strategies were selected to a match the demands of the situation. Be able to support your evaluation with information about the rhetorical situation (including source citations) and with examples from the rhetoric (by quoting directly or paraphrasing from the rhetoric).

After the Analysis

Once you have completed your evaluative reading, you may apply your findings by writing an essay, discussing your conclusions with others, formulating general ideas about what is effective in organizational rhetoric, or using the ideas to make decisions about the organization. You may also want to take your analysis one step further by conducting a critical reading (Worksheet for Conducting a Critical Reading; see p. 243).

WORKSHEET FOR CONDUCTING A CRITICAL READING

Remember that before moving to this step, you should complete the basic descriptive process of identifying strategies and describing the rhetorical situation, and should have completed the preferred reading (Worksheet for Conducting an Evaluative Reading; see p. 241).

Step I. Conduct an Oppositional Reading

Use the following chart to consider questions of choice and voice, and how rhetorical strategies provide support for your answers.

Questions of Choice and Voice:	Strategies That "Advocate or Defend" the Organization's View (Foss, 2004):
Choice: Is information presented in a way that allows audiences to make informed decisions? (Alvesson & Deetz, 2003)	
Choice: Are there any apparent contradictions that are ignored or de-emphasized, thus limiting the information available to audiences? (Giddens, 1979)	
Choice: Are there assumptions about power or shared values that are taken for granted? (McKerrow, 1989)	
Choice: What is left unsaid in the rhetoric? What information is omitted, and what topics are not addressed? (Cheney & Dionisopoulos, 1989)	
Voice: Who is "speaking"? Which groups' interests are revealed? Which are concealed? Can you clearly identify the rhetor? (Cheney & McMillan, 1990)	

(Continued)

(Continued)

Questions of Choice and Voice:	Strategies That "Advocate or Defend" the Organization's View (Foss, 2004):
Voice: Are the ideas or values of a few power parties presented as the ideas or values of the whole? (Giddens, 1979)	
Voice: Are there any apparent contradictions that are dismissed or reframed such that the voices of those identifying them are muted? (Giddens, 1979)	
Voice: Does the discourse invite participation from all interested parties? (German, 1995)	

Step II. Draw Conclusion About Power

Formulate conclusions about how power is constructed or maintained in the rhetoric. Answer some or all of the following questions as you consider what you found in Step I. The first two help you to describe in part the ideology or world-view of the organization.

1. What things seem to be most important to the organization? What things seem to be least important?

2. Which groups of people seem to "matter" to the organization? Who seems less important?

3. What possible implications for society grow out of this ideology? For example, does the ideology expand or limit opportunities for diverse groups of people? Does it reflect a tendency to focus narrowly on organizational interests, or to take a broader view?

After the Analysis

Once you have completed your critical reading, you may apply your findings by writing an essay, discussing your conclusions with others, formulating general ideas about the role of rhetoric in constructing or challenging organizational power, or using the ideas to make decisions about the power you give organizations in your own life.

References

Adamson, A. P. (2006). *Brand simple: How the best brands keep it simple and succeed.* New York: Palgrave Macmillan.

Albert, S., & Whetten, D. (1985). Organizational identity. In L. L. Cummings & B. M. Shaw (Eds.), *Research in organizational behavior* (Vol. 7, pp. 263–295). Greenwich, CT: JAI Press.

Allen, T., & Simmons, J. (2004). Visual and verbal identity. In R. Clifton & J. Simmons (Eds.), *Brands and branding* (pp. 113–126). Princeton, NJ: Bloomberg Press.

Altria Group. (2001, November 15). *Philip Morris Companies Inc. announces proposal to change name of parent company.* Retrieved June 16, 2009, from http://www.altria.com/media/03_02_pressReleaseArchive.asp#2001

Alvesson, M., & Deetz, S. (2003). Critical theory and postmodernism approaches to organizational studies. In S. R. Clegg, C. Hardy, & W. R. Nord (Eds.), *Handbook of organization studies* (pp. 191–217). London: Sage.

Argenti, P. A. (1998). *Corporate communication* (2nd ed.). Boston: Irwin/McGraw-Hill.

Aristotle. (1932). *The rhetoric of Aristotle* (L. Cooper, Trans.). Englewood Cliffs, NJ: Prentice Hall.

Ashcraft, K. L. (2005). Resistance through consent? Occupational identity, organizational form, and the maintenance of masculinity among commercial airline pilots. *Management Communication Quarterly, 19,* 67–90.

Ashcraft, K. L., & Allen, B. J. (2003). The racial foundation for organizational communication. *Communication Theory, 13*(1), 5–38.

Associated Press. (1989, April 12). Oil slick stalls near Kodiak; Crews will attack with nets. *New York Times.* Retrieved June 16, 2009, from http://www.nytimes.com/1989/04/12/us/oil-slick-stalls-near-kodiak-crews-will-attack-with-nets.html

Aune, J. (1983). Beyond deconstruction: The symbol and social reality. *Southern Speech Communication Journal, 48,* 255–268.

Aust, P. J. (2004). Communicated values as indicators of organizational identity: A method for organizational assessment and its application in a case study. *Communication Studies, 55,* 515–534.

Barker, J. R. (1993). Tightening the iron cage: Concertive control in self-managing teams. *Administrative Science Quarterly, 38,* 408–437.

Barnard, C. I. (1969). *The functions of the executive.* Cambridge, MA: Harvard University Press. (Original work published 1939)

Benoit, W. L. (1995a). *Accounts, excuses, and apologies: A theory of image restoration strategies.* Albany: State University of New York Press.

Benoit, W. L. (1995b). Sears' repair of its auto service image: Image restoration discourse in the corporate sector. *Communication Studies, 46,* 89–105.

Benoit, W. L. (1997). Image repair discourse and crisis communication. *Public Relations Review, 23,* 177–186.

Benoit, W. L. (2000). Another visit to the theory of image restoration strategies. *Communication Quarterly, 48,* 40–44.

Benoit, W. L., & Lindsey, J. J. (1987). Argument strategies: Antidote to Tylenol's poisoned image. *Journal of the American Forensic Association, 23,* 136–146.

Bergman, E. (1994). Crisis? What crisis? *Communication World, 11*(4), 9–13.

Bisel, R. S., Ford, D. J., & Keyton, J. (2007). Unobtrusive control in a leadership organization: Integrating control and resistance. *Western Journal of Communication, 71*(2), 136–158.

Bitzer, L. (1968). The rhetorical situation. *Philosophy & Rhetoric, 1,* 1–14.

Black, E. (1965). *Rhetorical criticism: A study in method.* Madison: University of Wisconsin.

Blackett, T. (2004). What is a brand? In R. Clifton & J. Simmons (Eds.), *Brands and branding* (pp. 13–26). Princeton, NJ: Bloomberg Press.

Bostdorff, D. M., & Vibbert, S. L. (1994). Values advocacy: Enhancing organizational images, deflecting public criticism, and grounding future arguments. *Public Relations Review, 20,* 141–158.

Botan, C. H., & Taylor, M. (2004). Public relations: State of the field. *Journal of Communication, 54*(4), 645–661.

Bridges, J. A. (2004). Corporate issues campaigns: Six theoretical approaches. *Communication Theory, 14*(1), 51–77.

Bullis, C. (1993). Organizational socialization research: Enabling, constraining, and shifting perspectives. *Communication Monographs, 60,* 10–17.

Burke, K. (1966). *Language as symbolic action.* Berkeley: University of California Press.

Burke, K. (1984). *Attitudes toward history.* Berkeley: University of California Press. (Original work published 1937)

Campbell, K. K. (1974). Criticism: Ephemeral and enduring. *Speech Teacher, 23,* 9–14.

Campbell, K. K. (1996). *The rhetorical act* (2nd ed.). Belmont, CA: Wadsworth.

Campbell, K. K., & Burkholder, T. R. (1997). *Critiques of contemporary rhetoric* (2nd ed.). Belmont, CA: Wadsworth.

Campbell, K. K., & Jamieson, K. H. (1978). Form and genre in rhetorical criticism: An introduction. In K. K. Campbell & K. H. Jamieson (Eds.), *Form and genre: Shaping rhetorical action.* Falls Church, VA: Speech Communication Association.

Campbell, K. K., & Jamieson, K. H. (1990). *Deeds done in words: Presidential rhetoric and the genres of governance.* Chicago: University of Chicago Press.

Center for Public Integrity. (1995a). Well-healed: Inside lobbying for healthcare reform, part I. *International Journal of Health Services, 25*(3), 411–453.

Center for Public Integrity (1995b). Well-healed: Inside lobbying for healthcare reform, part II. *International Journal of Health Services, 25*(4), 593–632.

Center for Public Integrity (1995c). Well-healed: Inside lobbying for healthcare reform, part III. *International Journal of Health Services, 26*(1), 19–46.

Cerner Corporation. (2009). *Web site home page.* Retrieved June 18, 2009, from http://www.cerner.com/public/Cerner_3.asp?id=129

Cheney, G. (1983). The rhetoric of identification and the study of organizational communication. *Quarterly Journal of Speech, 69,*143–158.

Cheney, G. (1991). *Rhetoric in an organizational society: Managing multiple identities.* Columbia: University of South Carolina Press.

Cheney, G. (1992). The corporate person (re)presents itself. In E. L. Toth & R. L. Heath (Eds.), *Rhetorical and critical approaches to public relations* (pp. 165–183). Hillsdale, NJ: Lawrence Erlbaum.

Cheney, G. (1995). Democracy in the workplace: Theory and practice from the perspective of communication. *Journal of Applied Communication Research, 23,* 167–200.

Cheney, G. (2005). Theorizing about rhetoric and organizations: Classical, interpretive, and critical aspects. In S. K. May & D. K. Mumby (Eds.), *Engaging organizational communication theory and research: Multiple perspectives* (pp. 55–84). Thousand Oaks, CA: Sage.

Cheney, G., & Christensen, L. T. (2001a). Organizational identity: Linkages between internal and external communication. In F. M. Jablin & L. L. Putnam (Eds.), *The new handbook of organizational communication: Advances in theory, research, and methods* (pp. 231–269). Thousand Oaks, CA: Sage.

Cheney, G., & Christensen, L. T. (2001b). Public relations as contested terrain: A critical response. In R. Heath (Ed.), *Handbook of public relations* (pp. 167–182). Thousand Oaks, CA: Sage.

Cheney, G., Christensen, L. T., Conrad, C., & Lair, D. J. (2004). Corporate rhetoric as organizational discourse. In D. Grant, C. Hardy, C. Oswick, & L. Putnam (Eds.), *The Sage handbook of organizational discourse* (pp. 79–103). London: Sage Publications.

Cheney, G., & Dionisopoulos, G. N. (1989). Public relations? No, relations with publics: A rhetorical-organizational approach to contemporary corporate communications. In C. H. Botan & V. Hazleton, Jr. (Eds.), *Public relations theory* (pp. 135–157). Hillsdale, NJ: Lawrence Erlbaum.

Cheney, G., & Frenette, G. (1993). Persuasion and organization: Values, logics, and accounts in contemporary corporate discourse. In C. Conrad (Ed.), *The ethical nexus* (pp. 49–73). Norwood, NJ: Ablex.

Cheney, G., & McMillan, J. (1990). Organizational rhetoric and the practice of criticism. *Journal of Applied Communication Research, 18*(2), 93–114.

Cheney, G., & Vibbert, S. L. (1987). Corporate discourse: Public relations and issues management. In F. Jablin, L. L. Putnam, K. Roberts, & L. Porter (Eds.), *Handbook of organizational communication* (pp. 165–194). Newbury Park, CA: Sage.

Clair, R. P. (1993). The bureaucratization, commodification, and privatization of sexual harassment through institutional discourse. *Management Communication Quarterly, 7*(2), 123–157.

Cloud, D. (2005). Fighting words: Labor and the limits of communication at Staley, 1993 to 1996. *Management Communication Quarterly, 18*(4), 509–542.

Condit, C. M. (1994). Hegemony in a mass-mediated society: Concordance about reproductive technologies. *Critical Studies in Mass Communication, 11*(3), 205–230.

Conrad, C. (1983). Organizational power: Faces and symbolic forms. In L. Putnam & M. Pacanowsky (Eds.), *Communication and organizations: An interpretive approach* (pp. 173–194). Beverly Hills, CA: Sage.

Conrad, C. (1988). Work songs, hegemony, and illusions of self. *Critical Studies in Mass Communication, 5*(3), 179–201.

Conrad, C. (1993a). Conceptual grounding. In C. Conrad (Ed.), *The ethical nexus* (pp. 7–22). Norwood, NJ: Ablex.

Conrad, C. (1993b). Introduction. In C. Conrad (Ed.), *The ethical nexus* (pp. 1–4). Norwood, NJ: Ablex.

Conrad, C., & Poole, M. S. (2005). *Strategic organizational communication in a global economy* (6th ed.). Belmont, CA: Thomson Wadsworth.

Consigny, S. (1974). Rhetoric and its situations. *Philosophy & Rhetoric, 7*, 175–186.

Coombs, W. T. (1999). *Ongoing crisis communication: Planning, managing, and responding.* Thousand Oaks, CA: Sage.

Coombs, W. T. (2004). Impact of past crises on current crisis communication. *Journal of Business Communication, 41*(3), 265–289.

Coombs, W. T. (2006). Crisis management: A communicative approach. In C. H. Botan & V. Hazleton (Eds.), *Public relations theory II* (pp. 171–197). Mahwah, NJ: Lawrence Erlbaum.

Coombs, W. T., & Holladay, S. J. (2002). Helping managers protect reputational assets: Initial tests of the situational crisis communication theory. *Management Communication Quarterly, 16*, 165–186.

Cooren, F., Taylor, J. R., & Van Every, E. J. (Eds.). (2006). *Communication as organizing: Empirical and theoretical explorations in the dynamic of text and conversation.* Mahwah, NJ: Lawrence Erlbaum.

Crable, R. E., & Vibbert, S. L. (1983). Mobil's epideictic advocacy: "Observations" of Prometheus-bound. *Communication Monographs, 50*, 380–394.

Crable, R. E., & Vibbert, S. L. (1985). Managing issues and influencing public policy. *Public Relations Review, 11*, 3–16.

Crabtree, S. (2007, November 18). Unitarians turned to ads in bid for recognition. *Washington Post.* Retrieved July 1, 2009, from http://www.highbeam.com/doc/1P2-10941128.html

Daugherty, E. L. (2001). Public relations and social responsibility. In R. L. Heath (Ed.), *Handbook of public relations* (pp. 389–409). Thousand Oaks, CA: Sage.

Deetz, S. A. (1992). *Democracy in an age of corporate colonization: Developments in communication and the politics of everyday life.* Albany: State University of New York Press.

Deetz, S. (2003). Corporate governance, communication, and getting social values into the decisional chain. *Management Communication Quarterly, 16*(4), 606–611.

Delia, J. G. (1970). The logic fallacy, cognitive theory, and the enthymeme: A search for the foundations of reasoned discourse. *Quarterly Journal of Speech, 56,* 140–148.

DeNavas-Walt, C., Proctor, B. D., & Smith, J. (2007). *U.S. Census Bureau, current population reports, P60–233, Income, poverty and health insurance coverage in the United States: 2006.* Washington, DC: U.S. Government Printing Office.

Douglass, M., & Wildavsky, A. (1982). *Risk and culture: An essay on the selection of technological and environmental dangers.* Berkeley: University of California Press.

Dutton, J. E., & Dukerich, J. M. (1991). Keeping an eye on the mirror: Image and identity in organizational adaptation. *Academy of Management Journal, 34,* 517–554.

Edwards, H. H. (2006). A rhetorical typology for studying the audience role in public relations communication: The Avon 3-day disruption as exemplar. *Journal of Communication, 56,* 836–860.

Eisenberg, E. M., Goodall, H. L., Jr., & Trethewey, A. (2007). *Organizational communication: Balancing creativity and constraint* (5th ed.). Boston: Bedford/ St. Martin's.

Elliot, M. (2003). Risk perception frames in environmental decision making. *Environmental Practice, 5,* 214–222.

Elsbach, K. D., Sutton, R. M., & Principe, K. E. (1998). Averting expected challenges through anticipatory impression management: A study of hospital billing. *Organization Science, 9,* 68–86.

Esman, M. (1972). The elements of institution building. In J. Eaton (Ed.), *Institution building and development* (pp. 19–40). Beverly Hills, CA: Sage.

Festinger, L. (1962). *A theory of cognitive dissonance.* Stanford, CA: Stanford University Press.

Fitzpatrick, K. (2006). Baselines for ethical advocacy in the "marketplace of ideas." In K. Fitzpatrick & C. Bronstein (Eds.), *Ethics in public relations: Responsible advocacy* (pp. 1–17). Thousand Oaks, CA: Sage.

Fleming, P., & Spicer, A. (2008). Beyond power and resistance: New approaches to organizational politics. *Management Communication Quarterly, 21*(3), 301–309.

Ford, D. J. (1999). *The rhetoric of the American Medical Association during the Health Security Act debate, 1993–1994.* Unpublished doctoral dissertation, University of Kansas, Lawrence.

Foss, S. K. (2004). *Rhetorical criticism: Exploration and practice* (3rd ed.). Prospect Heights, IL: Waveland Press.

Foucault, M. (1972). *The archaeology of knowledge* (A. M. Sheridan Smith, Trans.). New York: Random House.

Foucault, M. (1977). *Discipline and punish: The birth of the prison* (A. M. Sheridan Smith, Trans.). New York: Random House.

Freely, A. J. (1996). *Argumentation and debate: Critical thinking for reasoned decision making* (9th ed.). Belmont, CA: Wadsworth.

Freeman, R. E. (1984). *Strategic management: A stakeholder approach.* Boston: Pitman.

Freeman, R. E., Harrison, J. S., & Wicks, A. C. (2007). *Managing for stakeholders: Survival, reputation, and success.* New Haven, CT: Yale University Press.

Friedson, E. (1988). *Profession of medicine: A study of the applied sociology of medicine.* Chicago: University of Chicago Press. (Original work published 1970)

German, K. M. (1995). Critical theory in public relations inquiry: Future directions for analysis in a public relations context. In W. N. Elwood (Ed.), *Public relations inquiry as rhetorical criticism: Case studies of corporate discourse and social influence* (pp. 279–294). Westport, CT: Praeger.

Giddens, A. (1979). *Central problems in social theory.* Berkeley: University of California Press.

Gilpin, D., & Murphy, P. (2006). Reframing crisis management through complexity. In C. H. Botan & V. Hazleton (Eds.), *Public relations theory II* (pp. 375–392). Mahwah, NJ: Lawrence Erlbaum.

Gonzales, A. (2008, February 29). Animal rights group seeks AG action following lawsuit dismissal. *Phoenix Business Journal.* Retrieved June 16, 2009, from http://www.bizjournals.com/phoenix/stories/2008/03/03/story4.html

Gramsci, A. (1971). *Selections from the prison notebooks* (Q. Hoare & G. Nowell Smith, Trans.). New York: International.

Grunig, L. A., Grunig, J., & Dozier, D. M. (2002). *Excellent public relations and effective organizations.* Mahwah, NJ: Lawrence Erlbaum.

Haas, T. (2001). Public relations between universality and particularity: Toward a moral-philosophical conception of public relations ethics. In R. Heath & G. Vasquez (Eds.), *Handbook of public relations* (pp. 423–433). Thousand Oaks, CA: Sage.

Hart, R. P., & Daughton, S. (2005). *Modern rhetorical criticism* (3rd ed.). Boston: Allyn & Bacon.

Hauser, G. A. (1998). Vernacular dialogue and the rhetoricality of public opinion. *Communication Monographs, 65,* 83–107.

Hearit, K. M. (1994). From "we didn't do it" to "it's not our fault": The use of apologia in public relations crises. In W. N. Elwood (Ed.), *Public relations inquiry as rhetorical criticism* (pp. 117–131). New York: Greenwood.

Hearit, K. M. (1995). "Mistakes were made": Organizations, apologia, and crises of social legitimacy. *Communication Studies, 46,* 1–17.

Hearit, K. M. (1996). The use of counterattack in public relations crises: The case of General Motors vs. NBC. *Public Relations Review, 22,* 233–248.

Hearit, K. M. (2006). *Crisis management by apology: Corporate response to allegations of wrongdoing.* Mahwah, NJ: Lawrence Erlbaum Associates.

Heath, R. L. (1980). Corporate advocacy: An application of speech communication perspectives and skills—and more. *Communication Education, 29,* 370–377.

Heath, R. L. (1988). *Strategic issues management.* San Francisco: Jossey-Bass.

Heath, R. L. (1994). *Management of corporate communication.* Hillsdale, NJ: Lawrence Erlbaum.

Heath, R. L. (1997). *Strategic issues management: Organizations and public policy challenges.* Thousand Oaks, CA: Sage.

Heath, R. L., & Coombs, W. L. (2006). *Today's public relations.* Thousand Oaks, CA: Sage.

Heath, R. L., & Millar, D. P. (2004). A rhetorical approach to crisis communication: Management, communication processes, and strategic responses. In D. P. Millar & R. L. Heath (Eds.), *Responding to crisis: A rhetorical approach to understanding crisis communication* (pp. 1–17). Mahwah, NJ: Lawrence Erlbaum.

Heath, R. L., & Palenchar, M. J. (2009). *Strategic issues management: Organizations and public policy changes.* Thousand Oaks, CA: Sage.

Heider, F. (1946). Attitudes and cognitive organization. *Journal of Psychology, 21,* 107–112.

Hill, F. (1972). Conventional wisdom—traditional form: The president's message of November 3, 1969. *Quarterly Journal of Speech, 58,* 373–386.

Hoffman, M. F., & Cowan, R. L. (2008). The meaning of work/life: An analysis of corporate discourse on work/life issues. *Communication Quarterly, 56,* 227–246.

Hoffman, M. F., & Medlock-Kluyukovski, A. (2004). "Our creator who art in heaven:" Paradox, ritual, and cultural transformation. *Western Journal of Communication, 68,* 389–410.

Howard, L. A. (1997). Poetics and petrochemicals: Organizational performances of the Mississippi River. In J. D. Hoover (Ed.), *Corporate advocacy: Rhetoric in the information age.* Westport, CT: Quorum Books.

Ice, R. (1991). Corporate publics and rhetorical strategies: The case of Union Carbide's Bhopal crisis. *Management Communication Quarterly, 4,* 341–362.

Ihlen, O. (2006). Substitution or pollution? Competing views of environmental benefit in a gas-fired power plant dispute. In S. P. Depoe (Ed.), *Environmental communication yearbook* (Vol. 3, pp. 137–155). Hillsdale, NJ: Lawrence Erlbaum.

International Business Machines. (n.d.). *Pay and benefits.* Retrieved July 3, 2009, from http://ibm.com/services/us/gbs/bus/htnl/bcs_careers_workatgbs .html#section3

Jablin, F. M. (2001). Organization entry, assimilation, and disengagement/exit. In F. M. Jablin & L. L. Putnam (Eds.), *The new handbook of organizational communication* (pp. 732–818). Thousand Oaks, CA: Sage.

Jablin, F. M., & Krone, K. J. (1987). Organizational assimilation. In C. R. Berger & S. H. Chaffee (Eds.), *Handbook of communication science* (pp. 711–746). Newbury Park, CA: Sage.

Jerome, A. (2002). An argument field theory of organizational apologia: The case of Firestone and Ford. *Dissertation Abstracts International, 63*(10), 3538.

Jones, B. L., & Chase, W. H. (1979). Managing public policy issues. *Public Relations Review, 7,* 3–23.

Karlberg, M. (1996). Remembering the public in public relations research: From theoretical to operational symmetry. *Journal of Public Relations Research, 8*(4), 263–278.

Katz, D., & Kahn, R. L. (1978). *The social psychology of organizations* (2nd ed.). New York: Wiley.

Kent, M. L., & Taylor, M. (2002). Toward a dialogic theory of public relations. *Public Relations Review, 28,* 21–37.

Keyton, J., Ford, D. J., & Smith, F. E. (2008). A meso-level communicative model of interorganizational collaboration. *Communication Theory, 18,* 376–406.

Kirby, E. L., & Krone, K. J. (2002). "The policy exists but you can't really use it": Communication and the structuration of work-family policies. *Journal of Applied Communication Research, 30*(1), 50–77.

Koenig, D. (2007, February 26). TXU board OKs buyout offer. *Houston Chronicle.*

Kuhn, T. (1997). The discourse of issues management: A genre of organizational communication. *Communication Quarterly, 45,* 188–210.

Kuhn, T., & Corman, S. R. (2003). The emergence of homogeneity and heterogeneity in knowledge structures during a planned organizational change. *Communication Monographs, 70,* 198–229.

Larson, C. (2001). *Persuasion: Reception and responsibility* (9th ed.). Stamford, CT: Wadsworth.

Leichty, G. (1997). The limits of collaboration. *Public Relations Review* [Electronic version], *23*(1), 47–56.

Leitch, S., & Neilson, D. (2001). Bringing publics back into public relations: New theoretical frameworks for practice. In R. Heath (Ed.), *Handbook of public relations* (pp. 127–138). Thousand Oaks, CA: Sage.

Leung, W. (2007, October 15). *Strike! Globe and Mail* (Canada). Retrieved July 1, 2009, from http://libcom.org/forums/news/ibm-second-life-strike-update-17102007

Lewis, L. K. (2007). An organizational stakeholder model of change implementation communication. *Communication Theory, 17,* 176–204.

Maddox, K. (2007, September 10). Second Life has some firms second guessing. *B to B.* Retrieved July 1, 2009, from http://www.highbeam.com/doc/1G1-168679214.html

Mann, E. (2009, April 18). North Star Foods workers ponder the future. *Post-Bulletin* (Rochester, MN).

Marcus, A. A., & Goodman, R. S. (1991). Victims and shareholders: The dilemmas of presenting corporate policy during a crisis. *Academy of Management Journal, 34*(2), 281–305.

Mark, M., & Pearson, C. S. (2001). *The hero and the outlaw: Building extraordinary brands through the power of archetypes.* New York: McGraw-Hill.

Marx, K. (1978). Economic and philosophic manuscripts of 1844. In R. Tucker (Ed.), *The Marx-Engels reader* (pp. 66–125). New York: Norton.

Maslow, A. H. (1943). A theory of human motivation. *Psychology Review, 50,* 370–396.

Massey, J. E. (2001). Managing organizational legitimacy: Communication strategies for organizations in crisis. *Journal of Business Communication, 38*(2), 153–183.

McHale, J. P., Zompetti, J. P., & Moffit, M. A. (2007). A hegemonic model of crisis communication. *Journal of Business Communication, 44*(4), 374–402.

McKerrow, R. E. (1989). Critical rhetoric: Theory and praxis. *Communication Monographs, 56,* 91–111.

McMillan, J. J. (1987). In search of the organizational persona: A rationale for studying organizations rhetorically. In L. Thayer (Ed.), *Organization-Communication: Emerging perspectives II* (pp. 21–45). Norwood, NJ: Ablex.

McMillan, J. J. (2007). Why corporate social responsibility: Why now? How? In S. May, G. Cheney, & J. Roper (Eds.). *The debate over corporate social responsibility* (pp. 15–29). Oxford, UK: Oxford University Press.

Meisenbach, R. J., & McMillan, J. (2006). Blurring the boundaries: Historical developments and future directions in organizational rhetoric. In C. S. Beck (Ed.), *Communication yearbook 30* (pp. 99–141). Mahwah, NJ: Lawrence Erlbaum.

Merck & Co., Inc. (2008). *Public policy: Access to medicines.* Retrieved February 25, 2008, from http://www.merck.com/about/public_policy

Meyers, R., & Garrett, D. (1993). Contradictions, values, and organizational argument. In C. Conrad (Ed.), *The ethical nexus* (pp. 149–170). Norwood, NJ: Ablex.

Miller, K. I. (2006). *Organizational communication: Approaches and processes* (4th ed.). Belmont, CA: Thomson.

Mirel, B. (1994). Debating nuclear energy: Theories of risk and purposes of communication. *Technical Communication Quarterly, 3,* 41–65.

Mitchell, R. K., Agle, B. R., & Wood, D. J. (1997). Toward a theory of stakeholder identification and salience: Defining the principle of who and what really counts. *Academy of Management Review, 22*(4), 853–886.

Moreland, N., & Clark, M. (1998). Quality and ISO 9000 in educational organizations. *Total Quality Management, 9,* 311–320.

Mozisek, K. D., & Hoffman, M. F. (2005). *Taking stock of issues management: Policy argument theory and issues management in organizations.* Paper presented at the annual meeting of the Central States Communication Association, Kansas City, MO.

Mufson, S. (2007, July 31). Firm applies to expand nuclear plant in Maryland. *Washington Post.* Retrieved July 1, 2009, from http://www.washington post.com/wp-dyn/content/article/2007/07/30/AR2007073001881.html

Mumby, D. K. (1987). The political function of narratives in organizations. *Communication Monographs, 54,* 113–127.

Mumby, D. K. (1993). Critical organizational communication studies: The next 10 years. *Communication Monographs, 60,* 18–25.

Mumby, D. K. (1997). The problem of hegemony: Rereading Gramsci for organizational communication studies. *Western Journal of Communication, 61*(4), 343–375.

Mumby, D. K. (2001). Power and politics. In F. Jablin & L. Putnam (Eds.), *The new handbook of organizational communication* (pp. 585–623). Thousand Oaks, CA: Sage.

Mumby, D. K. (2004). Discourse, power, and ideology: Unpacking the critical approach. In D. Grant, C. Hardy, C. Oswick, & L. Putnam (Eds.), *The Sage handbook of organizational discourse* (pp. 237–2258). London: Sage.

Mumby, D. K., & Putnam, L. L. (1992). The politics of emotion: A feminist reading of bounded rationality. *Academy of Management Review, 17*(3), 465–486.

Murphy, A. G. (1998). Hidden transcripts of flight attendant resistance. *Management Communication Quarterly, 11,* 499–535.

Murray-Johnson, L., & Witte, K. (2003). Looking toward the future: Health design message strategies. In T. L. Thompson, A. M. Dorsey, K. I. Miller, & R. Parrott (Eds.), *Handbook of health communication* (pp. 473–495). Mahwah, NJ: Lawrence Erlbaum.

Neaves, W. B. (2005, June). Why the Stowers Institute supports stem cell research. *GCMS Journal.* Retrieved February 19, 2008, from http://www.stowers-institute.org/mediacenter/docs/Greene%20County%20Medical%20Journal%20June%202005.pdf

NRG Energy. (2007, September 24). *NRG Energy submits application for new 2,700-megawatt nuclear plant in South Texas* [News release]. Retrieved February 24, 2008 from http://investor.nrgenergy.com.

O'Keefe, D. J. (2002). *Persuasion: Theory and research.* Thousand Oaks, CA: Sage.

Packard, V. (1964). *The hidden persuaders.* New York: Pocket Books.

Pear, R. (2006, May 23). In Medicare debate, massaging the facts. *New York Times.* Retrieved March 1, 2008, from http://www.nytimes.com/2006/05/23/washington/23medicare.html

Petty, R. E., & Cacioppo, J. T. (1986). *Communication and persuasion: Central and peripheral routes to attitude change.* New York: Springer-Verlag.

Pfizer Inc. (2007). *Pfizer homepage.* Retrieved June 16, 2009, from http://www.pfizer.com/pfizer/do/index.jsp

Pharmaceutical Researchers and Manufacturers of America (PhRMA). (2007). *Homepage.* Retrieved December 7, 2007, from http://www.phrma.org/about_phrma/member_company_list/members

Poole, M. S., & McPhee, R. D. (2005). Structuration theory. In S. May & D. K. Mumby (Eds.), *Engaging organizational communication theory and research: Multiple perspectives* (pp. 171–195). Thousand Oaks, CA: Sage.

Pribble, P. T. (1990). Making an ethical commitment: A rhetorical case study of organizational socialization. *Communication Quarterly, 38,* 255–267.

Putnam, L. L., & Pacanowsky, M. E. (1983). *Communication and organizations: An interpretive approach.* Beverly Hills, CA: Sage.

Rovner, J. (2006, October 27). Missouri voters weigh stem-cell decisions. *NPR Morning Edition.* Retrieved February 2, 2008, from http://www.npr.org/templates/story/story.php?storyID=6391278

Rowland, R. C. (1991). On generic categorization. *Communication Theory, 1,* 128–144.

Rowland, R. C. (1999). *Analyzing rhetoric: A handbook for the informed citizen in a new millennium.* Dubuque, IA: Kendall Hunt.

Rowland, R. C. (2008). *Analyzing rhetoric: A handbook for the informed citizen in a new millennium* (3rd ed.). Dubuque, IA: Kendall Hunt.

Rowland, R. C., & Jerome, A. M. (2004). On organizational apologia: A reconceptualization. *Communication Theory, 14,* 191–211.

Russo, T. (1998). Organizational and professional identification: A case of newspaper journalists. *Management Communication Quarterly, 12,* 72–111.

Santa Clara County v. Southern Pacific Railroad Co., 118 U.S. 394 (1886).

Schiller, H. I. (1989). *Culture, inc.: The corporate takeover of public expression.* New York: Oxford University Press.

Schmitt, B., & Simonson, A. (1997). *Marketing aesthetics: The strategic management of brands, identity, and image.* New York: The Free Press.

Schuetz, J. (1990). Corporate advocacy as argumentation. In R. S. Trapp & J. Schuetz (Eds.), *Perspectives on argumentation* (pp. 272–284). Prospect Heights, IL: Waveland Press.

Schutz, W. (1958). *FIRO: A three-dimensional theory of interpersonal behavior.* New York: Rinehart.

Schwartz, M. P. (1993, November 29). Health insurance trade group rifts surface [Electronic version]. *National Underwriter, 97*(48), 3.

Scott, C. R. (1997). Identification with multiple targets in a geographically dispersed organization. *Management Communication Quarterly, 10,* 491–552.

Scott, W. G., & Hart, D. K. (1979). *Organizational America.* Boston: Houghton Mifflin.

Seeger, M. W., & Ulmer, R. R. (2002). A post-crisis discourse of renewal: The cases of Malden Mills and Cole Hardwoods. *Journal of Applied Communication Research, 30,* 126–142.

Sellnow, T. L., Seeger, M. W., & Ulmer, R. R. (2002). Chaos theory, informational needs, and natural disasters. *Applied Communication Research, 30,* 269–292.

Sethi, S. P. (1987). *Handbook of advocacy advertising.* Cambridge, MA: Ballinger.

Shabecoff, P. (1989, March 25). Largest U.S. tanker spill spews 270,000 barrels of oil off Alaska. *New York Times.* Retrieved June 16, 2009, from http://www.nytimes.com/1989/03/25/us/largest-us-tanker-spill-spews-270000-barrels-of-oil-off-alaska.html

Slevin, P. (2005, August 10). In heartland, stem cell research meets fierce opposition. *Washington Post,* p. A01.

Starr, P. (1982). *The social transformation of American medicine: The rise of a sovereign profession and the making of a vast industry.* New York: Basic Books.

Steele, E. D., & Redding, W. C. (1962). The American value system. *Western Speech, 26,* 83–91.

Stohl, C. (2001). Globalizing organizational communication. In F. M. Jablin & L. L. Putnam (Eds.), *The new handbook of organizational communication* (pp. 323–375). Thousand Oaks, CA: Sage.

Stohl, C., & Redding, C. W. (1987). Messages and message exchange processes. In F. M. Jablin, L. L. Putnam, K. H. Roberts, & L. W. Porter (Eds.), *Handbook of organizational communication: An interdisciplinary perspective* (pp. 451–502). Newbury Park, CA: Sage.

Sturges, D. L. (1994). Communicating through crisis: A strategy for organizational survival. *Management Communication Quarterly, 7*(3), 297–316.

Target. (2009). *Meet our team.* Retrieved July 3, 2009, from http://sites.target.com/site/en/company/page.jsp?contentId=WCMP04-035550

Taylor, M., Vasquez, G., & Dorley, J. (2003). Merck and AIDS activists: Engagement as a framework for extending issues management. *Public Relations Review, 29,* 257–270.

Tompkins, P. K., & Cheney, G. (1985). Communication and unobtrusive control in contemporary organizations. In R. D. McPhee & P. K. Tompkins (Eds.), *Organizational communication: Traditional themes and new directions* (pp. 179–210). Beverly Hills, CA: Sage.

Toohey, M. (2008, May 27). In landfill fight, little village had big ally. *Austin American-Statesman*.

Toulmin, S. (1958). *The uses of argument.* Cambridge, UK: Cambridge University Press.

Tracy, K. (2007). The discourse of crisis in public meetings: Case study of a school district's multimillion dollar error. *Journal of Applied Communication Research, 35*(4), 418–441.

Tyler, L. (1997). Liability means never having to say you're sorry: Corporate guilt, legal constraints, and defensiveness in corporate communication. *Management Communication Quarterly, 11*, 51–73.

Ulmer, R. R., Sellnow, T. L., & Seeger, M. W. (2007). *Effective crisis communication: Moving from crisis to opportunity.* Thousand Oaks, CA: Sage.

Vancil, D. L. (1993). *Rhetoric and argumentation.* Boston: Allyn & Bacon.

Vasquez, G. M., & Taylor, M. (2001). Research perspectives on "the public." In R. Heath (Ed.), *Handbook of public relations* (pp. 139–154). Thousand Oaks, CA: Sage.

Vatz, R. (1973). The myth of the rhetorical situation. *Philosophy and Rhetoric, 6*, 154–161.

Venette, S. (2008). Risk as an inherent element in the study of crisis communication. *Southern Communication Journal, 73*, 197–210.

Wallace, K. (1963). The substance of rhetoric: Good reason. *Quarterly Journal of Speech, 49*, 239–249.

Wal-Mart Stores, Inc. (2008a). *Featured video: Opportunities to grow.* Retrieved January 15, 2008, from http://www.walmartstores.com/GlobalWMStoresWeb/navigate.do?catg=218

Wal-Mart Stores, Inc. (2008b). *Homepage.* Retrieved July 1, 2009, from http://www.walmart.com

Waltzer, H. (1988). Corporate advocacy advertising and political influence. *Public Relations Review, 14*, 41–55.

Wander, P. (1983). The ideological turn in modern criticism. *Central States Speech Journal, 31*, 1–18.

Ware, B. L., & Linkugel, W. (1973). They spoke in defense of themselves: On the generic criticism of apologia. *Quarterly Journal of Speech, 59*, 273–283.

Waymer, D., & Heath, R. L. (2007). Emergent agents: The forgotten publics in crisis communication and issues management research. *Journal of Applied Communication Research, 35*(1), 88–108.

West, D. M., Heith, D., & Goodwin, C. (1996). Harry and Louise go to Washington: Political advertising and health care reform. *Journal of Health Politics, Policy and Law, 21*(1), 35–68.

Whetten, D. A., & Mackey, A. (2002). A social actor conception of organizational identity and its implications for the study of organizational reputation. *Business & Society, 41*, 393–414.

Wichelns, H. A. (1925). The literary criticism of oratory. In A. M. Drummond (Ed.), *Studies in rhetoric and public speaking in honor of James Albert Winans* (pp. 181–216). New York: Century.

Young, J., & Foot, K. (2006). Corporate E-cruiting: The construction of work in Fortune 500 recruiting Web sites. *Journal of Computer-Mediated Communication, 11,* 44–71.

Zemeckis, R. (Director), & Broyles, Jr., W. (Writer). (2000). *Cast away* [Motion picture]. United States: DreamWorks SKG.

Zoller, H. M. (2003). Health on the line: Identity and disciplinary control in employee occupational health and safety discourse. *Journal of Applied Communication Research, 31*(2), 118–139.

Zorn, T. E., Page, D. J., & Cheney, G. (2000). Nuts about change: Multiple perspectives on change-oriented communication in a public sector organization. *Management Communication Quarterly, 13,* 515–566.

Index

Accurate evidence, 43
Act/essence distinction, 200
Anticipatory socialization, to the
    organization, 211–212
Anticipatory strategies, 217–218
Antithesis, identification by, 36
Apologia strategies, in crisis
    rhetoric, 197–199
Argument, 38
Aristotle, 2, 26, 28–29
Artistic proofs, 26
Assets, 75, 124
    issue management and, 149–152
    organizational rhetoric and, 67–69
    risk rhetoric and, 171–174
Association
    identity building and, 124–125
    identity maintenance
        and, 129–131
Assumed "we," 37
Attitude change, 168
Audiences, 75, 123–124, 128–129
    crisis management and, 192–193
    diffused, 66, 147–148, 171
    enabling, 65, 147, 170
    functional, 66, 148–149, 171
    issue management and, 147–149
    normative, 66, 148
    organizational change and,
        214–215
    organizational rhetoric and, 65–67
    organizational socialization and,
        211–213
    reinforcement and, 213–214
    retention and, 213–214

rhetorical, 11–12, 58
    risk rhetoric and, 170–171

Barnard, Chester, 4–6
Bitzer, Lloyd, 57
Bitzer's perspective, on rhetorical
    situations, 57–59
Black, Edwin, 8
Bolstering, as apologia strategy, 198
Branding
    identity building and, 126–127
    identity maintenance and, 131
Burke, Kenneth, 34, 60

Canons of rhetoric
    of delivery, 47
    of invention, 25–44
    of memory, 48
    of organization, 44–46
    of style, 46–47
Categorical syllogism, 41
Causal reasoning, 40
Central route, leading to
    attitude change, 168
Character, 26
Claims, 38
    risk and, 177
Common ground
    strategies, samples of, 36 (table)
    technique, 35
Community, 28
Community participation, and
    risk, 177–178
Company storytelling, 129
Competence, 27

Consistency theories, 29
Constraints, 75, 124, 128–129
  crisis management and, 193–196
  issue management and, 149–152
  legal, financial, and societal
    limitations, 195
  organizational change and,
    214–215
  organizational rhetoric and,
    67–69, 194–195
  organizational socialization and,
    211–213
  reinforcement and, 213–214
  retention and, 213–214
  rhetorical situation and, 59
  risk rhetoric and, 171–174
Content, layers of, 153
Context, importance of, in
  rhetoric, 56–57
Corporate person, 27
Corporate rhetoric, in nonprofit
  organizations, 234–235
Corporate social legitimacy, 27
Corporate social responsibility
  (CSR), 27
Corporate voice, of organizational
  messages, 93–94
Counterattack, as apologia
  strategy, 199
Counterexamples, 40
Crisis
  defining rhetoric about, 187–188
  life cycle of, 188–191
  management, 191–196
  organizational rhetoric
    about, 201–202
  response stage, of organizational
    crisis, 190–191
  See also Crisis rhetoric; Crisis
    situations
Crisis rhetoric, 185–207
  apologia strategies in, 197–199
  defining, 187–188
  dissociation strategies in, 199–200
  foundations for understanding,
    188–191
  instructional strategies in, 196–197
  strategies in, 196–201
  See also Crisis; Crisis situations
Crisis situations

emotional nature of, 196
rhetorical strategies for, 221–223
timing of, 193–194
uncertainty in, 194
See also Crisis; Crisis rhetoric
Critical approaches, to
  organizational rhetoric, 77–101,
    109–113
Critical reading, worksheet for
  conducting, 117–118, 243–244
Critical status, of an issue, 145
Critical theory/perspectives,
  summary of key concepts in,
    96–97
Criticism, 106
Critique of concord, 93
CSR (corporate social
  responsibility), 27
Culture, organization and rhetoric
  in contemporary, 1–22
Current status, of an issue, 145

Decision premises, 41
Deductive reasoning, 41–42
Deetz, Stanley, 15, 81
Delivery, canon of, 47
Denial, as apologia strategy,
  197–198
Differentiation
  apologia strategy, as, 198
  identity building and, 125–126
  identity maintenance and, 131
Diffused audiences, 66,
  147–148, 171
Dissociation strategies, in crisis
  rhetoric, 199–200
Dormant status, of an issue,
  145–146

Early phase strategies, 218–219
Elaboration likelihood model
  (ELM), 166, 168–169, 172
Electronic medical records (EMRs),
  225–232 (case study)
Empirical research, 69–71
Enabling audiences,
  65, 147, 170
Enthymeme, 41
Environment, as situation
  and strategy, 236

Ethics, and organizational
    rhetoric, 97–100
Ethos, 3
    in organizational rhetoric, 27–28
    interdependence with pathos and
        logos, 42–43
    in traditional rhetoric, 26–27
Evaluative approach, to analyzing
    organizational rhetoric
    origins and goals of, 105–106
    procedures of, 107–109
Evaluative reading, worksheet for
    conducting, 115–116, 241–242
Evidence, 38
    accurate, 43
    objective, 44
    qualified, 43–44
    risk and, 177
    timely, 44
Examples, representative, 40
Exigencies, 57–58, 75, 123, 128
    anticipated or unanticipated,
        63–64
    crisis management and, 191–192
    issue management and, 146–147
    organizational, 62–65
    organizational change and,
        214–215
    organizational socialization and,
        211–213
    positive or negative, potentially,
        64–65
    reinforcement and, 213–214
    retention and, 213–214
    risk rhetoric and, 169–170
Exxon Valdez, 186

For the Record (newsletter), 227–228
    (figure), 229–230 (figure)
Foregrounding, 82
Forensic research facility, locating,
    180–184 (case study), 182
    (figure)
Formal rhetoric, 12
Functional audiences, 66,
    148–149, 171

Generalization, hasty, 39
Genre criticism, 106
Giddens, Anthony, 90

Globalized organizational world,
    rhetoric in, 233–234
Goodwill, 26

Hasty generalization, 39
Hegemony, 92–93

Identification, 34–37
    versus identity, 122
Identity
    building, 122–127
    organizational, 120
    rhetoric, 119–137
    rhetorical strategies for, 221–223
    versus identification, 122
Identity maintenance rhetoric,
    127, 130
    evaluating and critiquing, 131–132
    rhetorical maintenance and,
        128–129
Ideology, construct of, 88–92
Image repair strategies. See
    Organizational image
    restoration strategies
Imminent status, of an issue,
    144–145
Impersonal message, 12
Individual/group distinction,
    199–200
Inductive reasoning, 39–41
Instructional strategies, in crisis
    rhetoric, 196–197
Intelligent rhetor, 26
Internal messages, rhetorical
    strategies for, 216–223
Internal rhetoric, 209–232
Internet, identity and disaster relief,
    133–137 (case study),
    135 (figure)
Invention, canon of, 25–44
Issue life cycles, 143
    critical status, 145
    current status, 145
    dormant status, 145–146
    imminent status, 144–145
    potential status, 143–144
Issue management, 139–162
    audiences, 147–149
    constraints and assets in, 149–152
    exigencies, 146–147

foundations for understanding,
    143–146
identification and, 155–156
organizations and, 140–143
rhetorical situation in, 146–152
Issue rhetoric. *See* Issue
    management
Issues
    appeal of, 153
    claims and evidence, 152–154
    credibility strategies, 156
    evaluating and critiquing, 156–157
    evidence for, 153–154
    organizations and, 140–143
    rhetoric about, 139–162
    rhetorical strategies for, 221–223
    solutions to, 153–154
    strategies for rhetoric about,
        152–156
    subject of, 153
    values advocacy in rhetoric about,
        154–156
    See also Issue life cycles; Issue
        management

JetBlue, 202–207 (case study)

Life cycles, of issues, 143–146
Logos, 3
    interdependence with ethos and
        pathos, 42–43
    in traditional rhetoric, 37–38

Maintenance rhetoric, and identity
    creation, 119–137
Member advocacy, 215–216
Memory, canon of, 48
Menu labeling, 158–162 (case study),
    160 (figure)
Message
    characteristics of, external to
        internal, 13
    impersonal, 12
    internal, rhetorical strategies
        for, 216–223
    organizational, 93–94
    organizational rhetoric and, 12–14
    personal, 12
    public, 13
    universal, 13

Metamorphosis
    socialization process and, 213
    strategies following, 219
Mumby, Dennis, 81

Needs, 30–31
Neo-Aristotelian criticism, 106
Nonartistic proofs, 43
Nonprofit organizations, corporate
    rhetoric in, 234–235
Normative audiences, 66, 148

Objective evidence, 44
Open systems, 11
Opinion/knowledge distinction, 199
Oppositional reading, 110
Organization
    anticipatory socialization
        to, 211–212
    canon of, 44–46
    defining, 4–6
    studies of, key ideas in critical
        approaches to, 82–96
    See also Organizational rhetoric;
        Organizations
Organizational apologia, 197
Organizational change
    exigencies, audiences, and
        constraints for, 214–215
    rhetorical strategies for, 220–223
Organizational credibility,
    27, 175–176
Organizational crisis, 186–187
    crisis response stage, 189–190
    post-crisis stage, 190–191
    pre-crisis stage, 188–189
Organizational enthymeme, 155
Organizational entry, 212–213
Organizational exigencies, 62–65
Organizational identity, 120–122
Organizational image restoration
    strategies, 198
Organizational linkages, 65
Organizational rhetoric
    analyzing, approaches to, 104–113
    audiences in, 65–67
    canon of delivery in, 47
    canon of invention in, 25–44
    canon of memory in, 48
    canon of style in, 46–47

canon of organization in, 44–46
characteristics of, 10–14
constraints and assets in, 67–69
critical approaches to, 77–101,
     101 (table), 109–113
defining, 6–8
ethics and, 97–100
ethos in, 27–28
evaluating and critiquing,
     103–118, 201–202
evidence in, 43–44
in a complex organizational
     world, 233–236
internal audiences, for, 209–232
logos in, 38–42
message and, 12–14
pathos in, 29–37
process for analyzing,
     xvii (figure), 19–22
rhetorical situation in, 62–69
rhetorical strategies in, 23–54
studying, 15–19
understanding, 8–10
worksheets for analyzing, 237–244
See also Rhetoric
Organizational risk, rhetoric about,
     163–184
Organizational socialization,
     211–213
Organizational texts, worksheet for
     identifying rhetorical strategies
     in, 238–239
Organizations
contemporary culture, in, 1–22
defining risk in, 165–166
issues and issue management in,
     140–143
rhetorical situations in, 55–75,
     63 (table), 240
See also Organization;
     Organizational rhetoric
Original empirical research, 69–71
Outrage, and risk topics, 172

Pathos, 3
interdependence with ethos and
     logos, 42–43
traditional rhetoric, in, 28–29
Peripheral route, leading to attitude
     change, 168

Personal message, 12
Post-crisis stage, of organizational
     crisis, 190–191
Potential status, of an issue, 143–144
Power
construction of, 85–88
showdown over, in Texas,
     72–74 (case study)
Pre-crisis stage, of organizational
     crisis, 188–189
Preferred reading, 108
Primary research, conducting, 70–71
Proofs
artistic, 26
nonartistic, 43
Public, and critical descriptions,
     94–96
Public message, 13
Published sources, research
     from, 69–70

Qualified evidence, 43–44

Readings, 103–118
critical and evaluative,
     worksheets for, 115–118
oppositional, 110
preferred, 108
Reasoning, 38
by analogy, 40
by example, 39–40
causal, 40
deductive, 41–42
inductive, 39–41
Recurring situations, 75
Reinforcement of socialization
exigencies, audiences, and
     constraints for, 213–214
rhetorical strategies for, 219–220
Representative examples, 40
Research, of the rhetorical
     situation, 69–71
Retention of employees
exigencies, audiences, and
     constraints for, 213–214
rhetorical strategies for, 219–220
Rhetoric
canons of, 25–50
context in, 56–57
crisis, 185–207

defining, 2–4
ethos in, 26–27
formal, 12
identity, 119–137
in a complex organizational
    world, 233–236
in contemporary culture, 1–22
internal, 209–232
issues, 139–162
logos in, 37–38
risk, 163–184
traditional, 26–27, 37–38
See also Organizational rhetoric
Rhetoric, The (Aristotle), 3
Rhetorical artifact, 3
Rhetorical barriers, 68
Rhetorical criticism, 3
Rhetorical discourse, 3
Rhetorical methods, 3
Rhetorical situations, 11, 55–75
    Bitzer's perspective on, 57–59
    crisis management and, 191–196
    for identity maintenance
        rhetoric, 128–129
    in internal organizational
        rhetoric, 211–216
    perspectives on, 57–62
    researching, 69–71
    Vatz's perspective on, 60–62
    worksheet for describing, 75, 240
Rhetorical strategies, 23–54,
    49–50 (table)
    for identity building, 124–127
    for identity maintenance, 129–131
    for internal messages, 216–223
    special situations and, 48
    traditional, in contemporary
        forms, 235–236
    worksheet for identifying,
        51–52, 238–239
Rhetorical theory, 3
Risk
    defining in organizations, 165–166
    rhetorical strategies for, 221–223
    strategies for rhetoric about,
        174–178
    See also Risk rhetoric
Risk frames, expert and nonexpert,
    167 (table)

Risk perception frames, 166–168
Risk rhetoric, 163–184
    audiences and, 170–171
    constraints and assets in,
        171–174
    evaluating and critiquing, 178–179
    exigencies and, 169–170
    foundations for understanding,
        166–169
    rhetorical situation for, 169–174

Situation
    environment as, 236
    recurring, 75
    rhetorical, 11
Situational crisis communication
        theory (SCCT), 187–188, 196
Socialization, anticipatory, 211–212
Society, organizations as force in,
        15–16
Speaker, organizational, 10–11
Stakeseekers, 83
Status, of an issue, 143–146
Strategies
    anticipatory, 217–218
    apologia, 197–199
    combination, 200–201
    common ground, samples of,
        36 (table)
    dissociation, 199–200
    early phase, 218–219
    following metamorphosis, 219
    instructional, 196–197
    organizational image
        restoration, 198
    stylistic, 178
    See also Rhetorical strategies
Strategy, environment as, 236
Style, canon of, 46–47
Stylistic strategies, and risk, 178
Suspicion, discourse of, 85–88
Syllogism, categorical, 41

Texans for Affordable and Reliable
        Power (TARP), 73
    advertisement for, 53 (figure)
Texas Clean Sky Coalition,
    advertisement for,
    54 (figure)

Timely evidence, 44
Trade groups, 130
Transcendence, as apologia
    strategy, 198
Transcendent "we," 37

Universal message, 13

Values, 31–33, 154–156, 176
Vatz, Richard, 57, 60
Vatz's perspective, on rhetorical
    situations, 60–62

Wallace, Karl, 38
"We," assumed or transcendent, 37

About the Authors

Mary F. Hoffman (PhD, University of Kansas) is an associate professor and Chair of the Department of Communication and Journalism at the University of Wisconsin-Eau Claire. She has taught courses in organizational rhetoric, organizational communication, and rhetorical criticism, and currently teaches event planning and training and development. Her research is concerned with how individuals negotiate organizational demands that conflict with personal values. Her work on three organizations of Benedictine nuns has been published in *Communication Studies, Western Journal of Communication,* and *Journal of Communication and Religion.* Her work on how individuals and organizations negotiate the idea of work/life balance has appeared in *Qualitative Research Reports in Communication* and *Communication Quarterly.*

Debra J. Ford (PhD, University of Kansas) is Assistant Dean for Student Affairs and Research Assistant Professor at the University of Kansas School of Nursing. In addition, she is program director for the leadership major in the doctorate in nursing practice and MS in nursing degree programs. She also teaches in the University of Kansas Department of Communication Studies. She has worked for 12 years in recruitment, advising, and administration in nursing education, and has taught for 10 years. She teaches courses in organizational communication, organizational rhetoric, leadership, communication theory, and health communication. Her research focuses on strategies used by organizations to influence public policy, group communication processes in public–private partnerships, and the scholarship of teaching and learning. She has published articles in *Communication Theory, Health Communication, Western Journal of Communication,* and *Communication Studies,* among others. She is the principal investigator on a U.S. Department of Education GAANN grant.

Supporting researchers for more than 40 years

Research methods have always been at the core of SAGE's publishing program. Founder Sara Miller McCune published SAGE's first methods book, *Public Policy Evaluation*, in 1970. Soon after, she launched the *Quantitative Applications in the Social Sciences* series—affectionately known as the "little green books."

Always at the forefront of developing and supporting new approaches in methods, SAGE published early groundbreaking texts and journals in the fields of qualitative methods and evaluation.

Today, more than 40 years and two million little green books later, SAGE continues to push the boundaries with a growing list of more than 1,200 research methods books, journals, and reference works across the social, behavioral, and health sciences. Its imprints—Pine Forge Press, home of innovative textbooks in sociology, and Corwin, publisher of PreK–12 resources for teachers and administrators—broaden SAGE's range of offerings in methods. SAGE further extended its impact in 2008 when it acquired CQ Press and its best-selling and highly respected political science research methods list.

From qualitative, quantitative, and mixed methods to evaluation, SAGE is the essential resource for academics and practitioners looking for the latest methods by leading scholars.

For more information, visit **www.sagepub.com**.